WHAT PEOPLE ARE

EYES OF T

C000260829

In a heartfelt, eloquent tribute to the mysterious connection between human beings and wild animals, Eleanor O'Hanlon takes the reader on a remarkable personal journey of close encounters, including the "friendly" gray whales that migrate to Mexico's Baja peninsula, an account that is both riveting and deeply moving.

Dick Russell, author of *Eye of the Whale Epic Passage from Baja to Sibbria*

The beautiful writing perfectly captures the author's sense of wonder as she gazed into their lives of the gray whales. Without being religious I recognise that feeling of wonder and connectedness through immersion in the natural world where, at heart, we all belong.

Spirituality grew out of this I am sure and I know from experience that spending large amounts of time in the company of whales or wolves, bears or wild horses, whether as a biologist, a shaman, a writer or a filmmaker brings insights which science alone cannot yet fully describe. In this way we come to see that each animal is an individual with its own personality and moods, it's own strengths and weaknesses.

It has never mattered more that we should have empathy for the other living things with which we share the Earth. By showing us how she, and the other outstanding observers in this book, look at the animals who live alongside us, Eleanor has made us want to care.

John Aitchison, wildlife filmmaker,. BBC *Frozen Planet*, *Big Cat Diary* and *Yellowstone*

Eleanor O'Hanlon has written an exquisite insight into the majestic Gray whale. Mexico's San Ignacio Lagoon is the Sistine Chapel of Nature, where humanity can experience the blessing and miracle of interspecies communication. In her evocative prose, Eleanor takes the reader into that magnificent wilderness, allowsing us to experience the moment of awe when time stands still as humanity and the whale connect.

Her book awakens our responsibility to honour the sacred by recognising the intelligence and wisdom of our animal kin. Eleanor is a voice for Creation.

Sue Arnold, CEO, The California Gray Whale Coalition

Eleanor goes to the ends of all the Earth – the Bering Strait. Siberia. The Arctic pack ice. The Caucasus mountains. The deep Russian taiga forest. Her writing is full of knowledge, insight and emotion, telling you things you didn't know, showing you things you would never have noticed, even if you were there with her.

Staffan Widstrand, photographer and author, *Wild Wonders of Europe* and Managing Director of Wild Wonders of Europe, the world's largest photography initiative for conservation.

The writing is so beautifully sensitive and expressive, with great poetic clarity in the descriptions of willlderness and wildlife. The succinct descriptions of colors, the way that light creates dimension and visual contrast, the changing weather and sense of place echo the way I see as a photographer and try to express through my imagery. Eleanor's words are composed as poetry, as well as delivering the urgent message that there really is no separation between humanity and all other living things.

Pat O'Hara, wilderness photographer and author of *Washington's Mount Rainier. A Centennial Celebration*

The book looks delightful, with a good mix of personal experience, stories and natural history.

Dr Rupert Sheldrake, best-selling author of *A New Science of Life* and *Dogs that Know When Their Owners Are Coming Home and Other Unexplained Powers of Animals*

Eyes of
the Wild

Journeys of Transformation
with the Animal Powers

Eyes of the Wild

Journeys of Transformation
with the Animal Powers

Eleanor O'Hanlon

Illustrations by Natasha Hoffman

EARTH

BOOKS

Winchester, UK
Washington, USA

First published by Earth Books, 2012
Earth Books is an imprint of John Hunt Publishing Ltd., Laurel House, Station Approach,
Alresford, Hants, SO24 9JH, UK
office1@jhpbooks.net
www.johnhuntpublishing.com
www.earth-books.net

For distributor details and how to order please visit the 'Ordering' section on our website.

Text copyright: Eleanor O'Hanlon 2012

ISBN: 978 1 84694 957 9

A CIP catalogue record for this book is available from the British Library.

Design: Stuart Davies

Printed and bound by CPI Group (UK) Ltd, Croydon, CR0 4YY

We operate a distinctive and ethical publishing philosophy in all
areas of our business, from our global network of authors to
production and worldwide distribution.

CONTENTS

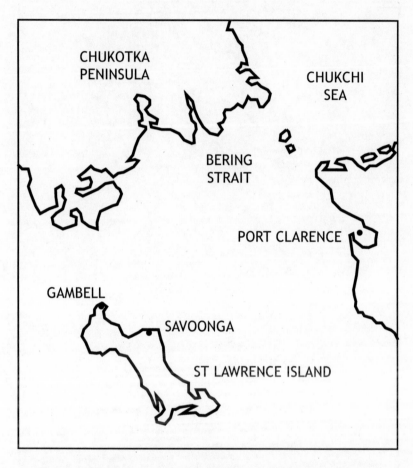

Map 1. Gray Whale Feeding Grounds in the Bering Strait.

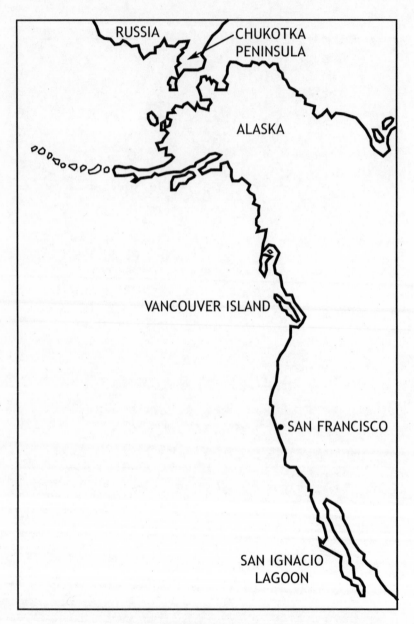

Map 2. Gray Whale Migration along the Pacific Coast of
North America.

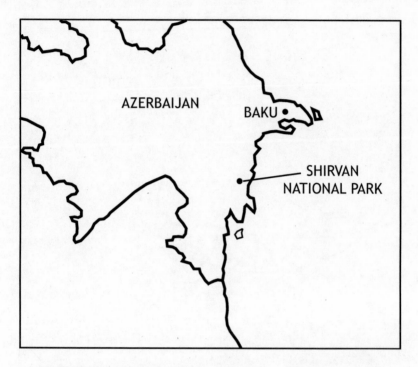

Map 3. Shirvan National Park at the edge of the Caspian Sea.

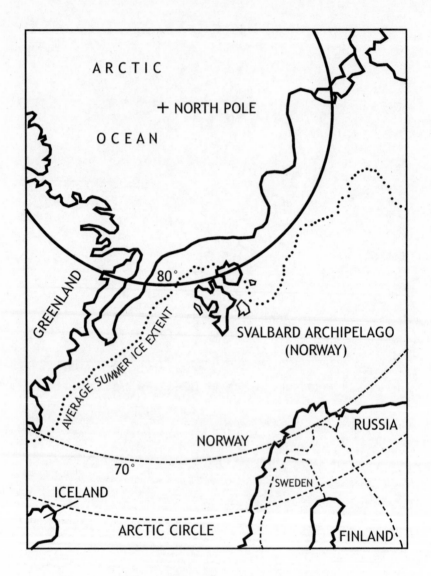

Map 4. The Svalbard Archipelago.

The Book of Whale

The Turning Whale
Whale. From the Old English Hval or wheel

1 The Opening

Among Gray Whales, Laguna San Ignacio
Baja California Sur, Mexico
March 2007

The gray whales come to us.

"*Tenemos amigos,*" the boat driver Cuco Fisher says. "We have friends."

He cuts the outboard engine as the two whales swim towards our small open boat, their smoothly powerful undulations rising and falling through the lagoon's clear green water: a gray whale mother with her young calf by her side.

The whales surface alongside, an eruption of life from the deep, the water rippling in shining falls from their backs as the mother exhales, a gust of warm spray that briefly hangs in a mist plume on the air. The calf lifts its head above the water and I glimpse the ancient, undersea face – the dimples on the dark skin of the upper jaw, each one with a single bristle of short hair; the long mouth with gently rounded lips, the top lip slightly overlapping. Then the calf sinks onto the strong support of the mother's back and the pair submerges, becoming little more than vague suggestions of enormous presence until they disappear into the green depths.

In the silence they leave behind, I wait, gazing into the water in the hope they will surface again.

Slowly, surely, with silken gliding, the mother returns to the surface. There is no stir, no ripple through the water as she rises, only the massive darkening of her body, coming more clearly into focus until she breaks through the surface beside me, and her blowholes pulse again with that same great *whoosh* of exhaled air.

The plosive power of the whale mother's breathing resounds with the expansive dimensions of her life. Her body extends forty feet or more beneath the water – twice the length of our open boat. The double curve of her tail flukes spreads around twelve feet wide. She weighs perhaps thirty tons, and the mottled white patches on her dark-gray skin, the absence of a dorsal fin, and the colonies of barnacles that cluster roughly on her back and sides distinguish her as one of the gray whales of the Eastern Pacific, also known as the California Gray, *Eschrichtius robustus*.

Each year the gray whales make one of the longest and most arduous journeys of any creature on Earth as they swim between their principal summer feeding grounds in the Bering Strait and the southern Chukchi Sea and the sheltered lagoons along the Pacific coast of Baja California where they mate and give birth between January and April. San Ignacio is the only one of the lagoons that has not been affected by development. It is set within the Vizcaino Biosphere Reserve, a UNESCO World Heritage site and the largest nature reserve in Mexico.

When this gray whale mother knew she was pregnant, she left Baja California and turned north, swimming an average of eighty miles each day and following the entire Pacific coast of North America within a few miles of shore until she reached the Bering Sea and Strait. Although she may have foraged along the way, the richly productive Arctic waters are where she was able to feed most intensively. In late autumn she began her journey south, to bring her calf safely to birth inside the lagoon's mangrove channels, where the sheltered waters helped her raise it to the surface for its first breath.

After twelve months curled inside its mother's womb, the newborn whale calf's first movements in the water are wobbly and uncertain. The mother rolls onto her back to hold her baby against her chest and strokes it gently with her flippers. When the calf has grown stronger on the extraordinary richness of her milk – gray whale milk is more than 50% fat and contains three times as much protein as human milk – she leads it to more challenging waters near the lagoon exit, to swim through the powerful currents and develop the stamina and coordination it will need to follow her north.

In the past year alone, this gray whale mother has swum perhaps 10,000 miles or more while carrying her calf within her body. She will feed it, teach it, love and protect it with unstinting, implacable devotion as they make their epic journey north together. By the time they both arrive in the Bering Strait, the mother will have been largely fasting for eight months and she may have lost a third of her body weight.

With the mother alongside, the whale calf raises its head above the surface – as curious, playful and eager for attention as any young mammal – and I splash it on the nose with handfuls of water, a sensation which it clearly enjoys.

Then the mother does something utterly extraordinary. She sinks beneath her calf and deliberately brings it closer to the surface by supporting it on her back, so that I can touch it easily on the head and nose. As I run my hands along the calf's lips, the mouth opens with an audible release of suction and my fingers brush the baleen fibers that line the upper jaw in place of teeth among the grays and all other baleen whales.

No wild creature can make a greater gesture of trust than to bring you her newborn and allow you to touch it. This mother is bringing me what is most precious to her, the calf she has carried for twelve months in her body and brought to birth a few weeks ago in this lagoon. The next time she surfaces, she lingers alongside and I begin speaking aloud to her, naturally and without thinking. I tell her how beautiful she is, how happy I am to meet her. She blows again, a short misty burst like a snort, and submerges. A moment later the wooden *panga* is rattled by the power of her more forceful underwater exhalation. It rises out of the water, rocks and settles back, and I realize with shock that she has just lifted us up on her back and placed us gently down again.

Mother and calf flow over and under and around each other; they circle the boat in long graceful turns, sink and rise again with the water sparkling on their wet sides like stars. At times the mother turns through the water in a slow, powerful rotation that takes her from her belly to her back. Again, the boat rocks as she pushes it with her head from below. Yet I never have a moment's fear of her great size and power. She moves with completely refined, sensitive awareness through the whole of her body.

When the mother surfaces next, she comes close enough for me to reach out and touch her. I run my hands along the skin of her side, which feels indescribably smooth, as though the texture has been endlessly refined by the washing of the sea. Her flesh is firm and cool beneath my hands. Through the physical contact with her body, a sense of the expansive dimensions of her being opens inside me like soundings from some vast interior sea. As the depth of the meeting grows, it becomes an opening through which something entirely new keeps pouring – a wordless sense of connection with a greater life.

Turning onto one side, the whale gazes up at me through the water; looking down into her dark eye, ringed with folds of skin, I meet the lucid and tranquil gaze of an ancestor, one of the ancient ones of the Earth. I feel her taking me out, far out, of thought and linear time, beyond the limited concerns of my ordinary mind, into a profound sense of meeting with another being, whose consciousness is not separate from my own.

When she surfaces next with her calf by her side, the whale mother places her nose directly against the side of the *panga* and becomes completely still. Her blowholes are closed; her immense power is utterly composed and quiet. I reach out and touch her on the head with my right hand, then I put my left hand on her calf and join with them both on the undivided sea.

That evening, back at our camp on the lagoon shore, I try to write down something of the power of what I have experienced with the whale mother and her calf. But all that comes to me are a few terse words: *what was, on the day of creation, is, now.*

Eden, I think, is not simply a mythical place, or a metaphor for original innocence, or an outworn and divisive religious symbol. Eden is a state of being, and we are free to return every time we know ourselves again in deep communion with the rest of life.

The gray whales began to seek out this communion with people in 1972. A Mexican fisherman, Francisco "Pachico" Mayoral, one of the small number of permanent residents of San Ignacio Lagoon, was fishing near Punta Piedra, the rocky point at the lagoon's mouth where it begins to open to the Pacific Ocean, when a gray whale surfaced alongside him and lingered by his *panga*. Like the other fishermen who moved between the whales in the small open *pangas,* he had always been careful to avoid coming near them. But this whale did not submerge again; it remained alongside for almost an hour, until, moved in some mysterious way, Francisco Mayoral reached out his hand and stroked its side.

Even his own family could not believe him at first when he told them about the encounter. The gray whales' reputation for dangerous aggression was simply too well founded.

Among nineteenth-century whalers, the California grays were considered to be the most deadly target of all. The whalers called them "devil fish" and they claimed that the gray whales had caused more deaths and injuries than all other hunted whales put together. Their pursuit began in the late 1850s when the American whaling captain, William Scammon, first located the birthing lagoons on the Baja California coast and managed to navigate the difficult entry through the shallow channels between the sandbars.

Once inside the lagoons, the whalers drove their small boats between the mothers and calves, separating them and bringing the frantic mothers close enough to harpoon. The whale mothers were fierce defenders of their young. While their strength lasted, they used their heads to batter and overturn the whaling boats. They lashed them with their tail flukes, broke the rudders and flung the men into the water. Scammon later wrote that these gray whale mothers "showed a power of resistance and tenacity of life that distinguishes them from all other cetaceans. Many an expert whale man has suffered in his encounters with them, and many a one has paid the penalty with his life."

From the beginning the commercial hunt for the gray whale followed the same bloody and destructive course it has done for every whale species – hunt the whales to the very edge of extinction, extract maximum profit from them until too few remain to make it economically worthwhile, then move on to another whale species and do exactly the same to them. Season after season, the unrelenting carnage continued inside the Baja lagoons until their waters lay almost empty between arid shorelines stacked with bones. Scammon, who was both the instigator and the clear-eyed and factual witness of the slaughter, wrote in 1874:

> The large bays and lagoons where these animals once congregated, brought forth and nurtured their young, are already nearly deserted. The mammoth bones of the California gray lie bleaching on the shores of these silvery waters, and are scattered among the broken coasts from Siberia to the Gulf of California; and ere long it may be questioned whether this mammal may not be numbered among the extinct species of the Pacific.

The pursuit of gray whales inside their birthing lagoons was no longer worth the effort. Slowly, the whales began to recover – only to meet the force of more powerful industrial whale catchers armed with exploding grenade harpoons at the beginning of the twentieth century. When they finally received formal protection in the early 1930s, the California gray whales had become so rare that they were rarely seen at sea and it seemed possible that they would follow their gray whale cousins in the North Atlantic to complete extinction – the first and, so far, the only whale population to have been completely extinguished by commercial whaling by the mid-1700s. The world's industrial whaling fleets turned to the pursuit of more profitable targets, particularly the blue whales in the southern ocean, which they slaughtered in hundreds of thousands between the 1930s and 1960s. The scale of that slaughter was matched by its extreme cruelty. One whaling captain wrote of the blue whale in 1962, "How few people realize the despairing fight it puts up before dying of convulsions with an explosive shrapnel grenade tearing at its vitals. It has to be seen to be believed."

Left alone at last, the shattered California grays began their long recovery to their current population, which is estimated at between seventeen and twenty thousand. Until the last few years, researchers believed this level roughly corresponded to their population before commercial exploitation. More recent research reveals that it is probably well below it: a study of genetic variation between individuals that was carried out in 2007 suggests that before commercial whaling there were four to five times as many gray whales in the oceans.

Walking along the white desert flats crusted with black algae, I find whalebones scattered on the shore – massive shoulder blades, vertebrae and hooped ribs. Exposure to the salt and bright sunshine, the wind and rain has worn and bleached the bones and they feel smooth and warm to the touch, as though they have taken on some of the heat of sunlight as they aged. I do not know how long they have lain here, but it is entirely possible that they once belonged to some of the whales that were slaughtered inside San Ignacio Lagoon.

For more than a week I have spent every day on the water among the gray whales. Every day the whales have approached with the same gentle playfulness and peace. Although I am never again alone in the boat with them, as I was with the mother and calf, I can see how consciously the whales choose their level of interaction. The boats are not allowed to follow the whales. The grays themselves choose when to approach, and how long to remain alongside. I have seen some whales return to the same boat until they have connected with every single person on board. I have returned to Eden. I do not want to leave.

In recent years, some of the researchers who study cetaceans – all whales and dolphins – have begun to look at them in a much larger way. They have discovered that individual whales and dolphins have a sense of personal identity and consider the needs of others. They have the ability to use abstract concepts and communicate them to the others in their close-knit social groups. They are intensely cultural – passing information, understanding and ideas between clans and individuals in ways that are still mysteries to science. As their scientific research erodes the artificial boundaries between humans and cetaceans, some leading specialists now argue that cetaceans should be granted basic rights as persons, which would mean that no whale or dolphin would ever be captured, slaughtered or confined.

The grays themselves use a wide variety of sounds to communicate and they can live to be seventy years old. It is entirely possible that the whales that came to this lagoon in the 1970s, when the first whale approached Francisco Mayoral, had experienced the carnage of industrial whaling, which almost wiped them completely from the Earth.

What could possibly motivate the grays to reach out to people in this way? How can they be so open and so trusting? How can they come to us in such peace, as though they had never known that welter of blood, anguish and death, and allow us to play with their young in the very same places where they suffered and died? These questions touch me all the more deeply because I have been with the gray whales before, at the northern end of their great annual migration. On that journey through their feeding grounds in the Bering Strait I saw the whales struck by hand-held harpoons and lances. I saw the waters of the Bering Strait run red with spurted blood from their blowholes and I saw them die.

There are scientists who offer pragmatic explanations for the whales' extraordinary openness towards people. They speculate that friendly whales may be attracted by the sound of the outboard engines on the *pangas*, which vibrate in a similar register to their own underwater calls. Or that new mothers are looking for a way to keep their lively babies entertained and take a little time off from the demands of motherhood. For others the whales' attitude and behavior have a profound spiritual dimension: they reach out in a gesture of forgiveness for the suffering and death they have known at human hands.

But forgiveness is a word that is loaded with the legacy of human pain, with all our emotional struggles and distress. Like

9

anybody who has ever struggled to find forgiveness and let go of the corrosive effects of bitterness and anger, I know how these feelings linger, how they surface again after the years in which they seemed to lie forgotten. We humans hold fast to the shadows of the past; we do not find it easy to forgive.

What I have experienced among the gray whales is quite different. The whales have shared with me something of that ineffable freedom which lies *beyond* the difficult human struggle to forgive the past – to truly forgive both ourselves and others and find release from the repetitive cycles of pain and suffering. The whales approach us from the other side of the human duality of guilt and forgiveness, reaching out to share that freedom with us – troubled, uneasy sleepers being nudged awake by some benign, enormous friend. They are awake and present on this Earth where so many of us have gone to sleep, and lost ourselves in separate dark dreams of emptiness and fear.

In the gray whales' company I have come to realize that we do not know what the whale really is. The usual categories of understanding, based on the separation between human consciousness and the consciousness of the whale, are made meaningless by the power of their presence – life meeting life, consciousness meeting consciousness, in recognition and in peace.

The first peace, which is the most important, is that which comes within the souls of men when they realize their relationship, their oneness with the universe and all its powers, and when they realize that at the center of the universe dwells Wakan-Tanka, the Great Spirit, and that this center is really everywhere, it is within each of us.

Black Elk, holy man of the Lakota people.

This book begins and ends among the gray whales, moving through a circle, which is perhaps the most ancient of all symbols for unity. The four animals – Whale, Wolf, Bear and Horse – hold the four divisions or directions, an image for the unity of diversity that is common to the shamanic, Native American, Celtic Christian and many other traditions. At the center of the circle, at the heart of the six directions – the four cardinal directions with the Heavens and the Earth – is the point that represents the spiritual heart within each one of us, where forgiveness and renewal well up freely from the depths of who we really are. Whale, Wolf, Bear and Horse are companions, guides and helpers on the journey towards the center, as the animals were in many wisdom traditions, before the ego-driven mind stripped all sense of sacredness from the Earth and reduced life to mere commodity, whose only worth resides in gain.

I traveled with these animals through places of great elemental power – the Russian *taiga* forest, the shores of the Caspian Sea, the Northern Rockies, the Siberian coast of the Bering Strait and the edges of the Arctic pack ice. The journeys gave me intense appreciation for the animals themselves, each one a marvel of living beauty and intelligence. They also brought me into contact with some of the most remarkable people I have ever known, men and women who have lived close to these animals in the wild, and come to known them intimately. Several are highly experienced field biologists; the others are sensitive and perceptive observers of the natural world. They all shared their deep knowledge of animal behavior and ecology with me. In addition, each one told me an extraordinary story of finding direct connection with the animals they studied in ways that profoundly affected them, and took them beyond the conventional boundaries between species.

There were many times when these journeys also affected me very deeply. I found that the power of the landscape, the presence of the animals and the dynamic flow of living energy through the wild were working on me inwardly. They were calling back aspects of my own being that I had long neglected or forgotten and driving me to explore the inner realities in ways I had not dared to do before. And this was drawing me into the deep current that has run through many human cultures for tens of thousands of years – the natural connection between the animals, the rhythms and cycles of the Earth and the waking of the soul within each person.

The idea that finding inner relationship with the animals and the elemental life of nature can help us to open up the deeper levels of awareness that usually remain dormant in everyday life, has become foreign in the West. Our culture has conditioned us to remain caught up in mental activity and the processes of analysis and judgment. But it is a fundamental aspect of many indigenous wisdom traditions, as well the original Christian teachings. The shamans of Siberia and the High Arctic, the spiritual elders of Native North America and the storytellers of the Pagan and Celtic Christian traditions of Britain and Ireland whose teachings appear in this book, were natural mystics who made no separation between the life of the Earth and cosmos and the spiritual light within the human heart. They lived among the animals; they observed their ways with great care and attention, like any field biologist. But their love and knowledge of the animals had another dimension: they understood them to have their own connection to the realities beyond physical appearance. To be present with the animals, beyond the limitations of the ordinary thinking mind, opened the way to these subtle realities and helped people to live in balance on the Earth.

The inner connection with the animals often found expression through storytelling, for stories convey patterns of meaning in ways that bypass the thinking mind and speak directly to the imagination and the heart. Throughout this book, you will find retellings of some of these traditional stories. I hesitated before including them: I did not want to simply appropriate them or use them disrespectfully. But the stories spoke so powerfully to me of what is constant in human experience, and the potential for authentic inner transformation, that I felt they wanted to live again in people's minds, in association with the magnificent creatures that originally helped to inspire them.

Although we inhabit a different reality, the essence of what the shamans and spiritual elders knew and taught remains true, and it can help us now. All the world's great mystical teachings are one in their simplicity. They tell us that the essence within all life is also the deepest reality within each one of us, at the very center. When we lose the direct connection with our own true nature, we drift into a mind-made world and become prey to all the fantasies of fear, vulnerability and greed. But the life of the Earth is far beyond the separate, egocentric mind and it can help us to wake up again, and live from the greater consciousness at the core, the true Self within the Divine, which is untouched by fear, need, and separation.

Throughout this book, I explore the way in which the animals and the life of the wild can help us *now* to make that awakening, which has never been more urgently needed. This is a journey into deeper connection with the life of the Earth, not away from it. And so in my mind I go back now, to those first encounters with the gray whales, as I travelled through the coastal waters of the Bering Strait, in a small open boat, with my dear friend Afanassi Makovnev as my guide, on the journey that marked the turning of my own life, the point where it began to change.

2 The Journey North

The Chukotka Peninsula
The Russian coast of the Bering Strait August 1997
There are places on the Earth where power goes through you like
wine through water and transforms your perception of the world
forever.
This is a journey through one of those places.

The Breathing of the Sea

The late afternoon light casts a band of blue-black shadow across the rocks; as the boat reaches the middle of the bay, the water ignites around us in the sunlight and burns with a cold green flame.

There is a sudden, plosive expulsion of air. *Whale*, Afanassi calls out urgently, as the water by the boat opens on the arch of the whale's turning back and closes over the thrust and cleave of its tail. He cuts the engine, allowing the boat to rock in silence on the water as the whale rises again, a fluent gray curve embossed with white barnacles and the scribbling of sea-lice. The name – gray whale – runs along the distinctive, knuckled curve of the rolling spine and is misted on the air as it submerges, leaving behind a distinctive oval print on the water surface. In the quiet I hear more gusts of out-thrust air as two whales surface side by side and roll together through the water by the mouth of the bay.

Each time the whales rise to the surface, they warm the rock bowl of the bay with the emphatic *whoosh!* of the out-breath, which smells of the seabed, like a breeze blown off warm ooze and the decomposing mulch of kelp. No other whale feeds as the gray whales do, down among the fertile sediments of the sea floor. The grays turn to the right side as they dive and skim above the seabed, creating a powerful suction by retracting their tongues and stirring the bottom sediments. These sediments are densely packed with crustaceans and other bottom-dwelling creatures; the whales suck them up in a great mouthful of mud and sand, which they filter by pushing it out again through their baleen. The small crustaceans that live among the sediments remain behind, trapped between the fine hairs that line the baleen and the grays lick them off at leisure with their tongues.

We leave the gray whales intent on feeding and pass from the sheltered waters of the bay into the open waters of the Senyavin Strait. A sharp cold wind ruffles the water, striping it navy and white, and Afanassi clambers past me and attaches a strip of canvas to the bow of the boat, which keeps the worst of the spray from drenching us. I fasten my parka more tightly and pull on a second, warmer pair of gloves; body temperature drops fast in a small boat at sea.

It will take us four or five hours to reach Yttygran, the island where we'll camp tonight, and three more full days at sea before we reach our destination – the small Native settlement of Lorino, on the Bay of Lavrentiya, where the Yupik Eskimo and Chukchi peoples have recently resumed their traditional hunt for the gray whales. There are no roads through this remote corner of north-eastern Siberia; without a helicopter or all-terrain vehicle to cross the tundra, the only way we can reach the Native villages along the coast is by sea.

Standing behind me with one hand on the tiller, Afanassi is completely absorbed; all his attention is focused on the movement of the wind and currents and the pitch and thud of the boat against the waves. Dark-haired and bearded, with very clear blue-gray eyes behind his glasses, his cheeks are faintly weathered from ten years of travel by boat and dogsled around the Russian Arctic.

Small islands roll and hummock as we continue north

through the Senyavin Strait, past the cracked and tilted pyramids of nameless outcrops, their rocks stained purple from the droppings of the bright-beaked puffins that whir overhead.

The russet and bog-brown flanks of Arakamchechen rise in the distance, the largest island in the strait, where thousands of walruses haul out in summer on the shore. Like the gray whales, walruses forage in the rich murk of the seabed, searching for crabs and clam and sucking on the shells to release their prey. When they leave the chilly water to rest and digest, they pile up together on the shores of Arakamchechen, while their skins flush pink with fresh blood in the relative warmth of the air.

A long mud plume stains the surface water brown and shows where another gray whale has recently been feeding. The seabirds wheel overhead on the weightless acrobatics of the wind, and plunge on the leftovers, which the whale has sucked from the seabed and spat out in rising. As they bring up food from depths which no seabird could reach, the grays are helping to support the lives of some of the millions of birds – northern fulmars, auks, murres, guillemots, shearwaters, kittiwakes – that migrate to the coast of Bering Strait each summer to nest and feed.

We are traveling through some of the richest seawaters in the world. Their creativity is born in storm and darkness, from powerful winds that scour the Bering Sea in winter and stir the nutrients from the bottom sediments, lifting them into the currents that bear them north towards the Bering Strait and the pouring light of the Arctic summer. Such upwellings are fundamental to the ocean's life. Like the beating of the heart in the human body, they circulate life by bringing nutrients from the depths to the light-filled waters near the surface.

Each spring, as the Earth inclines her head to the Sun, the tide of light flows north with such power that midsummer days beyond the Arctic Circle are never touched by darkness. Sweeping north in a soundless blaze, the light cracks open the ice cover and the nutrient-rich waters of the Bering Strait explode into life. Phytoplankton – microscopic algae that correspond to the green plants on land – blossom and feed the zooplankton – small animals that live in the water column. Still more plankton fall to the sea floor, where they nourish the dense benthic communities of small crustaceans on which the walruses and the gray whales depend. Land and sea take a great breath of light, filling with life and energy, and the birds and the animals travel north along the path of that abundance.

The gray whales have come four or five thousand miles to feed on amphipods, small crustaceans resembling shrimps which live on the seabed and feed on the plankton that fall to the floor when the sea ice melts in spring. An adult gray whale may consume one to two tons a day of the different amphipod species, along with mollusks, worms and other small denizens of the seabed. To find such great quantities of food they must search through huge areas and they disturb their feeding grounds more than any other animal – even the elephant – does. Great craters mark the sea floor where gray whales have been feeding, yet their intensive combing of the seabed is not destructive. On the contrary: like the wind-driven currents of winter that stir up the nutrients in the bottom sediment, the gray whales are participating in the series of dynamic exchanges which renews its life.

The grays live within a symbiotic – a mutually beneficial – relationship with their amphipod prey. As they till the seabed, the whales stir up the nutrients that spur fresh growth in the plankton on which the amphipods feed. They seed new areas with the juvenile amphipods that escape through their baleen. With their tongues and their baleen, the whales filter the heavy layers of mud from lighter grains of sand and so help to free the bottom of the Bering Strait from the heavy sediments that are constantly being discharged by the great Alaskan rivers. In this way they help to maintain the fine sand that the amphipods prefer, and they make the sea floor more fertile than it could ever be without them.

Standing on Sacred Ground

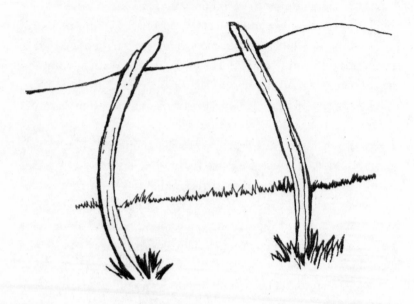

It is late evening, and the day is burning slowly down to a low red flame when we come around the north side of Yttygran Island and enter Siqluq Bay to land in a small cove backed by a range of low hills. Afanassi drops anchor in the shallow water and we wade to the shore, carrying supplies and a tent for the night.

A pale archway rises over the white heads of the cotton grasses on the tundra. The sides gleam as white as limestone in the dusk and curve for fifteen feet or more to a narrow gap at the top, making the outlines of an archway across the air. The white arch is made from whalebone: two great jawbones taken from bowhead whales have been set upright and opposite each other in the ground.

Walking along the shore to gather driftwood for a fire, we pass the massive bulk of bowhead whale skulls and jawbones rising whitely from the tundra or lying broken on the ground by their bases. The whole shoreline is an ancient sacred site, constructed entirely with the skulls and the ribs and jawbones of bowhead whales. In the gathering dark there is no time for exploration. Afanassi hurries to make the fire and we set up our tent on the shingle before the whalebone arch, and unpack some food from the waterproof storage boxes. A seal surfaces just offshore, sleek and whiskered, and makes a circle of scarlet ripples on the still water. Across the darkening mirror of the bay, the hills of Arakamchechen Island roll before the open waters of the Bering Strait.

Before we eat, Afanassi slices a small piece of dried meat and drops it onto the ground before the fire. *For the spirits,* he says. He is smiling, but the gesture was made seriously: he knows there are presences here, powers that are inherent in the hiss of the sea on the shore, the scouring and scraping of the winter ice and the unimpeded action of the air and by acknowledging them, he looks for harmony for our journey.

Then he proudly flourishes the bottle of red wine that he secretly packed to celebrate this first evening of our new journey together, which is also my birthday. We laugh and huddle companionably around our small driftwood fire, eating tinned beans and drinking the cold, thin wine as darkness slowly settles and all the standing whalebones vanish in the night.

When we wake, the morning is cloudy and still, with a pearly overcast that hangs between sea and sky like the inside of an oyster shell. With my back to the sea in the nacreous light, I look directly at the great whalebone arch that rises from the tundra behind our tent. To the right, the line of whale skulls follows the grassy ridge above the shingle and runs into the distance along the curve of the shore.

I walk over to where the skulls begin. They have been placed together in pairs so that the side bones of the skull rise in a half-moon curve around the hollow center. The skulls almost reach my waist. Yet, large as they are, they must have come from juvenile whales, for the bowhead *Balaena mysticetus* is larger even than the gray whale. Adults can reach sixty feet and the massive jawbone makes up one third of their body length. Today bowheads are among the most endangered of the great whales. Dutch, British and American whalers decimated them around the Arctic and the bowheads have never truly recovered from that assault.

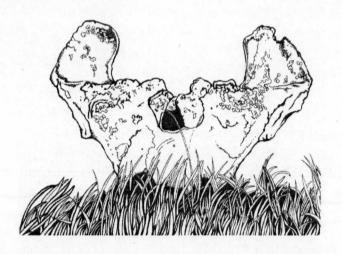

Two Russian archaeologists, Mikhail Chlenov and Igor Krupnik, found this site in the late 1970s and named it *Kitovii Allee* – Whale Alley. It is the largest and most complex sacred site that has ever been found in the Russian Arctic: fifty bowhead whale skulls and more than thirty bowhead jawbones have been arranged in geometric patterns along the shore, and a paved pathway through the hills leads to a circle of large stones.

The Yupik and Chukchi hunters who guided Krupnik and Chlenov to this place told them little about it. Either the significance of the site had been forgotten or it was a subject on which they preferred to remain silent. But the archaeologists sensed a power whose immediacy needed no explanation. They described it as "a sacred precinct... eerily reminiscent of a polar Stonehenge. Working among its strict, geometric lines, we soon found ourselves filled with a palpable sense of reverence."

They suggested that the whale skulls and bones had been placed in these intricate geometric patterns almost a thousand years ago, by the cultural ancestors of the Yupik Eskimo who live on both shores of the Bering Strait today, sustained by the life of the sea, fishing, gathering shellfish and hunting seals and walruses. The people who built Whale Alley were skilled marine mammal hunters who had also learned how to hunt the massive, slow-moving bowheads from their open skin boats or *umiaks* using ivory-headed harpoons and stone-bladed lances. They ate the meat and blubber; they rendered the blubber into oil to light their soapstone lamps; they made tools from the whale's baleen and supported the sod roofs of their semi-subterranean houses with its ribs. The body of the great whale was their food and warmth, their light and shelter but it was never a mere commodity or resource. They revered it as a spiritual being that had given up its physical body to sustain their life.

One aspect of Whale Alley makes the intensity of their reverence for the bowhead clear. Along the eastern coast of Bering Strait from Cape Dezhnev in the north to Saint Lawrence Island in the south, whalebones layer the ground around ancient villages and hunting camps and crumble slowly away into the soil. Whale Alley is different. According to the archaeologists, it contains only the ritual skulls and jawbones. The people did not hunt bowheads from this shore: they transported the massive bones by skin boat. They chose this place and set it apart from their ordinary habitation to be a place of meeting between the people and the spirit of the whale.

Later that day, I walk for hours through the entire site, following the tundra ridge above the shore. For part of the way, the whale skulls are placed opposite each other to make a walkway. The dark mouths of meat storage pits show between the hummocks and the tussock grasses of the tundra. They were dug from the permafrost – the ground of ice that lies beneath the surface of the tundra – and braced with whalebone.

The sea rasps and hisses over the stones. A ground squirrel slinks through a channel in one of the skulls, pads delicately around the hollow depression on top and darts away as soon as I move. I run my hands across the inner surface of the skull, this vaulted chamber of a brain as intricate in its folds and patterns as my own. Porous as limestone beneath my fingers, the skull has weathered to the feel of stone.

I remember the first time I ever came close to a whale. A gray whale had surfaced just off a steeply shelving, pebbled beach like this one and I ran down to the water's edge when I saw the blow. For a few minutes of pure exhilaration I was walking beside it, following its fluid undulations through the water. After the whale was gone, the sense of meeting remained with me – the felt presence of a great being, moving beside me through another element and sharing, on the gusts of its breathing, the beating heart and warm blood of my fellow mammal.

I remember that slow, rolling turn the whale's body made through the water; the intensity of my own, nameless feelings at the immense gentleness of its power and I wonder again at the depth of meaning this place, and all the gestures of its making, must have held for those people who built it, here at the northern rim of the turning Earth, between the fading and the blazing of the light, with their trust and constancy in the sustaining power of the sea.

Whale: the word appears to come from the Old English *Hval* for wheel – a wonderful image, which evokes the turning rim of the whale's body seen rolling through the water from shore or boat. "Most marvelous of monsters, the turning whale," wrote an anonymous Irish poet of the 8th century, as he remembered the whales and the coiling of the sea.

Whales move within great cycles of turning and returning. Their bodies are lifted up and fall back again in continuous circles on the immense swells of the open ocean. They move always between surface waters and the deeper sea, between the retention and the release of their breathing. They swim in great annual cycles between feeding and fasting, between the North and the South, the tropical and polar seas, desert and ice, stillness and storms.

Now some deep pattern of return in my own life has brought me back to their Arctic feeding grounds. I first came to this part of the Bering Strait three years before, with a cameraman to make a film about the walruses and the lives of the indigenous people. I came to know Afanassi well on that journey and he became a dear friend as well as a trusted guide as he took us to the most remote and inaccessible areas along the coast of the Bering Strait, in his own walrus skin boat or with the local walrus hunters in their open boats.

We often travelled among gray whales. The grays were feeding in small groups on the fertile stretches of seabed near the shore and when they rose to the surface, their breath smelled like the very exhalations of the sea. I had never seen or heard whales of any kind before, and something shifted in me inwardly as I listened to the warm pulsations of their breathing.

I began to sense a power that seemed to inhabit even the least conspicuous places – the roughly carved stones along the seashore or the damp brown bed of mosses by a stream. It was a power for which I had no name or knowledge. Then one afternoon in late September, walking alone on the tundra, I heard the voices of cranes ring through the empty sky. The birds appeared overhead on the long waves of their voices, flock after flock streaming in wavering, arrowhead lines. They were sandhill cranes, gathering to cross the Bering Strait and fly south to their wintering grounds in the American Southwest. *Echo makers* the Native North Americans call them for the resonant power of their voices, shaking the air.

Bare words for beauty. I knew little about the lives of the cranes that day, but in their hoarse bell and clangor, a sound so much older and wilder than the scattered and disjointed voices running through my mind, something deep inside stirred and woke. It was a part of myself I had put away long before and almost forgotten. I knew it only as absence – a pervasive sense of emptiness, inadequacy and loss. Or a sound like distant weeping, the voice of someone calling from a closed-off room, whose sorrow had lost the power to touch.

Suddenly I was waking again to the burning, enchanted life of the world. I stepped out of my ordinary self into the space of light, and for a time that radiance lingered and shone out through the surface of visible things. They became transparent in the light. Even when I was home again, ringed with the noise and concrete of a busy London street, I stood before the ordinary blaze of a tree in autumn and watched in astonishment the leaping, rooted, dance of its flame.

We often associate the word "mystical" with something vague and uncertain, with cloudy intimations that dissolve in the common light of the everyday. I can only say, in all honesty: that has not been my own experience. The reality of a greater dimension to life rose up, as immediate, immense and unmistakable as the rising of the whale and the pungent breath of its life from the deep.

I had been granted the experience of the indwelling presence at the core, the Self that is beyond form, beyond fear and separation. That sense of expansion came with the intensity of the uninterrupted fall of the light in the Arctic summer; it was simple and immediate in a way that words cannot convey and I never doubted its reality. But, as the first immediacy faded, it was more difficult than I could have imagined to integrate this into everyday life. The experience was not something that I could put easily into words or communicate to other people. It had nothing to do with conventional religious thinking, which has largely separated the sense of imminent Divine presence from the animals and the Earth. And though I had worked for several years in conservation, whatever I believed I knew about the living Earth was only a shadowy thought before this living radiance, this overwhelming presence – of *sacredness*.

The experience of expansion, intense joy and greater connection also had profound psychological effects. It stirred up sedimentary layers of painful experience, which I had never acknowledged, but kept dormant and half-forgotten beneath the surface. I began to realize consciously that my life, like that of so many others, was founded on the sense of separation from the rest of life, that it was full of the fear and loneliness, the loss and dislocation which that separation engenders. And so I swung between different states – between the intense joy of inner expansion and turbulent upwellings of the emotional pain which few people on this Earth will not experience.

It is said that all mystics come from the same country and speak the same language. That is, they have come to know utterly that their home is the country of union, the country of silence where no words are needed to know, and be known. They have gone beyond time and all the illusions of separation. The divisions which the egocentric mind makes between human cultures and tongues, between human awareness and the consciousness of plants and stones, animals and birds, the sun and all the other stars have become utterly meaningless. All that remains is the unity with life which we know when we turn from appearance to reality, from separation to unity and return to our true Being within the Divine Source, the Great Mystery from which the whole of creation has come.

Standing now in that sacred space within the Arctic landscape on Yttygran, I wonder, with some anxiety, what this second journey among the gray whales will bring. I wonder what these spiritual ancestors, the grandmothers and grandfathers of the Arctic, knew and taught that might help me find strength and guide me as I make it. Bending down, I pick out a stone from the shingle; it is russet and gray and it fits in the palm of my hand. When I close my hand around it, the strength it contains is palpable and it comforts me.

I look along the line of whale skulls again. This time I notice the way the rhythm of their curve and hollow seems to rise and fall, wavelike, with the hills of Arakamchechen Island on the other side of the bay.

Each one a crescent hollow, like the moon. A stone bowl. Or a boat of bone, lightly balanced on the ever-moving, undivided sea.

Hunters on the Sea

Heading back to camp, I hear the sound of a boat engine through the damp silence. A *baidarka* cuts across the bay – an open wooden hunting boat, with three cross benches. Three men are standing between the cross benches and I can see the heads and ivory tusks of the two walruses they have taken lashed to the side of the boat through holes cut in the thick hide. Afanassi waves to them to pull in and we walk down to the water's edge to greet them.

Dark-haired, with fine-boned Asiatic features, the men wear short canvas jackets and their rubber waders are rolled down over dappled, sealskin trousers. They tell us they have been hunting walrus around Arakamchechen and they're on their way back to their camp at Inakpuik Bay. Their dignified reserve and the soft tones of their voices meshes strangely in my mind with the puddles of walrus blood that dapple the bottom of the boat, the automatic rifles and the toggling harpoon heads that lie across the benches.

The men are Chukchi, descendants of a nomadic people who probably migrated north from Kamchatka to the Chukotka Peninsula. Some moved inland to herd the wild reindeer on the tundra while others joined the Yupik on the coast and became sea hunters of walruses, seals and whales. Before they were forcibly collectivized by the Soviet authorities, reindeer herders and sea hunters shared their resources and traded with each other, bartering reindeer meat and fur clothing for the meat of seals, walruses and whales, and waterproof cloaks made of walrus gut.

The hunters share food with us now: they leave us a gift of walrus meat before heading back to their camp. "Our survival food!" Afanassi says happily, as he slices the walrus with the knife he wears on his belt. He has a low opinion of the dried camping food I brought with me from Alaska. We need the Native foods like walrus and seal, he says, if we are to stay warm and travel safely for long days at sea. He cooks the walrus on the gas camping stove in the traditional way he learned from his Yupik father-in-law – boiled with pieces of the heart – and it tastes wonderfully rich and sustaining.

That walrus teaches me what food can be. Next to it, the preserved and dried foods I have brought are tasteless and empty. Dead foods, which have no relationship with the life of the land and sea.

To hunt and eat are acts of great significance for traditional Arctic peoples because they bring such intimate connection with the soul of the animal that, in dying, gives the people life. Until quite recently, this was a world where you depended entirely on animals to sustain you, keep you warm and fed and clothed. Utterly dependent on the animals, Arctic peoples do not take their relationship with them lightly, for they know them to have a soul and consciousness beyond the physical world. To take their life in greed and unfeeling ignorance would bring the hunter into great spiritual danger. "Life's greatest danger lies in the fact that man's food consists entirely of souls," an Igloolik Inuit from Greenland told ethnologist Knud Rasmussen. "We fear the souls… of the animals we have killed."

That fear is the manifestation of deep awareness and respect for life. At the heart of Arctic hunting traditions is the belief that the true hunter does not take life with violence. Within the web of consciousness we humans share with them, certain animals give up their physical bodies to help the people live. By the refined quality of his attention the hunter allows the animal to come to him, and through experience he becomes sensitive and skilled enough to receive that life, in all humility, as a gift. In the past, weapons were beautifully decorated and made with great care to please the animals' spirits. Women's skills were just as important: the clothing they made was richly decorated, elegant and beautiful because the animals are attracted to rich patterns and textures and colors, just as we humans are.

Traditional hunters often endured arduous periods of prayer and fasting to purify themselves of greed, violence and anger before the hunt. They were never to boast about their own skills or speak carelessly about the animal, either before or after its death, and they always treated its flesh and bones with great respect. As a further mark of respect, marine mammal bones were never taken inland to the tundra, but left by the shore where they remained close to the sight and sound and smell of sea. In this way the animal's spirit would carry their gratitude back to its ancestors and be born again on another tide of life.

Certain rituals were always carried out before and during the hunt: these were the patterns of behavior that reminded the hunter to be conscious of the magnitude of his actions, not to get caught up in arrogance, or the blind urge to kill, but to remain inwardly quiet so that he might become one with the flow of giving and receiving that governs all the relationships of life.

Every animal species was said to have a soul – a center of collective consciousness uniting the individuals – so that a meeting with one animal was also a meeting with all of its kind. And beyond the animals were the great animal masters – the archetypal powers that sustained the lives of many creatures and ordered their flow into, and out of, this physical world. One of the greatest of these powers was Sedna, the sea goddess who appears in different guises and under different names around the Arctic basin. The whales and all other sea mammals first came into physical existence from Sedna's hands, and she embodies the power of the ocean to give and sustain life.

I do not mean to idealize these traditions by suggesting that everybody always lived in harmony with them: that is clearly impossible. Yet this profound sense of connection with fellow creatures remains real, and for many traditional people, it has been a way to peace.

"There are many wonderful animals," one Yupik elder from Chukotka, Nikolai Galgaug'ye said in 1995, "but whales are the best of all. As they pass by your skin boat, great and quiet, you immediately come to understand your place on this Earth, and you become warm inside. It is very interesting to look at whales, but more importantly, it is necessary in order that you may become a fully fledged person – a hunter."

Masters of the Ice

It is raining when we take down our camp and leave Yttygran, heavy drops that spatter loudly on the hood of my oilskins. I look back at the whale skulls and the great arching jawbones, which remain like gray guardians along the shore until their outlines blur and fade between the sheets of rain; then we pull away from the island and Afanassi guides the boat back into the Senyavin Strait.

Green swell of water. Salt, cold air. In the distance, the misty spouts of feeding gray whales mingle with the slanting rods of rain.

Afanassi touches me on the shoulder, and points towards a gap in the mountains on our left: *Penkigney Bay*. The bowheads come there late in autumn, he says, on their way south from their summer feeding grounds in the Beaufort and Chukchi Seas.

I think of them gathering there, within the pleats and shadows of the mountains, before the coming of darkness and the hardening of the ice, at rest within a shared sense of life we humans can scarcely imagine, time presses so fiercely on our scattered minds, our shallow, uncertain breathing. On the slow, powerful drumbeat of her enormous heart, a bowhead may live for a hundred and fifty years; longer, it is believed, than any other animal, and her life unfolds within the pulsing of the light.

In winter, bowheads are largely hidden from human sight by the storms and darkness of the Bering Sea. They become visible again in spring as they gather along the southern edges of the seasonal ice pack that stretches from the Arctic Ocean, through Bering Strait into the northern Bering Sea. In the pure spring light, the pack ice rafts into a thousand, dazzling refractions of white and gray. The ice piles into pressure ridges or spreads unbroken beneath a white layer of flawless snow.

Imagine a group of bowheads rolling there by the edges of the ice, churning the black water white with foam as they glide their great bodies together in the buoyant rhythm that guides their mating: sleek black side touching side, on a midnight smoothness of skin so sensitive, the whale would sense the footfall of a bird.

A female rolls onto her back, and turns the white patches on her chin and belly to the sky. Another rises from the water and rests her chin on the ice, the dark brown eyes almost lost in the immensity of her head. Waiting. Suddenly a fifty-ton leviathan rockets half his body from the water with a muscular thrust of the tail and falls back in a thunder of breaking water. Watching. Searching for the first leads in the ice that will open the way to the north.

Bowheads are the master navigators of the Arctic pack ice. They enter the ice through the open corridors that part in spring, and move along the ice edges. When the ice hardens again, they sink beneath it and scan the underside for places that may splinter under the powerful thrust of their head and send out their voices to capture echoes of the way ahead, searching for the areas of open water that can spread like a lake in the country of ice.

The melting of the pack ice draws the bowheads further north, through the widening deltas of fragmenting ice, into the Chukchi Sea, and eastwards to the Beaufort Sea, gliding slowly through the dense clouds of krill that thicken the Arctic waters in summer. The bowhead allows her open mouth to fill with water; closing it, she expels the water with a tuck of the tongue and sucks the krill and other creatures it contained from the fringes of her baleen.

It seems like an extraordinary paradox that the baleen whales, the largest animals on Earth, should be able to live on mouthfuls of water. What makes this possible is the way that life concentrates densely in certain parts of the oceans. The phytoplankton, which are the marine equivalents of the green plants, capture and bind far more of the sun's energy into their tissues and they grow and die more quickly than the plants on land. Their productivity is intensified by the intense light of the polar summers, in the Arctic and Antarctic. Under the pouring light, in the presence of the nutrients, which the deep-water currents have swept from the seabed, the polar seas produce massive blooms of phytoplankton, which, in turn, feed the swarms of the krill and other small crustaceans on which the bowheads and the other baleen whales depend.

Their great size allows the bowheads, grays and other baleen whales to move in rhythm with these intense pulses of life through the polar seas in summer. Because their bodies are so large, their cells can live at a slower pace than smaller animals, and they are sustained by the energy stored within their blubber as they make their annual journeys from more temperate waters, where food sources are widely dispersed, into the concentrated abundance of the polar seas in summer.

And that is, perhaps, one reason for the immense peace of their presence – the whales' certainty of huge repose on rhythmic pulses of renewal that are older and more enduring than the restless human mind.

Moving between Worlds

In the afternoon, the sky clears and the steep coastal mountains of the Senyavin Strait fall to a long shelf of low cliff, fretted from below by the action of the sea. From there, the land spreads out more broadly into a series of shallow lagoons behind narrow spits of sand and gravel.

Towards evening, Afanassi takes the boat through an opening in one of the smaller sandbars. The tide is racing through the narrow exit and the boat is borne backwards and makes no headway until he drops into the shallow water and pushes it through into a small lagoon where the birds wheel and call in wide circles or drop to the sheet-metal spread of gray water and float among the reeds. Beyond the reed beds, and the soft-breasted birds, the muted expanse of green and purple-brown tundra spreads, brightened by the white tossing of the cotton grasses.

There's a small wooden cabin by the water, a shelter for passing hunters, with reindeer skins laid across a couple of wooden sleeping benches. We hang our wet clothes up to dry indoors and Afanassi cooks some walrus meat on the camping stove outside by the lagoon.

I've never known anybody quite like Afanassi. During our first journey together I learned that I could trust him completely. I never knew him to utter a false or unkind word. I never saw him lose his patience and good humor, his meticulous attention to every detail on the boat. He told me once that if he did make a mistake he would go back in his mind to the point where he had first lost concentration to understand it and make sure it did not happen again. An expert wilderness guide, he's also a talented photographer, with a sensitive eye for the subtle beauty of color and detail in the tundra plants, berries and delicate flowers. "When I first came here I couldn't work out how to photograph this landscape," he told me once. "Then I looked down and saw what was under my feet."

Afanassi's entire life has moved between different worlds – from the urban environment of central Moscow to the remotest parts of the Russian Arctic. As a boy growing up in Moscow he'd been fascinated by the Eskimo way of life. He built igloos in the snow around suburban Moscow and read every book he could find on them in the library. I'd grown up on a farm in the West of Ireland around the same time and I'd done the same – although it rarely snowed, I read everything I could find about the worlds of ice. I made him laugh when I told him that when I was five or six years old I couldn't understand why the farm dogs weren't being used for pulling anything, so I tried to train them. I harnessed them to a wooden crate using reins from the horses' bridles, and tried to make them run, but of course, they just sat and looked at me.

Afanassi had first come to Chukotka to work as a cameraman on a film. He stayed and married into the Yupik Eskimo community of Sireniki, a village that is more than two thousand years old, one of the most ancient settlements in the Russian Arctic. His father-in-law, Typykhkak, and the other hunters taught him how to work with sled dogs, travel on the ice and build the *umiak*, the traditional hunting boat made of walrus skin stretched and knotted on a wooden frame. As a mountain climber, Afanassi was used to working with rope knots, but the way these Yupik hunters could tie the boat frame together using slippery knots of bearded seal skin was something entirely new for him. "I loved to learn this from Typykhkak," he said. "And I showed him the rope knots that I knew from climbing which he also loved to learn. In this way we became good friends because we could share our knowledge."

When the skin boat was finished, Afanassi and Typykhkak fitted it with a wooden mast, rigged it with a square sail, and set out across the Bering Strait with several hunters from Sireniki and other villages to visit their relations in the Inupiat Eskimo communities of Alaska. It was a great occasion, the first time in more than fifty years that the indigenous communities on both sides of the Bering Strait were able to meet one another freely, as they had done in the past when they had often hunted and travelled together, united by common bonds of culture and kinship. These bonds had been severed during the enforced isolation of the Cold War, when the coast of the Bering Strait had become militarized.

Afanassi had taken me to meet Typykhkak when we visited Sireniki during our first journey together. One brilliant day in early October, he took us out from the village in his walrus skin *umiak*. A solidly-built man in his early sixties, he guided us along the cliff face and through a series of rock archways to a bay, where the tundra mountains were reflected in the still blue waters of an inland lagoon. This was Imtuk, the Yupik settlement, now abandoned, where Typykhkak had been born and lived as a boy. He lead us among the great bowhead jawbones set upright on the tundra, past the storage pits dug into the permafrost that still held dry shreds of old meat, to the shallow depression where his family's *iaranga*, or skin tent, had stood when he was a boy.

Typykhkak told me that he was eight years old when his father first began to teach him to be a hunter. At twelve he was already the youngest member of a boat crew that hunted the bowheads during their spring and autumn migration through the Bering Strait. On the day he had killed his first whale, he took small pieces from the flippers and dropped them into the sea, murmuring a blessing for the spirit of the creature that had given up its life.

We sat down with him among the grasses that had dried to the rustle of corn, while a gray whale surfaced repeatedly just offshore in a gust and glitter of heart-shaped spray.

The One Who Knows

"All that exists, lives," the Chukchi shaman said. "The lamps walk around. The walls of the houses have voices of their own. Even the chamber vessel has a separate land and house. The skins sleeping in the bags talk at night. The antlers lying on the tomb arise at night and walk in procession around the mounds, while the deceased get up and visit the living."

All that exists, lives. These words were recorded by a Russian ethnographer, Walter Bogoras, who traveled among the Chukchi in the early 1900s. They reach us now through layers of translation, and I suspect that their original humor got lost along the way. The shaman belonged to oral tradition, in which spoken words are vivid and direct, full of humor and charged with life through the breath of the speaker. He is speaking of the life in the most ordinary things – a stone lamp, a sod house half buried in the ground, a pot for pissing in – as well as the sacred altar of the reindeer antlers laid above the bodies of the dead. All these things, he says, whether they appear mundane or sacred, are *alive.* They are charged in their different ways with consciousness and this energy vibrates through the space around them, so that even the piss pot, the shaman adds jokingly, has *"a separate land and house."*

In the traditional vision of life along the Bering Strait, living forms were being constantly remade by the essence of life flowing through them. This transcended categories based on external appearance. When the orcas that hunt seals and gray whales left the frozen sea in winter, they were said to take form again in the wolves that hunted reindeer on land. Although they differ externally, orcas and wolves were understood to be connected inwardly, as hunters. Skin or fur or feathers were seen as temporary masks; behind these masks, we humans are not separate from the other animals. We share the same life and we can communicate and merge consciousness in states of heightened awareness.

A story from the Bering Strait oral tradition tells of such a moment of connection, piercing through the mask of external appearance. Once a hunter was walking alone on the tundra. A raven dropped from the sky and landed by him on the snow. The bird fixed him with its dark eyes and gave a harsh croak, then it lifted a black wing and, drawing back its beak like a mask, revealed behind it a face like that of a man.

The word *shaman* itself comes originally from Siberia, from the Tungus language family; it means "one who knows". Strictly speaking, shamans come from the Native cultures of Siberia, but the term *shamanism* is used more generally in the West to describe spiritual beliefs and practices which are common in many traditional cultures, and may date back to the Paleolithic peoples of Ice Age Europe, more than forty thousand years ago.

Shamanic cultures share the belief in different worlds, or dimensions of existence, which coexist with physical reality and interpenetrate it. These realms become accessible in states of heightened awareness. As the shaman expands in consciousness, beyond the physical body and the ordinary sense of time and space, they enter states of awareness that transcend the limitations of the everyday mind. These inner journeys take them through the upper or the lower worlds, guided by powerful helpers, which may be a wise ancestor or the spirit of an animal or plant. With their help, the shaman establishes direct relationship with the powers that underlie physical forms. They meet the spirits of the animals and the plants behind their masks of appearance and they return with the ability to share knowledge with others and bring them healing in mind and body. Most importantly, the shaman does not explore the invisible dimensions out of mere curiosity but in order to connect with the deep sources of knowledge and healing and so give help to others.

Shamanic practice is not a religion. It has no sacred texts, no dogmas and no formal structure. "Shamanism" is simply the collective experience of men and women who live in spiritual relationship with the Earth and the cosmos. The animals and plants and all the elemental forces that maintain life on Earth are understood to be conscious and finding inner connection with their power opens the way to the realities beyond physical appearance.

These fundamental aspects of shamanism are so widespread and so ancient that they seem to be natural expressions of living in intense relationship with the animals and the elements. The magnificent paintings that decorate the caves of Ice Age Europe were once thought to represent a form of "hunting magic" – a way of drawing the animals to the hunter. More recently, researchers have discovered that there was little correlation between the animals that were hunted and the animals that were painted. Scholars of cave art now suggest that the paintings were part of shamanic rituals of connection with the animal spirits and the other worlds.

There is a tendency to think of the shaman as an exceptional man or woman and it is certainly true that many shamans have undergone severe initiations and endured psychological break-downs before they could access different levels of awareness and mediate between them for the well-being of others. But the shamanism of north-eastern Siberia was not confined to special individuals. The practice was part of everyday life throughout the community. Until the Soviet authorities wiped out much spiritual practice by force – shooting shamans, even dropping them alive from helicopters with the taunting command to fly – men and women carried out their rituals in their skin tents and sod houses and made their own relationships with *kelet* – the elemental spirits that could help or hinder. Of course, some individuals were more gifted than others as healers and seers, but shamanic practice was not considered exclusive to them.

The shamans say that it is the spiritual light within each person that guides their way to the subtle dimensions. The Greenlandic shaman or *angakok* called this inner light their *quamaneq*, their shaman light, or enlightenment.

"It was not only I who could see through the darkness of life, but the same light shone out from me, imperceptible to human beings, but visible to all the spirits of earth and sky and sea, and these now came to me and became my helping spirits," the Greenlandic shaman, Aua told the Danish explorer and ethnographer Rasmussen.

The traditional shamans of inland Siberia described their expansion of consciousness as climbing a great tree, which unites the different levels of existence. The trunk and branches reach towards the Heavens and the tip of the tree is aligned with the Pole Star, along the central axis of the spinning Earth. This image of the great world tree, growing at the very axis of the Earth, is found in Native American and many other cultures to convey the branching unity of the different worlds or dimensions and the hidden structure that underlies visible reality. The tree's roots grow from the foundation of all things. The axis of the tree is everywhere, within each person and all things and the branches extend towards the infinite.

The shamans of inland Siberia said they nested like birds among the branches of the world tree, and were fed with knowledge and wisdom at the different levels – or degrees of consciousness – that they reached. But here, among the coastal peoples of northeastern Siberia, where no trees grow, the shamans used a different image for the inner journey: they said they travelled to the upper worlds on *light* – on the bands of the rainbow or the rays of the sun. For them too, the way to the subtle worlds was guided by the light of the Pole Star.

The Star that Never Moves

The Inuit call Polaris *the star that never moves*. It remains above the North Pole, aligned with the extended spinning axis of the Earth, so that when you gaze into the clear northern sky at night, it shines at the center of the great wheel of the heavens – the stars, the planets, the numberless galaxies which appear to turn around it through the sea of space as the Earth spins on its axis. The great significance of the Pole Star for the Siberian shamans is beautiful and profound: it was their guide to the light within, at the very center, where the rhythmic pulses and patterns of change that govern life's diverse unfolding are experienced in stillness that transcends the ordinary workings of the mind.

Whenever I look into the clear northern sky at night, I search for the Pole Star. *The star that never moves* shines as the cosmic reflection of the truth that is expressed within all the world's great mystical traditions. At the very core of our being is the Divine Self, at one with the formless essence of all that is, radiating through inner stillness and silence. That peace and stillness may intensify beyond what words could ever convey to become the ineffable awareness of Divine presence within the heart that the mystics know, but it is not strange or distant. From the very beginning, the connection with the deep Self feels utterly natural. It feels like coming home at last after long, unhappy wandering, to your true belonging in the stillness that fills every crevice of your being with peace.

Yet it is so hard to stay rooted in that light. Like most people, I fall back continually into the everyday states of confusion and anxiety; the inner light appears to flicker and dim or fade out completely, leaving me lost and bewildered, lonely and afraid, as I was before I ever knew the touch of its warmth and beauty.

To look up to the Pole Star, shining at the very center of the turning wheel of the stars, is one of the most beautiful ways I know to remember that the light of the Spirit does not shift and change and leave us. It is always the restless, uneasy mind that pulls away from the constancy of peace. The deepest reality within, the point of unshakable inner equilibrium, is the *one who knows:* the true Self within the Divine, shining in the purity and stillness that is undimmed by mental turmoil or the most raw and turbulent upwellings of emotion. And turning inwards, into the depths of peace and silence within us at the center, the way opens into dimensions of being that are far beyond the ordinary activity of the mind.

The Expansion of Open Spaces

The following day we round the outer rim of a large lagoon that extends deep inside the tundra. We enter through the narrow opening in the sand bar and draw the boat up on the shore. Afanassi wants to visit and photograph the remains of several ancient settlements on the inland tundra. This means a difficult hike of several hours across the boggy, uneven tundra and he decides to go alone while I wait on the beach by the boat.

The lagoon is a pewter sheet of reflected light. To the north, the tundra turns mountainous, stained with violet shadow. Underneath, the earth is bound in ice. Permafrost, permanently frozen soil, underlies the tundra surface: only the upper layers are released in summer when they help provide the plants with water for their short growing season. The soil that covers the permafrost is thin and poor in nutrients because the turnover of organic matter is so slow and the tundra's dwarf trees, grasses and flowering plants grow close to the ground for warmth and shelter.

The tundra's wolves and brown bears and the herds of wild and domestic reindeer must live through great annual changes in light and temperature from Arctic summer to winter as well as unpredictable tilts from milder to more severe weather. The great, open spaces of the tundra allow the land animals to survive such extreme changes. The reindeer, or caribou, as they are called in North America, may walk a thousand miles or more to find reindeer moss, the lichen that is their staple food. The range of a single male brown bear – the space that it needs to find food and partners – may cover five hundred square miles of Arctic tundra, far more land than the bear would need further south.

Indigenous philosophy and the principles of ecology meet in this awareness of the importance of expansive space. For the herders and hunters, the great, open spaces that sustain life on the Arctic tundra extended beyond the limits of the physical. A brown bear digging for roots, reindeer cropping lichen, the white

Arctic wolves moving like smoke across the snow – all these creatures were seen to flow into, and out of, the physical world from the immense spaces beyond. In the traditional indigenous vision, life moves between the worlds, constantly seeking dynamic balance in the continuous play of form and dissolution. Death is not seen as life's end: it is simply the boundary of another transformation, within the more subtle, formless space that allows that continual dance of transformation to be.

Alone in the vast and seemingly empty landscape, watching the play of light on the wide mirror of the lagoon before me, I feel a gentle opening and expansion. Awareness reaches out to the mountains, the floor of ice beneath, the graceful benediction of the light pouring weightlessly over the land. In that great spaciousness of nature, we find our own expansiveness again. The relentless activity of the mind, which is so habitual it seems normal, is really a form of acute contraction. When I am confined entirely within the mind, I lose that sense of space. My mind becomes crowded with opinions and arguments. It comments, judges, criticizes, compares. I find myself replaying emotional dramas. I lose myself in fantasies of past or future. Thinking becomes even more obsessive as the mind circles persistent emotions, unable to let them go and find release and rest.

The expansion that comes when the mind lets go of obsessive thinking and falls still at last, transcends what could ever be conveyed through words or writing. I can only say that it is the greatest gift that I have received in this life. Thoughts flicker and multiply, but the space of greater consciousness through which they move is still. As the mind falls still, space opens within. And that space is not separate from Eternal Presence, holding all life as one and allowing it to *be* – growing, blossoming, dying and reemerging in all its manifold diversity and grace.

The Voices of the Water

The next day is all gust and brightness. The boat bucks and

rocks, rising on a slap of green water that could burn with the salt of its cold. Gray whale ribs and jawbones arch from the shore like the skeleton keel of an upturned boat and mark the remains of ancient settlements where the gray whales come close to shore to feed or rub their backs and bellies against the pebbles and the sand.

I cannot call the landscape beautiful. The ordinary meaning of the word dissolves into this fertility of salt and fire. Land and ocean are simply alive in a way that transcends the usual mental judgments that I make about what is comfortable or uncomfortable, attractive or ugly, dangerous or safe. That life is one and it supports me. I feel it running like a river through my body. I am often cold, yet I am warm inside. I get tired, but not in the jangled, stressed-out way I know from city life.

That evening we make our camp on the narrow spit of sand that divides Mechigmen Lagoon from Bering Strait. Between those two bodies of moving water, our small driftwood fire flares up like a match struck in the single immensity of the darkness. The murmur of our voices, threaded on the fine line of the warmth between us, twists and tosses on the gusting of the wind, and as I lie in the tent unsleeping, I hear again, in the soft, ceaseless whisper and hiss of the water, the plosive breathing of the whales.

Everything in the world has a voice, the Siberian shamans said. "On the steep river bank, there is life. A voice is there and it speaks to me. The little gray bird with the blue breast... calls her spirits and sings her shaman songs."

At the boundary between air and ocean, I listen to the song of the moving water, one sound, always changing, always the same, the oldest continuous sound of our planet. Water breaks about us in the womb, where we are rocked in the amniotic fluid we share with the whales and all other mammals, similar in the composition and balance of its salts to seawater. The whale never leaves that rhythmic pull, but is born from the sea of her mother's womb into the great ocean that will always support her.

Now imagine going deeper, dropping beneath the surface wash of water on the shore and listening to all the voices that travel through the sea.

A great bassoon booms and rumbles: the voice of the bowhead whale, moving north through the crackle of ice and water. High-pitched wails spiral like soprano riffs on a saxophone: the calls of bearded seals. There is a rapid-fire burst of clicking as a pod of white beluga erupts in a high-pitched clatter of whistles and squeals.

Far to the south, another voice loops on the bass note of a cello, throbs repeatedly in a descending growl and then fans out in a sheen of sound, the high-pitched, overlapping harmonics as iridescent as the scales on the skin of a fish. Like a jazz artist, the singer twines his lines with grace notes and winds them into a single current that is broken only when he surfaces for breath – the voice of a male humpback whale, immersed in the changing river of his song.

With his head tilted down in the water, the humpback plays with musical themes and phrases, spinning them new variations in long sessions of continuous song that can last for a day or more at a time. His song is always changing and always the same: during the breeding season all the males in his community sing one song that continually evolves and changes its form. As each small variation in the song rises on the individual voice, it is adopted by the entire community of singers or allowed to fade away.

Nobody knows when certain whales began to sing or what part of their bodies they use to make their haunting music. The oldest fossil remains suggest that the first whale ancestors were small mammals that ate fish and shellfish in shallow rivers and estuaries and gradually moved back entirely into the oceans.

If you could watch the way that these ancestral whales changed form over tens of millions of years, you would see their body shape simplify as they lost their limbs and necks. They became massive, streamlined and sleek, and moved with powerful ease through the water on the thrust of their tail flukes.

At a certain point in their evolution, the ancestral line of all cetaceans – all whales and dolphins – separated into two main branches. The dolphins and porpoises, orcas, sperm whales, narwhals and belugas have teeth, while the baleen whales have baleen fibers hanging from the upper jaw, which they use to filter their food from the water column or the seabed. When they returned to life in the sea, these whale and dolphin ancestors entered a world in which sound was more powerful than sight. Light soon grows dim away from the coastal shallows, but sound moves further and faster through water than it does through air, and it keeps the trace of what it touches. The whales and dolphins live within a three-dimensional world that is structured through their perceptions of sound. They *see* their ocean environment with their ears. The dolphins and the toothed whales use high frequency clicks and whistles that bounce back rapidly enabling them to track fast-moving shoals of fish, while the baleen whales make calls at very low frequencies that travel on long corridors of sound through the oceans. These calls keep the whales connected across great distances, through a network of sound that allows them to pass information to each other about the dense breeding swarms of krill whose location varies from season to season.

At some mysterious turning point in evolution, some of these whistles, moans, whoops, and rumbles took on pattern and rhythm: sound became song. Sperm whales click together like a group of jazz drummers and each individual taps within the leading rhythm, which is carried by the leader of the pod. Many baleen whales sing at ranges far beyond human senses. Below the threshold of our hearing, the voices of fin whales pulse in patterned sequences that may be repeated for a day or more at a time. Deeper still, the calls of blue whales ripple in long, low frequency waves across hundreds or even thousands of miles of open ocean.

Humpbacks are different. These whales sing within the range of the human ear, and their compositions contain patterns that correspond to our own music. Humpback songs last between five and thirty minutes and the notes the whales use, the way they space their notes and alternate between percussion and tone are all familiar from human compositions. Humpback singers often follow a version of the classical sonata structure: they sound a theme, develop and elaborate it, then bring it back in a modified form. And the longer and more complex the song, the more likely it is that the singer will use elements that rhyme, just as humans use rhyme to make patterns in sound. Across millions of years of separate evolution, the voices of the singing humpbacks connect our two species in sounding echoes across the dark of the oceans, born out of the mysterious origin that shapes all music.

Male humpbacks engage in their long sessions of continuous song throughout the breeding season on their tropical mating grounds. The songs are associated with the rituals of courtship and mating, along with spectacular chases and occasional clashes between competing males. Divers among singing humpbacks describe the way the whales' voices reverberate powerfully through the water and ring inside the body of the listener, sending waves of music through blood and muscles and bones. Since each singer has a particular quality of tone and timbre that is recognizable to another, the male humpback's voice must vibrate like touch through the water towards the listening female and resonate inside her own body. When the pair unites, we can imagine their bodies still ringing with all the music that has been pouring into the sea. And when their calf is born twelve months later, it is the offspring of both light and song.

"They are hunters; we are hunters."

On the fourth day of the sea journey, we approach our destination, the small Native settlement of Lorino, on the Bay of Lavrentiya. The village appears as a small cluster of wooden houses rising between the mountainous tundra and the shore, the first sign of human settlement that we have seen in days. This is where the Yupik and Chukchi hunters have resumed their traditional hunt for the gray whales. I have come to observe the hunt for an international organization that makes reports to the International Whaling Commission, a forum originally set up to regulate commercial whaling. Today the IWC maintains the moratorium on commercial whaling and also regulates subsistence whaling by indigenous communities – a rather dark irony, since it was not Native whalers that brought so many whale species to the edge of extinction.

Watching the village approach, I remember the group of seal and walrus hunters that I met on my first journey with Afanassi when they gave us a lift along the coast in their open wooden boat. One, Andrei, was a Chukchi hunter and close friend of Afanassi's. Andrei bred Siberian huskies and he was carrying a puppy as a gift for a relative in another village, a black-nosed bundle of soft white fur that peered out from the shelter of his green oilskins. A second man, whose name I have forgotten, bearded, wearing a tunic with a hunting knife belted at the waist, had brought along a brown bear skin wrapped in canvas.

Then there was Sergei, his eyes creased with smiling behind the blue plastic glasses that he had mended with tape. "Are you frozen, Eleanora?" Sergei would gently inquire from time to time. I always assured him I was fine. Sergei wasn't fooled, though. He would simply smile and offer me another mug of the hot tea that he brewed up constantly in a blackened iron kettle over the small gas burner in the bow. The rest of the time he scanned the water, slowly sweeping his binoculars across the surface. Although they were not hunting at the time, he always signaled to the others when he spotted a seal in the water. The hunters shared a sign language and made different gestures for seal, or walrus or gray whale.

We were halfway through the journey when three dark triangles sliced the water surface – the dorsal fins of a small orca pod. Orcas, which are also known as killer whales, are the largest of the dolphins and they are remarkable for living in distinctive cultures. Some orcas remain in bays and estuaries, eating salmon and other fish. Others have developed a sophisticated hunting culture and they swim long distances in the search for seals. They also hunt gray whales, seeking out inexperienced juveniles or a mother and calf pair and working together to isolate the calf from the mother.

The bodies of young gray whales sometimes washed up on the shore, Sergei told me, showing the scars of orca attacks and missing parts of the jaw and tongue.

The thought of a gentle gray whale mother and her calf coming under such attack was painful, and the orcas' black dorsal fins seemed to slide more darkly through the water. What did he think of the orcas? I asked Sergei. Was he ever afraid of them?

His answer was very simple. "They are hunters. We are hunters. We understand each other."

After we had landed, Afanassi told me a remarkable story about orcas that he had heard from one of his other Chukchi friends. A hunter in this man's village had such a close friendship with one particular orca that it always came to his skin boat if he whistled or called. One day, as this man was returning with several others from hunting walruses, the sea rose and the heavily laden skin boat began to founder. The orca came to help them, bringing the others in its pod and the orcas surrounded the skin boat and swam beside it, supporting it with their backs and sides until they brought boat and hunters safely to shore.

That story of the bond between the hunter and the orca

reminded me of the traditional creation story from the Bering Strait that imagines the origins of this connection between people and whales.

Once there was a young woman who loved to sing. Her songs welled up from her as naturally as breathing and she often walked alone by the seashore singing.

Far out to sea a great whale heard her voice. He was so captivated that he came to the shallow water, scraping his belly against the pebbles and the sand and listened as the young woman sang about the small flowers that opened from the frozen ground in spring and the drumming of ten thousand wing beats above the seabird cliffs in summer. In the young woman's voice, the whale heard the continuous song of the turning Earth, whose only constancy is change and he was so moved that he raised his head above the water to catch a glimpse of the singer's face.

When the whale saw her, he thrust upright on his tail and cast himself onto the shore where she was standing. The moment the whale touched the ground his body was transformed: his great arched tail became his legs and feet; his flippers changed to human hands and he stood before her as a young and beautiful man.

So these creatures from two different worlds met and spoke and they found such love and mutual understanding that they lived together as man and wife by the shore. When their children were born, some came in human shape while others took the form of whales that grew inside the lagoons until they returned to the ocean.

The two lived together for a long time. Their human children grew into skillful hunters of seals and walruses with the deep knowledge of the sea that came from their father, but they knew that they were never to hurt or kill their whale brothers and sisters that had returned to the sea.

After the whale father had died, a season came when the walruses and the seals disappeared and the people were hungry and frightened. Then some looked at the whales that were breathing and breaching so close to the shore and they thought of hunting them. But only one man actually dared to take his skin boat and harpoon and go out to kill one. When he brought the whale's body back, the hunter went at once to his mother and he told her what he had done. She looked at him in silence for a while. "You have killed your brother," she said, and died.

That story is such a poignant expression of the pain of the hunter – the pain that comes from taking the life of a fellow creature, even to sustain your own. Remarkably, it suggests that even though their lives depended on hunting sea mammals, some of the people along the coast of the Bering Strait felt such a close connection to the gray and bowhead whales that they would not kill them even to ensure their own survival. It is little wonder that those who did hunt whales took such pains to purify themselves: they knew that the killing of a great whale was not to be done lightly or without great need.

"We are a People in Darkness."

Coming back to the present, Afanassi and I land by the lagoon outside Lorino village and set up our tent near the shore.

A few days later, in the chill dawn mist, I watch the whale hunters prepare their boats. They lay their rifles and toggling harpoons, which are attached with ropes to floating buoys, on the cross benches, and slide the boats into the water. I get into the boat with Geena, the tall, strongly-built Chukchi, who directs the hunt, and he sets a course that takes us fourteen miles offshore, towards the middle of the Bering Strait. The misty spout of a gray whale rises from the gray-green swell and the hunt begins.

Afterwards, when the long crack of the rifles has ceased, and the whale's body has been roped between two boats through holes cut in her tail flukes and pectoral fins, the hunters remain completely silent. Geena cuts inch-thick slices of skin and blubber, dices it and passes it to the other hunters. While the men eat in silence, images from the hunt throb like wounds across my eyes.

I remember the whale's blowholes pulsing blood through the water as she surfaced on a laborious breath. The way she became exhausted by the drag of the floats attached to the ropes of the toggling harpoons embedded in her flesh. How she lifted her head out of the water, and shoved it against the side of one boat trying to overturn it, while a hunter swayed above her, his lance in hand.

The journey back to Lorino is slow. The boats that tow the whale's body labor through the gray-green swell until the jumble of wooden houses rises from the shore, lit by thin shafts of glaucous light through rents in the heavy cloud. When the whale's body has been brought to the shore and flensed, the village women fill their buckets with the meat, while the children swoop around the remains of the carcass, sucking on strips of the baleen.

Two young girls draw me away from the great, ruined body and we walk together down the shore. One has her small sister by the hand, a little girl maybe four years old. I had seen her dance at a festival a few days before, her round face solemn and braided in her ceremonial fur and beads. "*Krasavitsa*," I tell her now, *Little beauty*, which makes her smile and smile. The older ones tell me stories and copy their names – Tamara, Marina – in careful Cyrillic capitals into my notebook. They tug at my heart, but their company can't dissolve the sadness that I feel.

I have seen seals and walruses hunted and killed before and been grateful when I ate their flesh. Although they use rifles and outboard engines, the people are as dependent on the gray whales for food as their ancestors were. Yet there is something hugely significant about the death of a great whale that cries out to be acknowledged and I long for some way to be reconciled inwardly with her death. If I knew how, I would pray to the whale for her forgiveness. But there are no rituals of consolation any more. No prayers are said in reverence for the whale's spirit. There are no quiet words of gratitude, no murmured benediction to the sea for the life that it has given, as Afanassi's father-in-law, Typykhkak, had made on the day he first killed a bowhead whale.

Later that day, as I sit drinking tea with Geena and Afanassi in the wooden hut where the hunters meet, I begin to understand this wrenching sense of loss and disconnection more deeply.

The Yupik and the Chukchi were the only Native Siberians to successfully resist the Russian Cossack troops which swept across northern Siberia from the late 1700s. They negotiated a formal treaty with the Russians which gave them a degree of independence which they retained until the Soviet government took over their lands from the 1930s. From then on, the Soviet authorities sought to bring these stubbornly independent people under state control: they closed down their small settlements and hunting camps and forced them to move to larger, purpose-built villages such as Lorino. The hunters were forbidden to travel freely or cross the Bering Strait to visit their relatives in the Native communities in Alaska. Instead they were forced to become workers within the state system – hunting walruses and seals to feed caged Arctic foxes that were being bred for their silver winter fur on industrial fur farms. The subsistence whale hunt that was bound up with their culture and their spiritual traditions was banned. Instead the whales were hunted by a Russian industrial whaling ship and their bodies were delivered to be ground up as food for the foxes on the fur farms.

Everything collapsed with the Soviet state. Native people were abandoned; their wages disappeared; deliveries of food and fuel to their villages diminished. Increasingly dependent on the foods they could hunt and gather, Geena and the other hunters had returned to hunting gray whales in order to sustain their communities, as traditional hunters have done in the Arctic for millennia, and to reclaim their dignity, their independence and their sense of self.

Afterwards I stand outside the hut for a while in the chilly gray overcast. The presence of death lies heavy on the beach. Old hanks of whale blubber litter the sand. The whales' blue and lilac intestines wash back and forth in the tide and the wind carries the continuous high-pitched yelping of the caged Arctic foxes from the fur farm that rises on stilts from the tundra behind the village.

It is blackly ironic, I think, that these people, who have the strength, the courage and the independence of spirit to live in one of the most challenging natural environments on Earth should have been made to serve a prison.

A woman, the Yupik elder and community leader, Lyudmila Ainana, takes me still deeper into the story. A slender, gray-haired lady, as fine-boned as a bird, with beautiful high cheekbones and large eyes behind her thick glasses, Ainana is the Chukotka delegate to the Inuit Circumpolar Conference, which brings indigenous people together from around the Arctic, and she works closely with Geena and the other hunters to help them to support their communities.

When I ask her about the significance of the Whale Alley shrine on Yttygran Island Ainana shakes her head and sighs. I believe that people went there once for the ceremony of the Blessing of the Sea, she says; but it is hard to learn anything about our traditions. Often we only learn about them from the foreigners.

"We are a people in darkness," she says. These words are uttered quietly, but with intense feeling. She takes me to the large map of the coastline that hangs on the wall of the office and shows me the network of small settlements that once occupied every cape and headland. The map reveals the original pattern of life along the Siberian coast of the Bering Strait, when the Native people hunted and gathered their food according to the rhythms of the year. Many of these sites had been continuously occupied, generation after generation, for more than two thousand years.

Nearly all were emptied when the people were forced to move into large villages and their lives ordered by the Soviet administration.

Ainana shows me the site where she was born; when the soldiers came they gave her family just one day to leave. The elders died rapidly, because they could not bear the loss of their old way of life and the customs and traditions that gave it meaning. The young children were taken from their parents and placed in boarding schools, where they were taught only in Russian, given new names and Russian food to eat. Separated from their families, the children were also cut off from their own language at a young age. This loss of intimacy with the native tongue is particularly traumatic for people living in oral tradition, in which words live on the breath of the speaker. The decline of the Native languages made a great rift between the generations. It broke the continuity of the cultural and spiritual traditions and set the young people adrift, unsure how to express themselves in either tongue.

Ainana tells me that her own uncle had been a spiritual guardian of the connections between the people and the animals. When he knew that he was dying, he requested that all his ritual objects be buried with him, for he saw nobody left to whom he could entrust his sacred knowledge or his gifts.

The story strikes me painfully and I turn and look directly into her face – this slender, gray-haired lady in her soft, woolen cap, with her graceful cheekbones and large eyes behind thick glasses. For a moment she seems to shift, to become light-boned and soft-breasted, feathered and plumed like a bird.

Owl-woman. Night woman. Watcher.

Then I turn my face away, trying to hide the strong upwelling of emotion and I look at the old place names on the map again.

Syllables of belonging. House without walls. Emptiness on the air.

"Everything that exists, lives."

A few days later, Afanassi and I head north to Akanni, one of those ancestral settlements which were forcibly emptied in the 1950s. But Akanni is being brought back to life: Geena and other hunters have begun to rebuild the abandoned houses and he has invited us to visit him there.

Akanni is set on a headland, where the steeply cut mountains step sharply out of the water. We land on a narrow strip of gravel beneath a path that winds up to the small cluster of wooden houses on the headland and the moment that I step onto the shingle, the weight of sadness I have carried since the whale hunt at Lorino begins to lift. The rising current of renewed energy is so immediate and so strong that I remark on it to Afanassi.

Akanni feels like a good place, I tell him. "The elders always chose their sites wisely," he agrees, waving to Geena, who is coming down the path with an older man, white-haired and bearded, who introduces himself as Sergei. They help us to unload the boat and bring our gear to one of the wooden cabins on the headland. Inside, Geena's mother lights the seal oil lamp, an oval dish of oil whose flame burns hotly, casting a dusky yellow light over the wooden table, the bare walls and the pressed earth floor. The walrus-gut parka she has made hangs in the corner shadows, hooded and translucent in the light of the seal oil lamp. She has stitched the parka's seams with seal ligaments and they will swell in water and make it completely waterproof when it is worn at sea.

A softly-spoken young hunter called Viktor has also arrived by boat and he sits down with us at the table. Viktor and I had met the first time I came here; after I left he wrote me a letter, and asked a British explorer who was trying to walk across the sea ice to Alaska to give it to me. Viktor knew only my first name, and that I lived in London. Months later, through a series of improbable coincidences, somebody actually delivered me his letter, which he had placed inside a beaded sealskin pouch.

I begin telling Viktor and the others how astonished I was to receive it, then stop. I can sense that none of the others finds this strange. His message was sent. It arrived. That is natural. I fall silent as Geena's mother puts fresh seal-meat, cooked in a stock of blood, roots and seaweed on the table, slices the meat on a wooden platter, and passes the broth to us in a bowl. It tastes, I tell her truthfully, like one of the most wonderful meals I have eaten in my entire life.

The following morning I walk down to the beach below the headland, wading across a fast shallow stream that runs into the sea. The small stones – blue, white, yellow – flash and dart through eddies of sunlight on the water. The banks of tufted grasses rise on layers of whalebone and I walk on crumbling shells bleached white as bone.

It is the beginning of September, the time the Yupik call *green shines golden*. To the north, the mountains are streaked with the purple, blue and gold of early autumn and a cool lavender light spreads across the sky.

This journey has taken me through such extremes. The sense of expansion and profound connection that began in the sacred space on Yttygran Island has collided with the harshness of reality – the pain of witnessing the gray whale's death, and seeing how the people themselves have been forcibly uprooted from their foundations. In my mind I can still see the faces of some of the men, raw with the industrial alcohol in which they seek refuge from the pain of emptiness and loss. I remember the look in Ainana's eyes as she told me the story of her uncle, that clear-eyed man facing death, who refused any of the false consolations of continuity and took his sacred knowledge with him when he died.

The stories of the Native people of Chukotka – the violent uprooting, the contempt for their knowledge and wisdom, the deliberate shattering of their language and spiritual relationship with the land and sea – are not unique. They are stories from the great dispossession that takes place where the indigenous nations are confronted with the arrogance and the ruthless force of the industrial powers. These stories of disconnection and loss are repeated where those people who still live in spiritual connection to the Earth and cosmos are confronted by the industrial powers that would turn it into a wasteland, a mirror of their own desolation.

In the end, indigenous nations around the world are being made homeless not only in the physical, but in the psychological and spiritual sense, because they are the ones who still hold the wisdom that is directly opposed to the plundering, egocentric mind that views the Earth as mere commodity and resource. If those of us who live within the industrial cultures could listen to their voices with some humility, we would see our present madness much more clearly. We would realize that treating the Earth and other living creatures as mere commodities to be traded and exploited is utterly insane.

In the indigenous wisdom traditions, the physical world – the sun and other stars, the Earth herself and all her creatures – is the manifestation of consciousness. *Everything that exists lives*, the Chukchi shaman said, as he tried to communicate this fundamental understanding. In the same way, the Kogi people, one of the indigenous nations of South America, describe the physical world as the trace of thought – of consciousness. They call this consciousness within nature *Aluna*.

In the indigenous wisdom traditions, the Earth and cosmos are sensitive and alive, imbued with the intense presence that we may call sacredness. The energies of creation continually pulse through the patterns and cycles of the physical cosmos and sustain them in their courses; in these energies there is no division. While we humans live in physical form the other creatures feed and clothe us. With gratitude and reverence for their gifts we are raised up in consciousness, out of the small egocentric self, into the space of light where life is known and recognized as one. In the space of light, the divisions the ordinary mind makes between skin colors and cultures disappear. We're all native here, in this realm of blossoming and becoming, where all our breaths hold birth and death and each one is indigenous to the Earth.

The sea breaks in a surf of foam and glitter on the shore and hisses over the white shells and bones. Slowly, with scarcely perceptible gentleness, I feel the boundaries that enclose my body and my mind dissolve, allowing the waves of the sea to foam and break inside. Sacred space is within; sacred space is without. Sacredness beyond the forms of culture and time; that can never be utterly lost however the forms in which it is received may change, because it lives in the essence of every stone, in the shells and bones, in the vanes on the feather of a bird, in the gray whale's mighty exhalations, in the intangible, everywhere light.

And in my heart, in my heart.

Presence, returning again with every breath, ripples of renewal borne in on waves, on the breaking sea.

Several days later.

The Bering Strait is a wide spread of dark water, tossing in steel-blue surges as we head back into the Senyavin Strait through high winds and a turbulent sea. I cling to the edge of the bench as the boat rises, hangs on a wave crest and lurches into the trough. The strip of canvas set across the bow is no protection against the wind and the salt spray stings with my face with cold. There is a choppy run of waves, and then another rises still more steeply.

The boat climbs, hovers, and drops into the trough with a thud that almost jerks me off the bench. Tossed between salt and darkness, for the first time I feel afraid of the immense indifference of the sea, uncoiling in a small part of its power beneath us.

Afanassi calls to me to stand up, telling me it will be easier. I shake my head at him, holding tightly to the bench. But he insists; keeping one hand on the tiller, he takes hold of my hand, draws me upright, puts the other arm around me and holds me firmly in front of him.

Bend your knees, he says, as another wave mounts. When the boat rises to the crest, I stagger back against him, but he holds me steady. The boat rises and falls with the pitch and drop of the waves, and he continues to hold me tirelessly, helping me to find balance with an assurance that is beyond any physical strength, aligned with the point of inner equilibrium that allows him to be carried with the motions of the sea.

Hours later, soaked through, shaken and very tired, we land at the small village of Yanrakynnot. And that's where I meet my friend Sergei again, with his cracked blue plastic glasses and his tolerant, accepting smile. He helps us to unload the boat and pull it higher up the shore. After we have talked for a while, he reaches into his jacket pocket, takes out a small piece of worked walrus ivory and hands it to me.

The walrus tusk is engraved with a polar bear walking over the sea ice. I can see that the bear is hunting – his head is lifted, smelling the air as he stalks a ringed seal lying at the edge of the breathing hole in the ice. The great ice bear himself, *Nanuq*, the most powerful of all the animal guides and helpers for the Arctic shamans. When I turn the tusk over, I see the figure of the human hunter engraved on the other side; he is cloaked and hooded, and he drags the seal's body home across the sea ice.

They are hunters. We are hunters, Sergei had told me. I thank him for his gift with all my heart and put the walrus tusk away in my own pocket. I have kept it with me ever since.

On the last day of our sea journey, Afanassi tells me that he has something to show me. Leaving the boat pulled up on the shore, we follow a track through the mountainous tundra until the strait and all the islands have disappeared from view. The ground becomes warmer as we climb. When we emerge on the slope above a fast-flowing river, hot thermal water is pouring from the mountain and filling a deep pool, lined with smooth sections of whalebone.

There is a second pool among the rocks on the riverbank, Afanassi says, where the hot thermal water flows into the river and mixes with the cold currents. "That place is a little bit mystical," he adds, with a smile. He is teasing me gently and I have to laugh. But he's right – the river's rolling, cold gray power draws me further down the slope and when I reach the rocks where the thermal water meets the river I take off all my heavy clothes until I am naked and shivering and enter the pool. Soon I can no longer tell which current feels hot or cold against my skin. There is only the one, gray river of fire, running past me forever, bringing the gift of aliveness in the taste of cold stone on the tongue.

3 Sedna's Story

Around the Arctic basin, the creative power within the sea has been represented by a female figure. Her name is Sedna and she is sometimes known as the Food Dish, because she is the source of nourishment for the people. The whales and the other sea mammals first came from her fingers. They were her gift and she could withhold them if the people did not respect their life.

Although Sedna embodies the life-giving power of the ocean, she is not a deity or goddess in the Western sense. She is a mortal woman who undergoes a powerful transformation, just as the shamans do when they pass through a profound experience of death and rebirth. Different versions of Sedna's transformation have been recorded around the Arctic and each person who told her story would have brought to it something of their own particular life experience. This retelling of Sedna's story was inspired by my own meeting with the gray whales in their birthing lagoons and the whales' willingness to meet us in shared peace.

I slept on the shingle by the hiss of the sea, and the night brought a dream on the breath that rose from that furnace of cold – Sedna's story, guardian of the sea mammals, the giver and receiver of life through the sea.

Sedna's hair rippled like a river through the darkness.

She lived with her father in a tent made of reindeer skin, and they followed the herds together across the great tundra plain. Her father was her constant companion and the only family she had left, for her mother had died when she was still a child.

While she lived, Sedna's mother had taught her daughter how to make skin clothes that were supple and warm and light. They carved fine needles from the delicate bones of the birds, and sewed parkas from the reindeer's summer hide and trimmed the hoods with the fur of wolverine and wolf. In summer they gathered red alder bark and yellow lichens to color the skins and they sat together outside the tent sewing, and braiding the seams with the auk and guillemot feathers which they had gathered together on the seashore.

Those summer days when the sun circled the sky and never touched the ground seemed endless. There were no divisions in the continuous fall of light to separate one day from the next, only the clear suspension of time in which the day turned through one circle of light. The changes came so slowly they could scarcely be seen at first. Each evening the sun slid a little closer to the ground before it rose again on another arc of the one, continuous day. Until the evening came when it sank for the first time, darkening the sky to violet and streaking the horizon red.

That was the day Sedna's mother told her that the clothes they were making together did not only keep the people warm. The animals' bodies are the clothes that they wear in this world, she said. By making something beautiful, we honor the gift and their spirits feel it.

Our own bodies are only clothes that we wear for while, her mother added. We put them on when we come here from the other worlds where the clothes are so fine, they could have been spun like spiders' webs from light.

The shapes of this world are always changing, Sedna's mother said then. They are like waves rising on the sea of light. She spoke quietly, but there was so much feeling in her voice that Sedna always kept that memory of her mother – sitting in a pool of late summer sunlight, her strong, graceful hands, stained with red alder, resting on the skins, while she spoke about the animals and waves rising on a great sea of light.

During the dark winter nights, when the rivers turned to

roads of ice and the wind made the skin tent shake, her mother told stories. She spoke about their animal ancestors, who had their own houses and lands in the other worlds, and she told stories of Raven, that enigmatic power that had first brought light into the world.

Raven was tired of shivering in the darkness, her mother said. The old man of the world had hidden the sun away and Raven resolved to trick him into releasing it.

But first he had to enter the old man's house. So Raven changed shape: he became a tiny seed and dropped into the cup of drinking water which the old man's daughter had just drawn from the stream. He slipped down her throat and settled in her belly, where he grew until he emerged as a baby from her womb.

The miserly old man was delighted with the child. He opened the box where he had hidden the sun away and gave him a brief glimpse of its warmth and beauty; but when the child tried to reach out and grasp the glowing treasure, the old man shut it away from him again.

Raven thought hard: how could he trick the miserly old man into releasing the sun? Finally he persuaded the old man to play a game with him, tossing the sun high into the air and throwing it back and forth between them like a ball. It was the first time the old man had played with a child in many years and he got so caught up in the delight of seeing the sun fly back and forth between them, that he let Raven catch and keep it.

As he held the sun in his hands, Raven was transformed. He became a mighty bird, with spreading black wings and a powerful beak. He caught the sun in his beak and flew with it into the heavens, where it became the fiery blaze that has lit the entire world since then and given light and warmth to every creature.

Sedna loved that story. She imagined the great bird Raven soaring through the night with the seed of all the world's sunlight held within his beak. But Raven was a tricky character in many ways, she thought. Seed or child or man or bird – how could you ever know what shape he would take next? He had such a gift for change that he could wriggle through the walls of the world like a fish through water.

As Sedna grew, the dark grief that opened at her mother's death seemed to close again. She became a young woman with a shining fall of long black hair, skilled at making richly-colored clothes. Many young men were drawn by her beauty and the skill of her hands, but she refused them all. She thought that she would always live like this, and she had no wish for anything else to change.

Perhaps that was why she never again went back to the sea. In summer her father always walked to the coast alone and he gathered the beaks and feathers of the auks and guillemots that she used to decorate her clothes. Until the day came when her father did not return from the coast alone: a stranger walked beside him, wearing a cloak of dried fish skin that gave off gray and silver shimmers in the sunlight as he moved.

The stranger's hair was black as a raven's wing and his voice was hoarse. But his words were so vivid and compelling that they conjured up all the forgotten wonders of the ocean – the mineral glitter in the scales of the fish and the rhythmic pounding of the sea against the rocks. That evening the quiet containment of Sedna's life sprung open and she promised to marry the stranger and live with him at the edge of the sea.

Sedna's father tried hard to dissuade her. The man was a stranger; how could she trust herself to him? But the pattern of her old life was broken and her father's words rang hollow. He promised that if she ever needed him, he would come to help her, and then he watched her walk away with the stranger until their figures merged with the tundra plain.

They followed the course of a stone-gray river towards the coast. Soon the air grew thick with the cries of the birds and they reached the shore where the waves broke with a hiss of foaming bubbles on the rocks. For a long time Sedna watched the changing flow of light and color in the water, then she turned to her companion – and stood in shock. For all around his body the outline of a great-beaked bird was taking shape on the air, with black wings spread wide across the day, and a light burning at its breast, so pure and bright it turned the daylight pale.

Sedna turned in fear from this vision of the Raven's power, burning through the curtain of the air and she ran between the jagged rocks hammered by the unending sea. On she ran until she came to a small hollow in the cliffs where she could hide and there she took the cold coils of seaweed and damp mosses for her bed and wept in loneliness and fear amid the endless screaming of the birds.

The wind carried her cries to her father and he came as quickly as he could to find her, paddling his small skin boat up the coast. When Sedna saw her father's boat on the water she waded out to meet him and they pulled away from the shore.

But the sky was darkening; the wind rose and lashed the wave tips white and their small boat began to pitch and heave. Her father felt the boat get heavy and labor in the swell, and the storm entered him with a piercing wind of fear. He seemed to feel his small boat sinking, the water rising to his mouth, and thinking only to save himself, he caught his daughter and threw her into the sea.

Sedna clung to the edge of the boat, bewildered by the shock and sudden cold. But her father had become mindless with fear, and drawing out his knife, he hacked through her fingers, one by one.

The waters closed over her head and Sedna sank beneath the waves. Down she went through the luminous clouds of drifting plankton, sinking through the water until the roar of the storm waves receded and all around her was the immense blue space and silence of the sea. Down she sank, further and still further, until she was met at last by a living presence like the warmth of sunlight in the water and she heard a voice speak softly in her mind.

The shapes of this world are always changing, her mother's voice said. They are like waves rising on the sea of light.

The sea of light.

The walls of the blue-gray water opened and Sedna entered the light on which the entire perceptible world is floating, drifting, dying and being remade. It held all the love that she had ever thought was lost, broken and betrayed, and letting go entirely, she gave herself to the light at the heart of the sea.

On the surface, the wind dropped. The small boat rocked between the wreckage of the storm and her father sat and wept, a lost, bewildered man who had woken to find his nightmare real. Seeing how he tormented himself with guilt and grief, Sedna reached across the worlds to touch and comfort him. But her father was so lost in grief that he could not feel her subtle touch and he thought only of the terrible betrayal he had made.

That impulse was not lost. It entered Sedna's severed fingers and quickened them with life and they began to change. They shifted and transformed – and a white-skinned, black-eyed beluga arched into the sea. A piebald orca followed. A narwhal appeared, with a great ivory tusk spiraling from its forehead. And then the waters opened around the bodies of the great whales – the blue, the fin, the humpback, the gray and the bowhead whales. The whales rolled through the surface and misted the air with the wind of their breathing. The water crackled, whooped and rumbled with the intense joy of their calls and greetings. Then, for one moment, it was still, before swelling for the first time with the long, undulating melodies of their songs.

The waves of whale song beat on the hull of the skin boat where Sedna's father sat and wept. They shook it. They made it resonate like a deep-toned drum. A whale rolled alongside him through the water, and moved by something he did not understand Sedna's father put out his hand and touched it on the side.

The touch pierced through his guilt and grief to enter his heart, and it woke the memory of the freedom that is beyond all separation and every thought of loss. And so it was that Sedna's father became the first person to find rest for his heart on the breath and gliding of the whale, for he had witnessed the power of transformation that is borne on the back of grace.

Sedna herself, it is said, went still deeper into the ocean of light until she became utterly one with its essence, and she dwells within it to this very day.

4 The Shaman's Journey

When I was a child I was afraid of drowning. The Atlantic breaks with a tremendous roar on the Irish west coast, and the gray-white waves are caustic with cold even in the brilliant wind-whipped light of summer. Unable to swim until much later, I stayed in the shallows and watched the ocean's immense reach and return. I loved the ocean, but I feared it too and that experience of growing up so close to its power made Sedna's story very real for me the first time I came across it.

Sedna's story also touches me for deeply personal reasons. I grew up in a family where alcoholism and other addictions caused a great deal of emotional suffering and I saw how suffering becomes a legacy that is passed on through the generations, until it can be transformed through finding the inner freedom from which true forgiveness comes. When I was young, I buried the hurt and anger and sought forgiveness through the will, by trying to forget the past. Although this was right and necessary at the time, it cannot last. You cannot open fully to the creativity of life when you have closed so much of your self away. True forgiveness is beyond the will alone – rising as the expression of inner freedom, it comes from the greater consciousness beyond the personality and the ego-driven mind.

What I found in this story is an archetypal account of that inner transformation. It is, for me, the story of any woman or man who transcends painful experiences by realizing the creative essence within, at the very core of their own being. Although it appears harsh in many ways, this is ultimately a profound story of renewal, losing something essential and finding it again, at a much deeper level than before.

When I read it first, I thought the story as severe and simple as coastal rock. As I looked more deeply, patterns emerged – a young girl, alone with her father, who clings to the familiar and does not want to change. A birdman who lives by the sea. A

storm and a terrible betrayal, driven by fear. A miraculous transformation that brings new life into the ocean.

Like an illuminated dream, all these figures and events evoke
aspects of inner experience and the workings of the psyche and
the soul. As a young girl, Sedna reacts to the pain of her mother's
death by trying to remain adolescent, protected by her father. But
she cannot close out change forever and when the mysterious
stranger arrives from the sea, he wakes her dormant life from
sleep, stirring the flow of sexual energy, which has been dammed
through her emotional reliance on her father. But this stranger is
more than human – he is as much bird as man. In some versions
he is associated with the fulmar, a powerful and wide-ranging
seabird, or with Raven, the power which first brought light into
the world.

The bird is a perennial image for the human soul and the
mysterious birdman represents creative energy at a higher level –
Sedna's own soul. By promising to marry him, she makes the
commitment to unite with it; in that moment of vision on the
seashore, she sees clearly what this represents – creative light so
bright the light of day itself seems pale. The magnitude of the
power frightens her and she runs from it, crying to her father for
help, the one person who represents safety and stability. But
when he is faced with the power of the storm that threatens to
capsize the boat, her father cannot be the strong parent she
wanted, and imagined him to be. He cannot find the inner calm
that would carry them safely through the storm. Overmastered
by his fear, he tries to save himself by casting his daughter into
the sea.

It is a lacerating image of disconnection – parent from child,
masculine from feminine. But as she sinks down, into the
immense blue space of quiet below the surface raging of the
storm, Sedna hears her mother's voice again, for the first time
since she was a child. *The sea of light* – the light of Eternal
Presence, which is her own deepest reality. As Sedna gives herself

entirely to the light, she is transformed. This transformation is so complete and powerful that her fingers, which had once stitched such beautiful, richly-colored clothes, become the living whales that move fluidly with the changing motions of the sea – consciousness taking new form, presence that shares peace.

One of the most moving aspects of Sedna's story is the unpredictable nature of this transformation. Who could have known that such pain and darkness could be changed into new life and beauty? The story expresses the freedom of the Spirit to bring healing and renewal from even the darkest places, overturning the categories and expectations of the ordinary mind.

The Journey to the One Who Knows

When Arctic peoples feared they had lost their own inner connection to life, they turned to Sedna for help. The Arctic shaman travelled inwardly to meet her, carrying the prayers of the people for the return of the animals and the renewal of connection with their life.

The shaman did not make the journey to Sedna alone. The spirit of the polar bear went with them, sharing its power and taking them down through the ocean until the shaman saw at last a great light shining through the water. This was the light where Sedna dwelt. When the shaman entered, she sat with her back to them, her gaze on the flame of a burning oil lamp, her long hair flowing unbound down her back. It was beautiful hair, rich and dark and shining, but since Sedna could not comb it without fingers, it had become tangled and knotted. The shaman sat at Sedna's back, and began to gently undo each knot and tangle. This was very intricate and demanding work; it took great sensitivity and concentration, for each knot represented a contraction in the human mind and heart that was blocking the free flow of life. The shaman worked patiently and carefully until every one of the tight knots had been released and Sedna's hair flowed freely again, a warm living river, down her back.

For me, the shaman's journey through the ocean to find and release the knots and tangles of Sedna's hair evokes the inner journey that each person makes to the deeper levels of awareness, to find and release painfully-contracted feelings in the psyche in the stillness of conscious presence. The shaman's journey also recalls the gray whales. When the grays go down to the sea floor to feed, they comb the sediments and filter them through their baleen, just as the shaman combs Sedna's hair to release the tangled and contracted energies of life. In the gray whales' wake, currents of fresh energy rise as the life that would otherwise have stagnated beneath the weight of drifted sediments is renewed.

This is the dynamic of every natural habitat. Nature is always in transformation. And the same dynamic is at work in the inner world, down among the turbid sediments where we lay away painful memories and feelings of guilt and anger. Without the touch of living consciousness in the depths of the psyche to release buried feelings and bring freedom, inner renewal is blocked and there is no way to find genuine release from the past.

The shaman's journey represents the conscious seeking out of that inner renewal. As you open up to greater life, buried emotions are also stirred naturally and they begin to rise to the surface. Sometimes they rise in powerful emotional storms and these releases of emotion can feel quite traumatic. It may even seem that part of the ordinary personality is unraveling. But the buried feelings are being brought to the surface so that the inner life may be renewed. Just as the currents and upwellings renew the life of the ocean by bringing nutrients from the bottom to the light-filled waters of the surface, so the upwellings of emotion may also bring renewal when they are brought to the light of the greater consciousness that is beyond the mind.

In the mystical traditions, the work of consciously recognizing and releasing the unconscious thought patterns and emotions is known as the way of the witness. The witness holds the inner space in which restrictive emotional patterns and the residues of painful experiences are acknowledged, released from guilt and blame and given freely to the light that brings complete healing and the freedom of forgiveness. The next journey takes the way of the witness, with the spirit of the wolf for help and guidance to see more clearly among the unconscious shadows in the mind.

The Book of Wolf

Eyes of the Wolf

There was once a great wizard who wanted to give all the animals human shape. He succeeded in making appear human only the eyes of the wolf.
A story from the oral tradition of the Bella Coola Indians of North America.
Have you ever looked at what's around you through the wolf's eyes?
Dr. Jason Badridze

1 The Man Who Lived among Wolves: The Story of Jason Badridze

Tbilisi, Georgia
There are times when you meet a person and immediately feel at ease with them. It was like that the first time I met Dr. Jason Badridze – an instant sense of familiarity and warmth. I was in Georgia, the small republic in the Caucasus, writing about the

country's efforts to protect its wilderness areas when some of the nature reserve staff suggested that I meet him. They told me he had trained as a neurophysiologist and been professor of Ecology and Vertebrate Behavior at Tbilisi University. He was also the leading researcher on wolves in the Caucasus region, and he had raised orphaned wolf cubs himself and returned them to the wild.

Jason picked me up from the friend's flat where I always stayed in Tbilisi: in his fifties, compact and bearded, with dark oriental eyes and a beaky nose, his gaze was open and direct behind his glasses, and there was a vivid sense of humor dancing in their depths. He kept a pile of small change on the dashboard of his jeep, and whenever an elderly man or woman knocked on his window to beg at the traffic lights, he always passed them a few coins. "Hard times," he said briefly, "especially for the old."

Driving through the narrow streets of Tbilisi's old city, past the houses of crumbling, saffron-colored stone with their enclosed, Moorish-style balconies on the upper levels, we soon discovered that we knew some of the same people.

"Ah, I am very happy that you know my blood brothers!" he exclaimed in his extravagant Georgian-Russian-accented English. Jason's "blood brothers" were several dedicated Russian biologists who raise orphaned bear cubs and wolf pups and return them to the wild. I had got to know them all when I visited their research center deep in the Russian *taiga* forest. The center had been founded by one of Jason's closest colleagues, the renowned brown bear biologist Professor Valentine Pazhetnov, whose son-in-law, Volodya, also raises orphaned wolf cubs. (We will meet all these people later.)

That evening, as we sat in his flat talking over a bottle of the excellent Georgian red wine, Jason told me an episode from his life which I found so extraordinary, so unexpected and compelling that it could have come from the pages of a magical story rather than the life of a scientist.

When Jason was young, he had gone alone to a remote part of the Borjomi forest, in the mountains of the central Georgian Caucasus. He was looking for wolves. He wanted to find a wolf pack that would become so accustomed to his presence he could approach them closely and observe their daily lives.

At the time, this was new territory for a wolf biologist. It is very difficult to observe wild wolves in a forest – their lives are hidden among the trees and dense undergrowth, and revealed through their tracks and droppings and the remains of their kills rather than direct observation. Until radio collars and telemetry made it possible to track wolves from a distance, researchers learned about forest packs by following their trails on foot or ski and trying to understand the traces that they found.

It was rare for them to see a wild wolf at all. Long persecution has made wolves wary of human beings and they are very skilled at avoiding us. One American researcher, Doug Smith – who later took charge of reintroducing wolves to Yellowstone Park, in North America – spent ten field seasons traveling on foot and ski through wolf habitat on Isle Royale. During that entire period, he saw wolves from the ground only three times. Many researchers into animal behavior – also known as ethologists – watched wolves in captivity instead and studied their body language and ways of relating to each other. However, this approach to understanding wolves had an obvious disadvantage – wolves are wideranging animals and when they are confined, certain aspects of their behavior become distorted. To watch wolves behave naturally in the wild, a few researchers traveled to remote parts of the treeless Arctic tundra where it was possible to observe the wolves openly in summer.

Jason, though, wanted to do things differently, and he began by trying to understand things from the *wolves'* point of view.

"At first I had no idea how I could possibly make contact with those wolves or even come close enough to see them. I knew they were being hunted by the forest rangers because the only information I could find on them came from a government pamphlet telling hunters how they could track and kill them, so I decided that the first thing these wolves absolutely *must* understand is that I am not a danger to them.

I went to the rangers and I told them they were to keep out of that part of the forest. That wasn't easy! I used bad words; I talked very tough to them. Secondly, I decided that these wolves must always know my smell. So the whole time I was living in the forest I always wore the same clothes."

Jason followed the tracks and scat left by a small resident wolf pack and he began to put out deer meat for them at certain places in their territory. Then, in one sudden, heart-stopping moment, he came upon the adult male and female, the pack's mated pair. His first, instinctive reaction was to try to distract their attention away from him – he tossed the meat he was carrying before them on the ground.

The wolves ignored the meat, and the male took a few steps closer.

"When the male was a few yards away from me he stopped. I saw him look at me and it seemed to me that he was puzzled, that he could not understand what I wanted, why I did not seem to be a danger to him. Then the two wolves ran off into the trees and after they were gone I realized how frightened I'd been. I was shaking."

Some connection had been made during that brief meeting; in the months that followed it Jason regularly came upon the mated pair with the three others in their pack. The wolves, it seemed, were just as curious about this strangely benign, always solitary man whose presence had sent the hunters away. Finally Jason left the ranger's hut, which had been his base until then and began to live among them. He ran with them when they hunted and he slept near them on their *rendezvous sites* – the places where wolves gather while the pups are too young to travel very far with the adults.

"When these wolves had fully adapted to me, I lived with them. I took no tent. I had only the Caucasus shepherd's coat, which is made from felt. You can sleep outdoors even in rain and cold and stay dry and warm. I lived and worked alongside the wolves and when they accepted to let me follow them hunting, we often went for 30 or 40 kilometers a day together. I was young then, and I was very strong.

I lived for two years with these wolves in the Borjomi forest. During this time, I spent around 1,500 hours actively relating to them, sometimes at night, sometimes during the day. I never touched any of the wolves – I always stayed some distance away from them – and never once were they aggressive towards me. After some time, they let me take deer meat for myself from their kills – once they had eaten themselves, of course.

Those wolves were my teachers. Before I lived with them, I had been trying to analyze animal behavior even though I didn't know enough to understand what the behavior was really about."

I'd never seen a wild wolf when I first met Jason, and I had no direct experience of what he told me that evening, but I often thought about his story after I left Tbilisi. He had gone to the forest as a scientist: he wanted to observe as closely and accurately as he could how wolves really live in the wild. While he was among them, he'd been careful to respect the wolves' own space and keep certain important boundaries – he'd never come too close and he'd never made any attempt to touch them. Yet his work had taken him beyond the limits of scientific observation of wild animals and plunged him into the stream of living relationship with them.

There was one image in particular that kept recurring in my mind – the figure of Jason asleep on the ground, alone in the darkness among the animals which, almost more than any other, have embodied certain human fears of the uncontrollable, instinctual, unpredictable wild. Few of us will ever see a wild wolf, but their presence still carries a powerful elemental charge into dreams and storytelling, and that image of Jason asleep on the ground among wolves, with its dreamlike, fairy-tale quality, spoke powerfully to me of trust and the possibility of making a new connection across the barriers of fear.

War on Wolves

Tver, Western Russia 2003

It was not long after that first meeting with Jason that I got an email from one of the biologists at the Russian research center, which had been established by his "blood brother" the brown bear biologist Dr. Valentine Pazhetnov. Valentine's son-in-law Volodya wrote that tens of thousands of wolves – around one-third of the entire population – were being killed across Russia each year. Volodya called the mass cull Russia's *War on Wolves* and he'd begun to rescue some of the orphaned cubs and raise them himself in the hope they might someday return to the wild.

It was late January when I went to Russia to write about the wolf cull; the dense *taiga* forest was wrapped in deep snow and all the lakes were frozen. Volodya took me across the ice by sled to the island where he kept the four young wolves he had rescued as cubs from the hunters and I stood on the bank and watched them race shoulder to shoulder across the ice. Around ten months old, from the same litter, the wolves all had the boisterous enthusiasm of young adolescents. They would skitter to a sudden halt, roll around each other on the ice, play-wrestling and jaw-biting, and tug at neck and shoulders with their teeth in rough expressions of affection which showed how much pleasure they took in physical contact with each other.

The wolves were maybe fifty yards away on the ice when one of them stopped tussling with his siblings and looked towards the bank where I was standing.

I felt the change in his attention – it was like a prickling on the surface of my skin. The wolf began to walk towards the bank, moving slowly at first, then more confidently as he picked up the elastic trot which is a wolf's most characteristic gait. Unsure how to respond, I simply stood and watched him approach. About ten yards away, his body language changed completely: he lowered himself towards the ice and crawled towards me with his ears flattened. He was giving me the signals that convey deference among wolves and I realized that he was simply young and curious about the human tribe.

Before the wolf could reach the bank, Volodya came across the ice on his snowmobile and chased him off: he wanted to keep the wolves away from visitors who were not used to being around them. Volodya was their parent and their teacher, the emotional center of their life in captivity; he'd spent days and sleepless nights with them when they were small and helpless; he'd fed them and kept them warm.

He sat on the sled, absorbed in watching them, a medieval-monkish figure in a belted brown tunic and boots, and when the wolves were tired of playing, they clustered around him in open displays of wolfish adoration. They were keenly interested in other people too. A few days later, one of the females came close to me and leapt up, placing her front paws against my shoulders. A wolf's feet are huge. I felt her weight press on me and stood still, mindful of Volodya's warning to remain in a dominant position above the wolves at all times and never back off from them. Looking down, I met bright amber eyes not far below my own.

A wolf's gaze is very searching, with the energy of attention that you do not often meet in human eyes. I wanted to reach out my hands and touch her, but I knew this was no dog to be petted or caressed. Then I felt something entirely different: a subtle point of warmth that opened at the center of my chest and expanded towards her in warm waves of invisible connection.

There were many wild wolves in the immense *taiga* forest and when I went out walking in the evenings I sometimes heard them howl. One evening I walked out at dusk with Volodya's father Viktor, a laconic, slightly melancholy man, with an ironic sense of humor that I enjoyed. Viktor had spent much of his life around wolves and one of the things he liked best was to howl and hear them respond. We walked together to a bluff from which his voice would carry and he cupped his hands around his mouth and howled – a long, wavering swell, breaking off from the high pitch and slowly tipping into silence.

"You try," he suggested. "Sometimes they prefer a woman's voice."

I didn't know if I could at first, but almost without effort, the howl came through me, as though some part had picked up one of the voices of the Earth and allowed it rise into the distance, into the night and faintly, far off, the voices of the wolves rose in answer.

That voice, with its piercing, untempered pitch and wavering slide – it touches you with a sense of something you once knew much more clearly, something essential which you've forgotten between the flickering distraction of your thoughts.

The howling of wolves could have been heard once across much of the northern hemisphere. Fed on European fairy tales, the imagination places wolves in the dark, tangled forests of the North, but living wolves are far larger than the ideas and images we have of them in the West. Wolves do not belong to one landscape, culture or climate: they know how to thrive in many places and they hunt a great variety of prey. Their original range spanned much of the northern hemisphere above 35 degrees of latitude, all the way from the High Arctic tundra into the deserts of Arabia.

Flexible, adaptable and enduring, wolves are superb travellers that have padded across the Arctic sea ice to reach remote islands, such as Wrangel off the north coast of Siberia. They hunt lemmings, hares, caribou and muskox across the Arctic and sub-Arctic tundra; they track through dense northern forests to bring down elk, moose and deer, and they hunt swift gazelles in the deserts of Central Asia, Saudi Arabia and Northern India.

Biologists distinguish a number of subspecies or geographically distinct populations of gray wolves (*Canis lupus* to give them their scientific name) throughout this range. Nevertheless, all the world's gray wolves can breed freely with each other, making them the most widely distributed of all the wild mammal species of the North.

Until we humans began to fear them, to hate them and to find their presence on the Earth intolerable.

"Are wolves really so dangerous for people?" I asked Viktor, when we sat in his house drinking tea.

"No. Normally, wolves are not dangerous to people. Nearly always they try to avoid us."

"We are certainly dangerous for them, though," he added dryly, after a short pause.

"To look into the eyes of a wolf is to see your own soul – hope you like what you see," the great American conservationist Aldo Leopold wrote in the 1940s. As a young man Leopold had killed many wolves. Until the day he walked towards the body of the female he had just shot and saw "a fierce green fire dying in her eyes. I realized then, and have known ever since, that there was something new to me in those eyes – something known only to her and to the mountain." Leopold never killed another wolf.

There were many places in the Russian forests where that fierce green fire was dying. The carcasses of dogs or domestic stock were being laid out to attract wolves, laced with a deadly poison that caused the wolf to expire in agonizing convulsions. Eagles, ravens, magpies and other birds and small mammals fed on these carcasses, as they naturally do on wolf kills in the wild, and they were dying too. The use of poison, as well as shooting and trapping, was being encouraged by government payments for the wolf pelts.

"However, wolves are extremely useful," Viktor concluded, with a dark edge of irony. "We need something to blame for our failures and mistakes."

The Devil's Dog

This demonization of wolves became prevalent in late medieval Europe. The wolf was "the devil's dog" for medieval churchmen who conjured it as an image of the original, sinful darkness of the physical world, which they claimed had closed around the human soul. Like the women condemned and tortured as witches, who had drawn similar projections of the demonic because of their knowledge of birth and herbs and healing, wolves were burned at the stake or hung by the neck in village squares by people who sought relief for fears which they could not bring themselves to see and understand.

Wolves were also condemned as ruthless competitors for land and food because they took the deer that the human hunters wanted exclusively for themselves; when the forests were cleared and the deer were gone, wolves took domestic sheep and cattle. However, the fear and hatred that were directed against them bore little relationship to the real need to prevent them from killing domestic stock. Instead, wolves became scapegoats for the deprivations of common people; they were the creatures that could be blamed for the poverty and insecurity that resulted from the appropriation of land, game and timber by the wealthy and powerful. So killing wolves became an outlet for fear and anger at the consequences of predatory relationships between *people*. It is significant that so many of the metaphors associated with wolves evoke relationships in which people are exploiting and abusing one another: we still refer to poverty as the *wolf at the door*, a lying hypocrite is *a wolf in sheep's clothing*, an unfeeling seducer a *wolf with women*.

Across Europe teams of hunters with specially trained dogs worked so effectively to clear the land of wolves that they were rapidly eliminated from many northern European countries or only survived in small numbers far from human settlement.

European settlers carried this legacy of hatred, fear and intolerance with them to North America. Before the arrival of European settlers some two million wolves had ranged the continent from the Arctic tundra to Mexico, living freely alongside the continent's First Nations. The night air was full of their haunting voices; their tracks and scat covered the plains. Yet there was no excessive fear of them.

Native Americans honored wolves as their kin within the sacred totality of life. *Wolf* was one of the four great totem powers of the peoples of the Pacific Northwest, along with Eagle, Bear and Raven. On the Great Plains, the Pawnee lived in such close kinship with the wolf that others called them the "Wolf People". The Pawnee hand-signal for wolf was the same as their hand-signal for each other and they wrapped their sacred bundles and medicine pouches in wolf fur to protect their power.

The new settlers made no attempt to coexist with wolves or to understand their ways within the whole, as the Native communities had done: they simply set out to exterminate them. Wolves were hunted down relentlessly using guns and steel traps, and huge quantities of strychnine, a deadly poison, were placed in poisoned carcasses and laid across hundreds of miles of territory.

A sense of righteousness accompanied acts of great cruelty. "Wolfers", as the professional hunters were known, staked out den sites and left chunks of meat studded with razor blades, glass or nails for the pups. They captured the pups and set them on fire, or wired their jaws together and released them to slowly starve.

Clearing the land of wolves was one of the ways the settlers asserted ownership and control. The destruction wrought on wolves ran concurrently with that inflicted on the First Nations – robbed of their dignity and independence, the buffalo which had sustained them slaughtered, their sacred ceremonies outlawed, confined at the last to reservations within the arching magnificence of the land where they had walked in freedom. And it was carried out for similar reasons – to assert ownership and power by demonizing and excluding the other.

This hostile relationship with wolves in the West reveals far more about the distortions of the egocentric human mind than it does about wolves. It shows clearly how the shadow images in the mind are projected outwards. The wolf images which have emerged from the most fearful and tormented aspects of the unconscious mind – savage and ruthless, driven entirely by instinctive aggression – are not the animal itself, but outer reflections of inner fear and anger. While these images and emotions remain as unconscious shadows they seem to take an external shape in other creatures or in people which themselves are only dimly seen, as in the warped and freckled surface of an old mirror. Not another being, breathing and changing, but distorted images that are made and maintained with the power of the mind.

2 Attention is the Natural Prayer of the Soul

Yet among many indigenous traditions the presence of wolves evokes not fear but the healing power of the elemental energies of the wild. The Chukchi people of north-eastern Siberia would wrap their sick in wolf fur to surround them with its aura; the Hidatsa women of the American Northwest placed wolf fur on their bellies to support them as they gave birth. And I was about to come into contact with that healing power myself, in the most unexpected way.

I had been drawn to work with wolves at a time of emotional struggle and distress. The light that brought such transparency to the world was also illuminating aspects of my emotional makeup that I found very difficult to face. Currents of fear ran below the surface of my relationships: the fear of not being good enough; the fear of losing the other person's love and being left abandoned and alone; fear of being exposed and meeting judgment in their eyes; fear of facing and truly the feeling layers of pain and anger that had been laid down since childhood and adolescence.

One night the figure of a wolf appeared to me in a powerful and unforgettable waking dream. I saw the wolf come towards me out of the formless dark, his stride steady and purposeful. Behind him, a raven was perched on the shoulder of a woman whose face I could not clearly see. The woman stood completely still and silent, with the raven on her shoulder. I was not dreaming – the scene was unfolding before my inner eyes – but I had the strange immobility you sometimes have in dreams while you are sleeping.

The wolf approached; reaching into the center of my chest he drew out from it an iron bar. He carried the bar away in his mouth and buried it, then came back to me and packed the open wound with a mouthful of mosses. For days afterwards, the place that had been touched throbbed and ached, like the site of an old wound that had been uncovered.

I had never thought of wolves as healers. And that woman who stood so still and silent with the raven on her shoulder – who was she? I recalled how precise the wolf had been; how he'd known exactly where to find that iron bar and which herbs and mosses would help heal the wound it left, and I began to understand what it represented – some of the pain that had been compacted in my heart.

The ineffable touch of the Spirit does not make life easier in the superficial sense. When you receive some experience of who you really are, your true nature which is beyond physical form and the limitations of the ordinary mind and personality, you also begin the difficult task of bringing into lucid consciousness everything that you're *not*: the unthinking reactions, judgments and prejudices that swirl through the everyday mind and, deeper still, the unhealed hurts and angers that burn beneath the surface. Sooner or later, the light of the Spirit touches all the pain that is hidden away beneath the surface, not to bring more suffering but to bring true healing and complete release.

The wolf had come to me as a healer at a time when some of the hurt and anger that had been stored below the threshold of conscious awareness was rising strongly to the surface. Although the pain was buried it had never been entirely dormant. Without realizing, I often projected the unconscious emotions outwards, onto other people or circumstances, hiding from what I felt at a deeper level by swinging the weight of responsibility around: that person's attitude makes me feel anxious, inadequate or afraid. Or this man fills me with longing and intense desire – I've placed on him my unconscious desire for healing, and what he represents is the promise of release from the emptiness I feel inside.

The habit of projecting unconscious emotions – positive or negative or quite often both at once – makes life very stressful.

When you project onto another, you cannot truly meet them in the present, because your consciousness is conditioned by past experiences and beliefs or expectations about what the future should or will be. The other person becomes an actor in a mental and emotional story that you're telling yourself about life.

As long as I placed the responsibility for what I felt onto others, the underlying emotions could not be healed: they churned in repetitive cycles and fed the accumulation of anxious and compulsive thoughts. One reason it is so difficult to be truly honest, and face emotional patterns without blaming others, or expecting others to resolve them, is that the act of projection is so immediate that it is unconscious. It's a trick of the mind that is so habitual you don't even notice as it happens.

All the spiritual ancestors, the ones who have found the way through the turbulence and the instability of the ego-driven mind to the stillness of the deeper self, say the same. Watch. Stay awake. Be the lucid guardian of your inner space. From the point of inner stillness, observe your thoughts and emotions. As you watch you begin to understand how they work together to make dramas that appear to take on increasing reality as other people are drawn into them. Or, in the words of the Gospel, "Watch and pray so that you do not fall into temptation."

"Attention is the natural prayer of the soul." When I found those words, by the French philosopher Malebranche in the work of the German-speaking poet Paul Celan, they made a deep impression on me. All my life, as long as I could remember, giving attention to the beauty and diversity of the natural world had brought a sense of expansion and greater connection.

Now I began to realize the critical importance of giving attention to the *inner* life. The psyche speaks in images and dreams: the woman who appeared beside the wolf, standing in silence with the raven on her shoulder, represented the deeper level of consciousness that witnesses the inner life from a point of lucid stillness. In many spiritual traditions, this lucid clarity is known as the watcher or the witness: a state of intense conscious presence, in the moment, that transcends the reactions and judgments of the everyday mind.

The witness holds the space of stillness in which thought patterns, feelings and reactions come into conscious awareness and find release. This has nothing to do with any form of religious belief: simply paying attention to what is passing through the mind in each moment while remaining aware of the subtle sensations in the body develop clarity and peace. As you witness the motions of the mind, without judging them or labeling them mentally, you come more deeply into yourself; the sense of stillness deepens and you find the expansion of inner space.

But maintaining the awareness of the witness is not easy because it brings up what is *really* going on below the surface of the everyday mind and psyche – and this often means allowing volatile and uncomfortable feelings to rise to the surface. Like the shaman who must work gently and carefully to unbind the tight knots from Sedna's hair, witnessing the fear and pain that have been locked away within the psyche is intricate and demanding work. It can only done slowly and carefully, with great kindness and compassion for one's self and others.

But it is immensely worthwhile. As you witness patterns of emotional pain from a point of greater stillness, you no longer identify with them completely: you gain a sense of inner expansion and begin to know, from the truth of experience, that who you *really* are is far beyond them.

Attention is a healing art. The wolf that had appeared to me in that waking dream and the woman who watched in silence with the raven on her shoulder were showing the healing power the attention of the witness holds. By seeing the shape of my own psyche more clearly and witnessing the pain and anger that were stored in the unconscious, rather than suppressing them or projecting them onto others, they could be released at last and healed in the light of consciousness which is beyond the human conception of time.

After I returned from the wolves in Russia Jason emailed me a photo. It showed him lying on his back on a bed of dry leaves, with a wolf at his shoulder. Man and wolf appeared completely relaxed with each other, secure in their own space. The wolf was a female, Jason wrote, an orphan that he had raised himself and released into the wild. Although she had been living independently for several years, she remembered his voice and she always came when he called.

The photo reminded me of something Jason had said to me. "It is one of the best feelings in the world when the wolf knows you are not an enemy." Seeing how relaxed he was with the wolf made me realize how much I wanted to see him again, spend time in his company and learn more from him about wolves.

Wolves were appearing in my own life as guides through some difficult territory and I had begun to realize what fine companions they are when you are trying to develop inner strength and find emotional balance. Wolves don't waste their energy in repetitive thinking or regrets for the past or imaginary fears for the future. They simply pay full attention in the present; they are alive in the body, connected to the elemental energies of the Earth and extremely alert to all the messages of the senses.

So I rang Jason in Tbilisi and asked him about his next field trip. He was going to a nature reserve in southern Azerbaijan, he said, at the edge of the Caspian Sea where he was running a field study on the relationship between wolves and a rare and beautiful species of desert gazelle. Of course I could come with him, he said, and welcome.

3 A Pasture for Gazelles

The Shirvan Nature Reserve
Azerbaijan
April 2004

"Have you ever looked at what's around you through the *wolf's* eyes?" Jason asks me as he gets down on all fours in the scrub and peers at the pile of wolf droppings he has just spotted lying on top of a small wormwood bush.

I am not sure what he means, but I squat down beside him in the low scrub, among the spicy odors of the wormwood and the chalky smell of the sun-beaten ground. The wolf droppings have dried gray-white in the sun and when Jason probes them carefully with a small twig, they crumble and show splinters of white bone and some matted clumps of russet hair.

Between the clumps of wormwood and other saltwort scrub bushes, the bare ground is netted with dry cracks and crusted with salt in the sunlight. It holds the line of prints left by the pressure of the wolf's four toes and shows the deep points dug by the claws.

These prints are large – three-quarters the size of my extended hand – and they bear an unmistakable impression of power. Jason tells me that they were made by the adult male who had left these droppings on the bush. The wolf had also left a message with his droppings, he explains; they tell other wolves that the area is occupied. Wolves constantly mark their territory with urine and droppings as they travel, particularly along the borders between neighboring packs.

"I get down on all fours so that I can see at the same level as the wolf." Jason continues. "Do you see how this bush where the wolf left his droppings is taller than the others and has more space around it? These things matter to the wolf."

Jason collects the droppings in a plastic bag for analysis later in the laboratory, and rises to his feet and we get back in the jeep and take a rough dirt track across the semi-desert plain.

A great bloom of spring flowers lays a wide band of dusty rose across the sage-gray scrub; to the north, the saltwort scrub thickens into longer waves of russet and oat-colored grasses, rolling between exposed patches of terracotta soil. From there, the land rises abruptly in a line of sandstone ridges, their stark stone folds stripped bare as desert dunes and stippled with violet shadow. Ten thousand years before, the waters of the Caspian, largest of the world's inland seas, were lapping beside these ridges. The Caspian has receded inland since then, exposing this flat stretch of semi-desert along its western shore, which has become the Shirvan nature reserve.

Whenever he spots a fresh line of wolf tracks, Jason gets out of the jeep and examines them carefully; he measures each print and paces out the distance between them. He looks closely at the places where the prints are spaced further apart and the toes have dug in more deeply as the wolf picked up speed, and he examines the traces left by other animals – trails scratched by foxes and jackals, the prints of a wild cat, a line of wild boar tracks that runs straight as a highway over the sand. Beneath his ancient khaki field hat, bleached by long exposure to the sun, his gaze is warm and vivid with interest behind his glasses.

"I try to be as alert as possible when I'm in the field," he tells me, while he is mixing up dry plaster with water and pouring the mixture over one pair of wolf prints to make a cast of them. "I try to notice everything – *everything*. The science – the reflection and the analysis – that always comes afterwards, when I'm at home again or in the laboratory."

At the sound of our jeep engine, a group of gazelles starts suddenly into flight. They flee from the jeep in bounding, muscular leaps, a long ribbon of movement that rises and falls away across the plain. The warm chestnut color of their backs and haunches turns white along the belly and a white oval patch marks each rump beneath the short dark whisk of the tail.

Through binoculars, I can see that the entire group is male, with horns that bend in a lyre-shaped curve. They are goitered gazelles, a rare species now, but once abundant across Asia until habitat loss and mechanized hunting almost wiped them out. Around four thousand gazelles live here in the Shirvan, and the reserve is the single most important refuge that they have. Yet even this limited space is threatened: some of the reserve has already been opened to oil drilling and up to a third has been licensed for future exploration, constricting the gazelles' space even further. Jason comes to the Shirvan because he plans to make another refuge for them; he will reintroduce a small group to the Georgian territories where they lived before they were eliminated through overhunting. To do this successfully, he needs to understand their lives here, and study their relationship with the six or so wolf packs that hunt them inside the Shirvan.

Some female gazelles are browsing on the bushes, their dark eyes making pools of shadow on either side of the delicate, hornless heads, which are marked with two black stripes between forehead and nose.

From the way their round white bellies hang I can see that many of these females are pregnant. Within the next week or so, Jason says, they will begin to birth their young. During the first days of the birthing season only a few calves drop to the salt-cracked ground. Then the pulse of generation intensifies as the gazelle mothers bring their calves to birth in almost simultaneous accord. This concentrated rhythm of reproduction has evolved to protect the young gazelles from excessive predation by the wolves. As they flood their range with newborn calves during one short period in spring, the herd mothers not only benefit from the new growth of spring, they also overwhelm the capacity of the wolves to take too many of their calves by shortening the period in which they are most vulnerable.

We leave the jeep among the sand dunes that rim the Caspian shore and walk down to the empty sweep of dun-brown sand. The water is slightly saline: the Caspian has retained some of the salt tang of the ocean to which it was once connected millions of years ago through the Black Sea. It is a clear mineral blue, like lapis lazuli, and bounded offshore by long sandbars grown wiry with grasses, which enclose white flocks of feeding swans.

We find a sheltered place to sit among the dunes and Jason takes out a cigarette from his pocket and lights up.

"A few years ago two wolves suddenly ran out in front of my jeep," he recalls. "The female swerved off to the side, but the male kept running ahead of the jeep. I think he was trying to draw my attention away from her."

Jason is reliving the encounter as he speaks and the changing expressions of his emotions – surprise, delight, intense, focused interest – flicker rapidly across his face.

"The male ran straight towards a group of gazelles, and the gazelles just stood and watched him! It was astonishing; you've seen for yourself how quickly they flee when they feel threatened in any way. Those gazelles stood calmly and watched the wolf approach because they knew immediately that he wasn't hunting them. They knew because predator and prey are always reading each other's emotions and intentions. They continually study each other. They watch and learn. You see – animals are the best ethologists!" he concludes with one of his vivid smiles, tucking the remains of his cigarette in his pocket and rising to his feet.

As we walk back to the jeep by the mineral blue water I notice gazelle prints on the sand beneath the shallows – heart-shaped marks the gazelles left when they were drinking. The hoof prints make a repeating pattern in the sand, a temporary mosaic of overlapping hearts that shifts and wavers beneath the shallow wash of light and water.

A line of wolf prints runs along the sand, just above the gazelle prints in the water, deep enough to pool with shadow in the powder-white light of the afternoon. These wolf tracks are recent, and they follow the gazelle prints for some yards along the waterline before bending back into the dunes.

One page from a relationship, the meeting of salt and flesh, printed on the shifting, mineral surfaces of sand and water.

On the way back, a wild boar surges from the scrub with her young, her earthy denseness of dark flesh low-slung and powerful.

A hawk hovers and alights, a hooded watcher, on the scrub.

The afternoon darkens. A cold wind rises. A thick purple band spreads across the horizon and there are distant mutters of thunder.

A current of movement flows across the edge of sight.

Jason halts the jeep, grabs his binoculars and leaps out. I find the focus in my own – and there is the wolf, the gray fur streaked with red along the shoulders, the legs moving in that fluid, elastic trot. Each foot springs off the ground and meets it again with a steady fluent swing through the shoulders and spine and haunches.

"It's a male," he says. "And he is carrying something in his mouth. It looks like part of a gazelle shoulder."

"Ah, he is a very fine guy!" Jason exclaims warmly, after watching the wolf in silence for a few minutes. "He is working hard now to feed his family."

We watch the wolf move along the ridge until he disappears; even after he has gone the current of his passing feels electric and I scan the scrub again, eager to catch another glimpse of him.

"Maybe I can begin to understand the landscape now," I tell Jason back in the jeep. The words feel clumsy, but he simply nods as though he understands what I am trying to say.

"Yes. In that wolf's coat I saw the mix of colors from this place – sand and gray, red and brown. It is always a very emotional experience to see a wild wolf. They live with such intensity! I always hear this intensity in their voices. Even now, after all these years, every time I hear a wolf howl, the feeling is so strong that I almost feel that I cannot breathe. Especially in late winter, which is the time of courtship and love, they howl often then and with so much feeling! But I have also seen wolves just sit quietly and look at the sky, look at the colors of the sunset."

Lightening cracks and flashes and the rain pours down in a sudden burst of drenching cold that rattles the roof of the jeep and beats across the salt-baked ground. The dry surface crust dissolves; the clay beneath is churned and melted to thick slurry that gives the jeep no purchase. It skates from side to side and Jason puts all his attention into keeping it from veering off the track.

A Family of Wolves

Back at the wooden hut near the reserve entrance which we share with Levan, Jason's student from Tbilisi University, Jason cooks dinner for us all, crouching over the small gas camping stove on the hall floor, and after we have eaten the talk returns to the lives of wolves.

"I don't like to use the word pack," Jason says. "It is more accurate to say that wolves live in families. There were six adults in the wolf family I lived with in the Borjomi forest. The male and female I first met in the forest were the parents; there were three younger adults from a previous litter, and another male who was much older. He had arthritis or some old injury, because he was limping. I don't know what his relationship was to the others, but they took care of him. He always had food from them.

When the parents had new pups, I lived with the whole family on the rendezvous sites. I never touched the pups but I could be around them without any problem, and I was able to observe exactly how the parents taught them about food and hunting.

When wolf pups are born, they already have strong instinctive reactions. Even when they're very young they pounce on mice and small rodents. But the parents must teach them the relationship between these instinctive reactions and their food. At first the pups don't know that they can eat that mouse they instinctively want to seize. The parents must teach them, and they do it step by step – first they show them the prey, then they teach them the connection between this animal and their food."

Their close family relationships are among the most fascinating aspects of wolves' lives for me. These powerful predators, whose bodies and instinctive responses have been honed by evolution to give chase and kill, take hold of flesh with their powerful canine teeth and rip their prey, live in families where there is intense loyalty and support. Group harmony is maintained through physical displays of affection, and demonstrations of deference and respect towards older and more influential members.

Wolves are very skilled at communicating emotions through body posture and facial expression. Look closely at a wolf's face and you often see marks that intensify the expressions of feeling: a subtle darkening of the fur around the eyes emphasizes the gaze; the changing patterns of color along the nose and around the ears highlight the expressions of emotion and intention.

Family life is centered on the relationship between the wolf parents, the mated pair which biologists call the *alpha* male and female. The mated pair is usually monogamous, not necessarily in the sexual sense, but in the quality of their emotional bond, which may endure through a lifetime as they mate and raise their pups together. The size of the wolf family varies with the age of the parents, the type of territory that they occupy and how rich it is in prey. It may just be one young wolf pair with their first litter of new pups or a much larger extended family which includes different generations – yearlings, young adults, older wolves – and wolves that are unrelated by blood.

The mated pair has the authority of elders and parents and the male usually exercises this authority more directly over the other males, the female over other females.

Individual wolves have distinctive personalities and different strengths: one wolf may lack speed in the chase but be very observant of small signs that betray age or sickness in the prey. A timid and unassertive youngster might be especially playful and attentive to the pups and help to raise them. The parents must be able to harmonize these different ages and temperaments and keep a check on the aggression that is an inherent part of any predator's emotional response, so that a sense of wellbeing normally prevails.

Wolves demonstrate – and celebrate – their relationships with eloquent gestures and postures. A younger or less assertive wolf conveys deference to an elder when she carries her tail lower, flattens her ears or rolls over to expose her belly. The more senior carries her tail higher and she may make her authority very clear by pinning a junior to the ground and clamping its jaw firmly between her own.

It is easy to project human ideas about authority, submission and appeasement onto these gestures and assume they must be accompanied by fear or resentment in deferential animals. But that is not necessarily how wolves themselves experience them. The submissive animal is repeating movements first made as a pup towards the parents. Unless emotional tensions are high, the gestures must carry memories of affection and nurture and evoke security. When one American researcher measured heart rates in captive wolves, (using them as an indicator of arousal) he found they were lower when the wolf watched with relaxed interest the motions of falling leaves, or the sunlight glinting on the water. Equally, the wolf's heart rate declined when it was engaged in a ceremony of friendly greeting with an elder, and it stayed low even when the wolf lay in a passive position beneath the older animal on the ground.

It takes intelligence and insight to maintain this kind of emotional balance in a group of animals that must hunt and kill to make a living. "Wolves," as Jason told me, with one of his characteristic outbursts of scientific enthusiasm, "have fantastic cognitive possibilities."

Families come in many forms. Wolf families do not always follow a fixed pattern. Long-term partnerships break up when one partner dies or takes a new mate. A young female meets a solitary male passing near her territory; after they mate, she returns to her own family and raises her pups with their support.

But it is usual for the alpha pair to mate during the brief period in early spring when the female is fertile. While the emotional bond between this mated pair remains strong, they will actively prevent the other adults in the group from breeding. As a result, the period in late winter that leads up to mating can be a very volatile one among wolves: sexual and emotional currents are running strong and levels of tension and aggression can rise sharply as the mated pair assert their authority more forcibly over the others.

Once this point has passed, relationships usually become calmer. Around sixty days after mating, the mother gives birth to her pups in an underground den, which may have been excavated from a natural opening or the lair of a fox or badger. The pups are born blind and deaf, and for the first few weeks the mother must remain with them constantly. She relies on her mate and the rest of the family to bring her fresh meat or regurgitate what they have already swallowed before it has been fully digested.

When the pups are strong enough to leave the den, the entire family helps to raise them. One wolf stays behind to babysit the pups when the mother and the others leave to hunt. Wolves clearly enjoy the company of their lively and demanding young; the pups are treated with great affection by all adults and allowed to yank at their tails, chew on their ears and play-wrestle with them to their hearts' content.

"The strongest impression remaining with me after watching the wolves on numerous occasions was their friendliness," the American scientist Adolph Murie wrote in the 1930s after observing one such wolf family on the treeless, sub-arctic tundra around Mount McKinley in Alaska. "The adults were friendly towards each other and were amiable towards the pups... This innate good feeling has been strongly marked in the three captive wolves which I have known."

Some wolves spend a lifetime with their original family. Others leave, and they may travel for hundreds of miles into the unknown on long, solitary journeys in search of a partner and a territory of their own. These solitary journeys are dangerous and uncertain, for without the support of the family and the knowledge they have gathered of a particular territory and prey, the dispersing wolves are vulnerable to hunger and they risk injury or death from other wolves defending their territory against intruders. These hostile encounters are among the leading causes of death among wild wolves.

It must, I think, be one of the central tensions in wolves' lives – the tug between family and solitude, exploration and security, the known and the unknown.

Odors of Belonging

When Jason and I go out into the reserve again, the arid scrub is soaked in freshness after the heavy rain.. The heady odors that rise in waves from the grasses and wormwood bushes are a reminder that the world speaks even more directly to wolves through scent than it does through sight and sound. Wolves have very keen eyesight and their ears are finely tuned to frequencies beyond what humans can hear, but smell is the most acute of all their senses.

Wolves live in a world where emotions cannot be concealed behind a social mask: they are communicated directly through bodily secretions of hunger, satisfaction, aggression, joy. Wolves communicate through smell in many different ways. As they travel, they charge the land with the musk of their bodies – the reek of hormones from scent glands, the smells of urine and droppings, the oils they roll into the ground from their coats. The entire territory is layered with body scents – the aromatic identity that leaves the imprints of their passing on the ground and in the air.

Wolves pay great attention to these odors when they travel. They often pause to examine the places that are most thickly scented and they usually add another layer of smell by rolling or urinating. These scent marks communicate their claim to territory in a way that cannot be mistaken by other wolves. A wandering male that crosses another pack's territory and meets a female would know that she belongs because the land smells of her family. Since scent is rooted in the part of the brain that presides most directly over emotion, the two wolves would learn a great deal about each other through body odors alone. The stranger might be warned to make a quick retreat by the acrid spike of her aggression, as well as her threatening body posture. Or he might smell her intense desire for a mate and respond to it with his own bold odor of confidence and well-being.

"My relationship with the wolves in Borjomi went through different stages," Jason says that evening after we've had dinner and moved outside to sit on a couple of sawn-off tree trunks by the hut.

"I learned to communicate certain things to them using my body." He gathers his body together and slowly twists his head to one side; when he gazes at me with tilted head, the expression in his eyes is strangely different and very disconcerting.

"But I learned that the most important connection of all is with the mind," he adds, sitting up again and relaxing into his normal posture.

"What do you mean, Jason?"

"I will try to explain. At first, I was very nervous when the wolves were behind me because I could not see what they were doing. I was always turning around and trying to make sure that I knew exactly where they were. After some time with the wolves, this completely changed. I could *sense* exactly how much space there was between us without looking around to see where they were. I cannot explain how this was possible but after that I felt much more relaxed around them.

The thing that really made our relationship strong was when I helped the wolves to hunt. I closed off a path so that the deer they were chasing could not escape. The wolves were so excited when they saw this! They understood very well what I was doing. Even more importantly – they also understood exactly *why* I was doing it. After that, our relationship became very close."

One night, asleep on the ground, wrapped in his heavy felt shepherds' cloak, Jason woke and heard what he thought was rain pattering down. Poking his head out of the cloak, he saw the male wolf urinating on top of him.

You smell of us now, the wolf's gesture said. *You belong.*

"I have told you that those wolves were my teachers," Jason continues. "But I also survived because of them. Yes, I think those wolves saved my life."

Jason's usual vivid expressiveness becomes still. I sense him going inward to a deeper level of memory and his voice becomes so quiet that I must lean forward to catch his words.

"It was late one evening and I was running back with them from hunting. We had covered so much ground together that day and I was so exhausted that I barely knew where I was going. Suddenly, right in front of me, there was this bear. The bear stood upright, not much further away from me than the distance between us now.

We were both startled, we were both afraid... and a frightened bear is very dangerous. I must have shouted out loud because the adult wolf came running, the male, and straight away he ran at the bear and the bear turned away. Can you imagine this? The bear could easily have killed that wolf with one blow of his paw, yet the wolf didn't hesitate for one moment. This was the experience that really made me understand how wolves help each other. This was really altruism."

The next day, we leave the jeep among the dunes and go for another walk along the Caspian's empty, primeval shore. Jason squats by the water's edge, his dark eyes creased and thoughtful, listening to the slow liquid breathing of the sea. In his battered, bleached-out hat and worn khaki fatigues, he is an unpretentious figure, who gives no external sign of the depth of his experiences or the intensity of his life.

I leave him to his contemplations, and walk down the sweep of dun-colored sand, thinking about the extraordinary story he has told me. In zoology, altruism is behavior by an individual animal that directly benefits the members of its own species. But the wolf that defended Jason had endangered himself to protect one of the humans that had hunted and killed his own kind. There was no possible benefit to his species from his action; it was an act of simple allegiance with another life.

In his way, Jason was also a witness, although, as a scientist, he would not have used that term. He had gone to a remote forest alone, on a quest to see beyond the collective image of wolves as savage and dangerous creatures. He wanted to relate to wolves as they really are and not as people have sometimes imagined them to be. He had striven to be honest and observe the wolves without imposing his own preconceptions on them. In doing so, he had come to know himself more deeply and found a depth of relationship with the wolves that could never have been predicted by the mind.

Over the next few days, we follow the pregnant female gazelles as they move away from the Caspian shore to more arid inland terrain, where the sparse grasses and the saltwort scrub bushes grow between cracked pavements of gray sand, seared by salt and sun. Although they appear barren and unwelcoming, these inland stretches are where the gazelle mothers go to birth their calves for the newborn will run more easily on the open ground when they are ready.

On the bare, almost featureless plain, the refinement of the gazelles' beauty, their sculpted lightness and the perfect grace of their bearing in movement and stillness become even more starkly apparent. Driving by the line of oil drilling rigs that rim the edge of the reserve one evening, I notice one adult male lying on the ground alone. He doesn't stir and there is time to see the depth of the great dark eyes and the fine molding of the head beneath the curving, lyre-shaped horns. The oil well dips and swings and the gazelle keeps his stillness, a silent music of proportion and line from which everything superfluous has been stripped away.

The next day we find a female standing alone among the scrub; she walks slowly away when Jason stops the jeep. "I think that her calf has just been born," he mutters after examining her carefully through binoculars. "The females leave the others when they are about to give birth. Her newborn has no smell yet, so she hides it among the bushes to keep it safe from the wolves until it is strong enough to run in the open by her side. And she stays close by to feed it."

He gets out of the jeep and walks ahead through the scrub. Then he is waving to me, beckoning me over and when I stand beside him I see the newborn gazelle calf lying on the sheltering ground: legs folded, quivering, a little dappled bundle of light-boned breathing with enormous eyes, long ears twitching as it flares its new senses to the divergent world.

"Give me news of the Pastures of the Gazelles."

Back in the saffron-colored old city of Tbilisi, where the streets exhale mineral warmth from the thermal springs that bubble to its surface, Jason gives me two plaster casts of the wolf and gazelle prints he made while we were in the Shirvan. One shows a gazelle print in the shape of a heart, the other holds the two front paw prints of a wolf.

Going through my notes in a Tbilisi cafe, I take the plaster cast of the gazelle print from my rucksack and sketch it in my notebook. Beneath the drawing I write the word *earth* and then *heart*. Without thinking I move one letter over, and realize that *earth* has become *heart*.

At first I think there must be some mistake. I'm so convinced I got it wrong that I keep writing the words out and shifting the letters around. But there is no mistake. As I write them out the words transform. They become different versions of each other, the fluid statements of some original unity that is confusing for my mind.

It is strange how life speaks to you sometimes in the most unexpected ways. I sensed there was some meaning in that chance pattern of letters on a page. It felt like something pressing insistently on my mind but I could not understand at first what it might be. It would be many months before I remembered that the gazelle is the image for pure love and perfect beauty. In the poetry and song of Central Asia, Persia and Arab Andalusia, the image of the gazelle evokes both the beauty of the beloved and the beauty of the feelings that have woken in the heart of the lover. These associations are contained in the name of one of the great forms of Islamic love poetry: the *ghazal*, whose literal meaning is *the mortal cry of the gazelle*.

Among certain Sufis and other mystics that sense of beauty was expanded. The gazelle came to signify the beauty of the spiritual light within the heart and the perfect refinement of love – not the turbulence and instability of desire, but love as pure consciousness beyond fear or wanting, pouring freely, like living sunlight, through the heart of the awakened human being.

For the Sufis the work of the witness opens the way to the light of love and beauty within the heart. They have a wonderful expression for the work of inner watchfulness: they call it *polishing the mirror of the heart*. In this tradition, the mind is the mirror of the spiritual light within the heart; through the sustained work of inner attention, the mind is gradually cleansed of the unconscious shadows that bring such turbulence and emotional distress and it becomes lucid, still, perfectly clear.

Then it is free to reflect the beauty of the Spirit and work in harmony with the creative patterns through which life unfolds in such extraordinary richness, diversity and beauty. As the mind returns to the light within the heart, it comes into balance. It serves life's creativity and can no longer work for its destruction.

"Give me news of the pastures of the gazelles," the great Islamic poet and philosopher of Arab Andalusia, Ibn Arabi, wrote in his collection of mystical love poetry *The Kaaba of the Heart*. Speak to me of the spaces of the heart, the pastures where living beauty resides.

> Now my heart can take on any form
> It is a pasture for gazelles and a cloister for Christian monks
> A temple for idols and the pilgrims' Kaaba
> The tables of the Torah and the book of the Koran
> Whatever way love's camel takes
> That is my religion and my faith.

I had heard Ibn Arabi's lines some years before, chanted by a Moroccan singer in a restaurant in the old city of Jerusalem. It was an extraordinary place to hear them. They came like a message from the other Jerusalem, not the stone city that is torn by the long struggle for the ownership of truth, but the Jerusalem that is symbolic of the innermost heart of the human being – in Hebrew, the *place of peace*.

After my time in the Shirvan, those lines came back to me. I began to realize more clearly that the journey with wolves had been leading me beyond emotional struggles to the opening of the light within the heart: pure awareness, beyond form, that heals all sense of separation and dissolves the fear and pain that are carried from the past. And the wolves had been helping me by reminding me to stay alert, pay attention in the present moment and step away from the consuming activity of the everyday mind. They had helped me to understand the mind's tendency to project images born from its own unconscious fears. They had shown me that the real predator is within, in the workings of the ego-driven mind that fragment our wholeness and consume the energy of life.

As we witness the patterns of thought and feeling, spaciousness opens that is beyond the mind. The radiant light of the real spreads throughout the entire being, from the very core; it brings true healing, release from guilt and judgment and all the mental habits that keep us trapped in smallness and illuminates the indwelling presence within each person and all the creatures of the natural world.

This intimate connection between the spiritual light within the human heart and the life of the Earth, which has been almost lost in the West, is integral to the sacred teachings of the North American First Nations, where wolves have begun to return to the landscape at last, after enduring more than a century of persecution and fear.

4 The Wolf's Road

*I am blind and do not see the things of this world, but when the light
comes from above, it enlightens my heart and I can see, for the eye
of my heart sees everything; and through this vision I can help my
people. The heart is a sanctuary at the center of which there is a
little space wherein Wakan-Tanka dwells and this is the eye. This is
the eye of Wakan-Tanka by which he sees all things and through
which we see Him. If the heart is not pure, Wakan-Tanka cannot be
seen...The man who is thus pure contains the universe within the
pocket of his heart.*
Black Elk, Holy Man of the Lakota people

The Lamar Valley, Yellowstone Park in the Northern Rockies
North America
April 2005

The Lamar River winds in shining loops through the grasses of
the valley floor, and braids in shallow pools among the gravel
bars. A bull elk stands in the frigid river water to his knees, his
head held upright beneath the branching horns; a fawn-gray
wolf lies nearby on the bank and rests its head on outstretched
front paws. From where I stand, looking through binoculars
from the slope above the river, the wolf might be sleeping if it
were not the watchful attention that is apparent in its body. The
wolf has chased the elk to this refuge in the river and now it
waits. In the hours to come, as dusk closes on the valley floor, the
wolf may see the elk's resilience and strength of body and will
and leave, or it will watch him weaken and bring him to his
death.

This is only one brief passage in the continual dance of life and death between the creatures of Yellowstone's high, volcanic plateau and I will not see how it concludes. It is late April – early spring at this altitude, more than 7,000 feet up in the Northern Rockies – and the evening light is cool. The sagebrush and the grasses thread a ruffled tapestry of different greens – silver-olive and dry sage – across the meadows that slope away from the river's shining loops. Through binoculars I follow the sweep of the open meadows to the night-green border on the mountains where the dark masses of lodgepole pine and fir begin and then look higher still – up to where the trees give out on cliffs and peaks, the bare rock faces molded by violet shadow and coated with snow beneath towers of steel-gray, cumulous cloud.

The mountains' roots reach down towards fire. The Lamar valley runs near the northern rim of the great volcanic caldera that lies beneath the center of Yellowstone Park. Molten rock blooms from the deep Earth and rises into the chamber that is only a few miles below, holding one of the largest reservoirs of magma anywhere on Earth. The tides of molten rock rise and fall through the chamber, like the breathing of some elemental creature whose life pulses according to no human conception of time and they have erupted many times to the surface in massive releases of pressure.

Major eruptions occur in cycles of around 650,000 years, like a slow pulse beating deep within the Earth, and these outpourings of burning lava have built Yellowstone's peaks and high plateaus. Over eons of geological time, glaciers have molded them beneath icy tides, only to melt again beneath renewed eruptions of molten rock. The dynamic interplay between these potent and apparently destructive natural forces has formed the land; Yellowstone has been shaped and made by the repeated conjunctions of ice and fire.

The Lamar's long curves were pressed through the rugged peaks of Yellowstone's Northern Range by the weight and movement of the ice during the last glaciation. The Lamar is where the last wolves remaining in Yellowstone were shot dead by park rangers in the late 1920s, at the end of the long and bloody campaign that almost eradicated wolves completely from the US outside Alaska. Seventy years later, the Lamar is where the wolves were returned, deliberately reintroduced to restore the lost balance to the land.

Bringing Balance to the Land

It was just after dawn, on a snowy, overcast morning in March 1995 when the first wolf stepped back into Yellowstone. Three months earlier he had been living freely in the Canadian Rockies; he was captured and brought south to a holding pen at Rose Creek, above the Lamar Valley, along with some of the other wolves that had been taken to repopulate Yellowstone.

The wolf was a mature male, an exceptionally handsome animal with silver-blond fur, whose assurance and natural authority were apparent even in captivity. The other captive wolves were extremely nervous around people and they shrank away from the biologists who brought them food. Not this one: he never lost his confidence; his gaze never dropped or faltered, and that morning in March, when the biologists cut the wire, he was the first to leave.

The wolf stood on the ridge above and gazed down at them through the falling snow. Then he began to howl. It was "the most soulful, yearning howl imaginable," as team leader Doug Smith wrote later. The long, wavering swell and incline of his voice pierced the waves of gusting, wind-blown sleet; the light grew and the wolf continued to pace the ridge and howl.

He howled to call out the black female, his mate, who was still trotting nervously back and forth inside the wire; the two had become partners in captivity and the female was already carrying pups. And he howled, I believe, to assert his presence, to send his voice resonating across this landscape, which had lost so much life in the absence of its wolves.

Without wolves – the top predator – to keep them in check, Yellowstone's elk herds held many aging and undernourished animals that were pressing hard on the land's resources. With no need to remain alert and keep a careful watch for wolves, the elk browsed freely in sensitive areas along the riverbanks and trampled repeatedly across the same ground as they nibbled the new aspen and other young shoots to stubble.

Only a few hours after leaving the holding pen, the wolf and his black partner had brought down one of these aging bull elks weakened by poor nutrition; then, along with the female's year old daughter, the pair disappeared. When the signals from their radio collars were located, the daughter had left them to travel by herself, and the pair had settled together on a mountain slope some forty miles away.

Four weeks later the male was dead – deliberately shot and killed by a local man who dropped him with a single bullet. His heavily pregnant partner anxiously circled the same small area of the mountain as she waited for him to return. When she could wait no longer, she scraped out a hollow in the ground beneath a Douglas fir, and gave birth to eight pups.

Wolf mothers have not evolved to raise pups alone. They are always supported by a partner or family and the black female could never have fed herself and cared for her pups as well. Forced to intervene, the biologists recaptured the entire family and returned them to the Rose Creek pen until autumn. Just as they were about to be released, a young male showed up by the pen and courted the mother. The two wolves bonded and the young male became the instant father to her large family which he accepted and cared for as if they had been his own. The pair remained together until the female's death, and their family thrived – so well that in 1999, nearly four-fifths of Yellowstone's new wolf population were descended from that black female, Yellowstone's matriarch, with her two mates.

When the wolves returned, the land was made whole. All the

large animals that inhabited Yellowstone before Europeans ever set foot in North America are here today – the grizzly bears, the mountain lions and the coyote, the elk and deer and moose, the pronghorn antelope and the buffalo. The park and the surrounding territory of Greater Yellowstone are among the richest temperate ecosystems on Earth.

A year after being with Jason in Azerbaijan, I've come to see this act of restitution for myself and hike and camp in Yellowstone's Northern Range with a small group from the Yellowstone Institute, an educational trust that is based in the Lamar Valley. We get up at four in the morning to find the wolves; by dawn, we're standing on a bluff overlooking Soda Butte Creek, a few miles from the Lamar, guided by Yellowstone ranger Rick Macintyre, a tall, softly-spoken man with gray-blond hair, who has seen more of the wolves around the Lamar than anybody else.

This morning, like every morning, Rick was driving through the valley before dawn, locating the wolves by tracking the signals he receives from their radio collars. Even in the most severe winter cold, he's out watching them and taking copious field notes. "Every day there's something I've never seen before," he tells me, standing by his yellow van, which is a magnet for Yellowstone's wolf watchers.

Like all good field researchers, Rick knows that there is always something new to learn. Wolves are dynamic, adaptable animals, with distinctive personalities and their lives are not determined by fixed patterns of behavior. In the last ten years, Rick has come to know many Yellowstone wolves as individuals, and he has a particular affection for one of the black female's sons with her second mate.

All Yellowstone's wolves have been assigned numbers; this particular male is known officially as 301, but Rick refers to him wryly as "an agent of chaos and destruction" because this wolf is a trickster and he overturns all the rules. Others call him

Casanova. For most of his life, he has liked females far too much to settle down with just one and become a responsible alpha male. They like him, too: this wolf's numerous fleeting encounters with young females have left single mothers across Yellowstone raising pups with the help of their own families. He'll seduce the senior females as well, whenever he can lure them away from their mate. And he won't fight – in a confrontation with another wolf he simply throws his dignity to the winds and runs.

Rick helps me to get the spotting scope aligned on the den site beneath a fallen pine on the other side of the creek. At first all I can see in the scope's round window is the pattern of light and shade on fallen trunks and broken branches. There's a stirring, then a wriggling of small round bodies in the shadows and two fawn-brown pups crawl from under the fallen tree; one clambers along the trunk, while the other finds something more compelling to explore in the brush. A third pup appears, a fourth... and they're sniffing through the undergrowth and making cat-like pounces and playful rushes at each other. Finally, I spot the adult watching from the shadows – a slender wolf with a dark-gray coat, the babysitter who cares for the pups and keeps them out of trouble while the others are hunting.

Three more wolves approach the den site from across the valley, sharpening into focus in my binoculars, the fawn-brown bodies moving in that buoyant, almost floating trot that is so typical of wolves, all their energy and well-being swinging through every fluid and confident stride. They are vivid, vital, utterly compelling; simply being around them gives you a bigger sense of what it means to be alive.

The return of the wolves to Yellowstone is also giving biologists a greater understanding of how wolves relate to the other creatures in the community. The elk are the wolves' main prey. But a healthy adult elk can break a wolf's leg or back with one well-aimed kick and wolves know this well. So they watch their prey very carefully; they examine them for every sight or smell of weakness, age or sickness, and by taking mainly the aging and the sick, they help to keep the whole elk community healthy.

"The caribou feeds the wolf, but the wolf keeps the caribou strong," the Inuit proverb says. And the same is true of the wider natural community as well. Biologists have been astonished to discover the many different ways that wolves make the web of natural relationship more resilient and diverse.

When wolves make a kill, the meat does not feed wolves alone. Many other creatures feed on the carcasses – grizzly bears, foxes, coyotes and eagles, magpies and other birds, especially ravens, which live in close, almost symbiotic relationship with wolves. Wolves help the ravens and the other birds and animals to survive through lean times because they make food available to them throughout the year, not only when the weaker elk die naturally in late winter.

The return of wolves to Yellowstone is sending a cascade of renewal through the entire natural community. Without the wolves, the elk grazed freely along riverbanks and put the vegetation under constant stress. As the wolves stalk and challenge them, the elk have become more watchful and they avoid the riverbanks where visibility is poor. These vulnerable areas, which the elk had previously stripped of vegetation, have begun to regenerate and provide more nesting sites for songbirds. The aspen shoots that the elk had browsed low are getting the chance to grow again. And more tree growth will allow beavers to build more dam pools that provide habitat and nutrients for other river life.

It is little wonder that many indigenous peoples have honored wolves as healers, that the Chukchi people of north-eastern Siberia wrapped their sick in wolf fur to surround them with the wolf's power and the Hidatsa women of the North Pacific placed wolf fur on their bellies as they gave birth. The wolves are healers for the land. They are renewing the vibrant circulation of life, restoring the dynamic balance between living and dying, building up and breaking down, renewal and release.

Walking the Way of the Wolf

The next day we hike a trail across upland meadows, by rushing streams coursing with spring melt-water from the mountains and through cool stands of pine and fir. The open meadows are scented with sagebrush and delicate spring flowers and I find the leg bones of an elk, hung with tattered rags of hide, lying among clusters of the small pink-white flowers known as western spring beauty, whose root bulbs nourish Yellowstone's grizzlies when they emerge lean and hungry from months of fasting in the winter den.

A raven gives a hoarse cry and lands on the nest, a jagged creel of twigs at the top branches of a pine, where a raven chick begs for food, the beak wide open to show a mouth as red as arterial blood beside the shining blackness of the adult's head.

I am watching a female elk grazing alone on a riverside meadow when two wolves appear above her on the ridge, outlined against the sky. They turn into the meadow, and they're heading towards some fallen timber on the bank when she lifts her head and charges, pushing them into the trees. But they turn back and start nosing through the fallen timber on the bank where she may have concealed her newborn calf. Again she charges, energy and will evident in every determined line of her body, and this time she harries the wolves so fiercely they give up and trot away.

This magnificent trail, winding across the upland meadows may have been used by some of the many Native Americans who traveled, hunted and camped throughout Yellowstone. When Yellowstone was first established as a national park in the 1870s the administrators claimed that Native Americans avoided it because they feared the spirits that lived around the geysers and hot springs. The claim was meant to reassure early tourists; it bore no relationship to reality. The Tukudika – or Sheepeaters as the settlers called them – had hunted bighorn sheep in the mountains for a thousand years or more. Others came at different seasons: the Blackfoot people, the Shoshone and the Nez Perce and others, gathering plants and hunting and camping among the hot springs.

They conducted sacred ceremonies in places of great elemental power, and they may have entered these mountains on their arduous spiritual retreats, sitting alone in prayer and spending four days without food or water to purify themselves, "crying for a vision" that would strengthen the connection to the Great Spirit and enable them to help their people. Alone with themselves, and the powers of nature, they sought self-knowledge and, ultimately, the experience of that profound inner silence, which is said to be the very voice of the Great Spirit.

A small band of buffalo is grazing on the meadow, shaggy, great-shouldered females clustered around the leggy calves, which have curling, rust-orange coats. Through binoculars, their eyes are deep black pools in the weighty bearded heads. Some buffalo hairs have snagged on a bush, a fine brown tangle that I carefully unpick, and when I hold the soft brown buffalo hairs and see them grazing... it touches me with what I can only call reverence, for these are the last pure-bred, wild descendants from all North America's vast buffalo herds. There were tens of millions of buffalo in the American West until the mass slaughter of the late 1800s left barely a few dozen wild survivors to find refuge here, in one of Yellowstone's most remote valleys.

I hold the soft brown buffalo hairs and remember the words of the Kiowa woman, whose name was translated as Old Lady Horse, when the land was empty and the buffalo were gone. The buffalo were the life of the Kiowa, she said. The buffalo loved their people as much as the Kiowa loved them.

"Our tipis were made of his skin," Lakota healer John Lame

Deer said of the buffalo in the 1970s. "His hide was our bed, our blanket, our winter coat. It was our drum, throbbing through the night, alive, holy. Out of his skin we made our water bags. His flesh strengthened us, became flesh of our flesh."

The traumatic shock and disorientation the Kiowa and the other Nations must have experienced during the mass slaughter of the buffalo can scarcely be imagined. The buffalo were not simply their source of food and warmth and shelter – the buffalo were the living manifestation of the love of the Great Spirit. Through the gift of their bodies, the buffalo shared their love with the people. They became flesh of their flesh, and the people shared their love with the buffalo in prayer and sacred ceremony.

Black Elk Speaks

In the autumn of1947 two men met in a canvas tent in a migrant potato-picking camp in Nebraska. One was a young scholar of religions, still in his twenties, called Joseph Epes Brown. The other was in his eighties, ill and almost blind. His name was Black Elk, *Heyáka Sápa* in his native Lakota, the visionary, healer and holy man of the Oglala Lakota, whose life and visions had been recorded by the poet John Neihardt in a remarkable book called *Black Elk Speaks*. Joseph Brown had been so captivated by that book that he had set off for the West, determined to find Black Elk.

When he entered the tent, he offered Black Elk the traditional gift of tobacco and the two men sat and smoked together in silence for a while. Then, Black Elk spoke; in a soft and kindly voice he told Brown that he had been expecting him, for he had much to say before "he would pass from this world of darkness into the other real world of light."

Black Elk had been born into the traditional life of the Lakota. He had lived through the slaughter of the buffalo and the loss of the Lakota's traditional lands and he had witnessed the killing at Wounded Knee. Now his greatest desire was to pass on the sacred teachings of his people, so that the "flowering tree at the center of the nation" might bloom again. Joseph Brown moved with Black Elk and his family to the reservation, where he lived with them for over a year, learning the teachings and rituals of the Lakota and recording them in a classic book *The Sacred Pipe: Black Elk's Account of the Sacred Teachings of the Oglala Sioux*, a work which clearly conveys the profound depth and beauty of these traditions.

Joseph Brown was deeply affected by Black Elk's presence. He wrote later that Black Elk radiated the sanctity and wholeness of a great saint, an enlightened human being. Yet, coming from a Western background, he found it difficult to understand at first why Black Elk spoke so much to him about the animals and the natural world rather than speaking directly about the spiritual teachings of the Lakota. Finally he realized that Black Elk was, in fact, explaining his religion through everything he said about the natural world.

When Black Elk spoke of the life of nature, he was speaking directly of what he held sacred. In these teachings, there are no meaningless hierarchies, no abstract concepts to divide humanity from the life of the Earth and cosmos. All things and all beings are interrelated and equal within the Great Mysterious, the sacred totality that is beyond our mental images, words and concepts. The sacred totality is present in all the forms of nature, and in the essence, the spiritual power that inhabits all living beings and natural processes. The animals and the plants, the elemental powers of thunder, wind, sun and rain – all these are aspects of the sacred totality. The mountains, trees and running streams and living creatures are not inferior. They are far older than we humans on the Earth; to receive their gifts with gratitude and contemplate them with reverence and humility *is* prayer and communion with the Great Spirit.

The sacred relationship that unites all beings within the wholeness of the Great Mystery, was wonderfully expressed by

Luther Standing Bear, who was born into the Lakota people of the Great Plains in the 1830s.

> "From Wakan Tanka, the Great Spirit, there came a great unifying life force that flowed in and through all things – the flowers of the plains, blowing winds, rocks, trees, birds, animals – and was the same force that had been breathed into the first man. Thus all things were kindred, and were brought together by the same Great Mystery."

The negative associations of the word *wild* in Western cultures, evoking the threat of uncontrolled natural forces, were meaningless to the Native Americans who first came into contact with the settlers. "We did not think of the great open plains, the beautiful rolling hills, the winding streams with tangled growth, as "wild". To us it was tame." Luther Standing Bear wrote. "Earth was bountiful and we were surrounded with the blessings of the Great Mystery."

Every created being and thing is holy, *wakan*, and has power according to the level of the spiritual reality that its life reflects. It is essential to remain attentive and discriminate carefully between these levels, and so relate to the animals and the elemental powers of the natural world in ways that can help each person to deepen the connection to the Great Spirit and live in balance with other people and the entire natural community.

Observing the life of the wolf, Native Americans see a creature that is intensely watchful and present in the moment, alert to all the messages from the senses. Wolves form close relationships; they enjoy each other's company and they share food with others. At the same time, the young wolf will leave the family and familiar territory to find a partner and a territory of its own, showing that a time comes for the individual to leave the familiar in order to gain strength and self-knowledge. This aspect of wolves' lives mirrors the fundamental pattern of the Vision

Quest, one of the most important sacred rites among many tribes.

"We regard all created beings as sacred and important," Black Elk said, "for everything has a *wochangi*, or influence, which can be given to us, through which we may gain a little more understanding, if we are attentive. We should understand well that all things are the work of the Great Spirit. We should know that He is within all things, the trees, the grasses, the river, the mountains and the four-legged animals and the winged peoples; and even more important, we should understand that He is above all these things and peoples."

The symbol that directly expresses Native American understanding of the Great Mystery is the cross within the circle. The circle is present in almost every significant aspect of Native American life: the traditional shape of the tipis, set in a circle when the people camped; the image of the nation as a hoop or circle, the movements of the Sun Dance around the sacred cottonwood tree at the center of the circle, and other ceremonies, rituals and prayers.

The cross that is set within the circle unites the four divisions or directions with the Earth and the Heavens. At the very center, at the heart of the six directions, is the point of sacred unity and the innermost heart of the human being: "the center that is really everywhere" in Black Elk's words. The purpose of our human lives on Earth is to move from the periphery to the center and live consciously from that essence at the very core, which is one with the essence of all that is.

That evening we camp on the banks of a river that is running fast and turbulent with spring melt-water. The clearing is loud with the roar of white water and the clank of stones in the rush of the current, and I find a shallow pool and step into the river to wash, scooping the water up in handfuls and letting it run down my body. The water is electric with cold, charged with the power of its flow from the heights and the touch on my bare skin brings a powerful sense of waking. All night the sound of the river pours through my tent, so close that it makes me think of liquid thunder. The continual rush of water through the dark wakes me from sleep and I get up and stand outside for a while looking up at the clear sky. In all my life I have never seen any night burn so thickly with stars. The familiar constellations seem to disappear, consumed by the white intensity of the blaze.

The Wolf's Road – that is the name of the Milky Way among the Blackfoot people: the road of stars on which wolves travel freely between the spirit worlds and the flesh. When the star Sirius rises and falls, the Cree people say that it marks the passage of the wolves between the worlds, as they move between the Earth and Heavens, the ground and stars.

I think that is the note that I have always heard in wolves' voices from Russia to Azerbaijan – a piercing animal expression of the continual passage of life into, and out of, physical form. In this very moment, life is forming and dissolving in one great river of making and unmaking and the formless power that sustains this continual transformation has been rightly called the Great Mystery for there is nothing that the mind can grasp and hold: only Presence, hushing words and thinking, in the very depths of our being.

In the wisdom traditions of Native America, the animals are willing to help the person who sincerely chooses to walk the way of unity and peace. There is a wonderful story from the "Wolf People", the Pawnee of the Great Plains, about the Animal Council that is continually held in a cave beneath one particular mountain. The animals are aware of the actions of humans on the Earth above, and if a man or woman is in great need, and looks for help in humility and openness, the Animal Council chooses one of its members to find them. The animal brings guidance and healing and it shares something of its power.

The story that follows is inspired by a Native American tale of a woman who leaves the husband who has been unkind to her and wanders alone into the wilderness. Although inspired by Native American oral tradition, this version is not intended to evoke any particular culture. It is simply a story for anyone who walks away from the collective human dream of fear and pain to find what is most real, deep within.

5 The Woman Who Walked Away

They scarcely knew who she was at first, the woman walked so lightly through the street. Her clothing was torn and the dust was tangled with the scents of sage and cedar in her curling black hair; but she wore her patched and faded raggedness with unself-conscious ease and the skin that showed through the rents in her garments was warm as amber in the sun.

The villagers stared as she passed. She had left them so abruptly that night, and the husband, too, had vanished not long after. People had talked for months about their sudden disappearance and they'd never expected she would return. If the woman read the silent questions in their eyes, she showed no sign of it; she simply resumed her life in the village as quietly as if she'd never left. People felt awkward with her at first: they remembered what had driven her from the village and some were ashamed that they had done nothing to prevent it. But when the woman's eyes met theirs without a shadow, they realized that she was not as they remembered; then her old name felt strange and when they spoke of her among themselves, they simply called her *the woman who went away*.

As time passed, some of the villagers began to come to her alone, bringing feelings that were knotted painfully up inside them – anger and old grief, the scalding pain of having failed someone they loved. The woman herself said little. She asked few questions and she gave no remedies for pain. She simply listened and she gave them space to be and the words that were spoken in that space brought a relief that was as simple and welcome as a glass of cool water and green shade after the heat of the day.

The woman never spoke about her own life after she had left the village until some years had passed. She often sat with her friends in the evening, telling stories as the firelight danced between them in the darkness. On this winter evening they were telling stories about how certain animals had touched them and lifted them out of the ordinary round of their thinking.

"We were not always strangers, the way we are now," the woman commented at the end. "There was a time when the people and the animals shared their being with each other." Something about the words she had used struck her: she looked up at the faces of the men and women around the fire, these people who had shared their own stories with her and shown her some of the raw and tender places in their hearts. Then she gathered herself and began to speak.

The Story of the Woman Who Lived with Wolves

It rained the night I left him. The rain had found an old leak in the roof above one of the windows and the water trickled down the wall and pooled inside on the ledge. I was sitting in a chair by the window and listening to the water drip onto the sill.

Have you ever sat up like that? Do you know what it is to start awake in the silent darkness of the night as though some voice you cannot hear has been calling you from sleep? Every night for weeks I had woken, suddenly, as though I had been summoned. I left the bed where he still lay sleeping and I sat all night in that chair, taking small sips of shallow breath. Oh, I knew I had to leave... but there was such a haze in my mind, such a darting confusion of different thoughts...

A gust of wind rattled the roof and flung the rain against the glass. I heard him groan and turn over onto his back in the bed and I rose and crossed the room to look at him. Some dream was troubling his sleep; when I touched his forehead it was clammy with sweat. He muttered to himself and I caught the reek of the night's whisky on his breath. But I knew he wouldn't wake; he'd drunk enough to sleep until morning. I would lie down by his side, I thought, and rest for a few hours.

The water pooling on the ledge spilled over and clattered to the floor. At first I thought the window had blown open and let the wind sweep through the room. But that wind was inside me, setting my heart hammering like a sleepwalker on a narrow ridge who's woken to see the drop beneath her feet. If I lay down now I wouldn't get up again. I'd wake beside him in that bed tomorrow and all the tomorrows that came after it, and something in me that was struggling to stay alive would never again find air to breathe while I was walking on the earth.

The wind dropped. I stood in a pool of silence and now I knew what I had to do. I stepped back from the bed. I took some food from the kitchen and I was taking a few clothes from the drawer when my fingers brushed the beaded edges of a leather pouch pushed against the back.

It was a small sewing bag beaded with flowers and leaves. My grandmother had made it for me not long before she died and I'd put it away in that drawer and never touched it. I couldn't leave it... I tucked it into my bag with the rest, slung it over my shoulders and stepped out through the door.

The wind came in drenching gusts and every house in the village was dark. I thought of the disturbance if I knocked, the sleepy-eyed confusion of the children, the barking dogs. No – I couldn't bear the anxious stir and the questioning. But where could I go? That was when I remembered the hunters' cabin on the mountain. There would be a stack of firewood, maybe even a little food. I could shelter there for a few days and feel safe.

The thought renewed my courage. I walked on through the village until I found the turnoff to a path I knew from picking berries and climbed all night between the pale trunks of the birches. I stopped at dawn to rest and eat, and walked on to reach the cabin before dark.

Late that afternoon the air thickened with cold. A few light flurries melted on my hair and hands, then the snow came down in sleety waves that closed the world from sight. The cold gray light began to dim and the only shelter I could see was a couple of dry-stone walls stacked with rough timber planks. I crawled into a narrow gap between the planks and walls where I sat all night, dozing and shivering, until the first gray light came and my hands took shape out of the dark.

Not a bird stirred outside in the blank white wilderness. The pines were black beneath the low gray cloud and there was no sign of the path that I'd been following. For a moment my mind was as blank as the cold white waste, then a coil of fear turned through my gut. I could die up here alone, and nobody would ever know, until they found my body on the ground.

I stumbled on through the slush, looking for some path that I could take between the trees. Pictures flashed so vividly through my mind that they took shape before my eyes. I saw my body lying on the ground. I felt the seasons turn as my clothes wore to rags in the wind and my flesh shriveled to the enduring bones. I saw my own bare bones on the snow. The empty skull with empty eyes. A few poor threads of brittle hair.

Like a barrier cracking before the force of water, the pain and anger I'd held back for so long surged up and flooded me completely. It came like a roar of white river water, rising in wave after wave, as I remembered my husband's lies and betrayals, his bouts of reckless drinking. I saw him lying with the other women in the bed he'd shared with me. I heard the sound of his voice running through my head, slurred and jeering. I heard my own voice, tight and choked with pain, as I railed back at him with a force I'd never dared to use before his face.

While the storm of feeling lasted I cried out. I spoke my bitter words to him out loud and sobbed shamelessly, like a child. It shook me so hard I stood by one of the pine trees, trembling and leaned against it. I felt the tree rooted deep within the earth, the trunk and branches reaching to the light and a different thought came in. *All these voices in my mind… the anguish, the jealousy, the rage… that is not who I really am.*

The words came on a breath as pure as the first cold flowers in spring. For a moment I was sheltered in a stillness that had never been touched by that hot misery and shame and all the inner voices fell silent in its grace.

I found the courage to keep walking then, although the way grew steeper and I had no idea where it was leading me. Shafts of light broke through the overcast and melted the snow to slush as I climbed on until I came at last to a small meadow among the pines at dusk. There was a rock outcrop at the edge, with a crevice just wide enough to let me crawl inside, pulling my pack behind. I found the space to lie full-length, and then I put my head on my pack and was instantly asleep.

That night I dreamed that I was folded in thick fur. I ran my hands down through the dense undercoat, and felt the quick throb of a pulse beneath my palms. For a moment my heart was burning with its fiery touch, then I pressed the cloak of fur around me and I slept.

It was strange to wake in the darkness of the cave, with only the feel of the stone floor to tell me where I was. The dream feeling of being wrapped in warmth and comfort had remained and I lay there half-sleeping until the first blush of light appeared outside the mouth of the cavern. When the sunlight entered the passageway, and glowed on the walls of yellow rock, I rose and crawled outside, into the bright white morning.

I stood up in a small bowl of open meadow among thick stands of pine and fir. The trees climbed along the jagged ridges and the sunlight glanced off the nearest mountain peak and poured into the meadow across a white field of snow.

A small stream was humming through the rocks. It filled a stone pool and I cupped my hands and drank, to rinse the stale taste from my mouth. There was a small thicket at the other side of the stream and I glanced over – then stopped, seized by a still, gray shape lying beneath the bushes. A warning prickle crossed my skin. The animal rose in one flowing motion from the ground and stepped into the open.

She – I knew later the wolf was female – looked at me, her head lowered and I stared back, caught inside her gaze. I saw the long, fawn-colored jaws with the gleam of teeth just visible between her parted lips. The black fur that ringed her amber eyes. The triangles of her ears. I flushed with sudden warmth and sweat trickled down my sides, but I could not look away from her.

She shifted her gaze from me as a second wolf slipped out behind her from the bushes. This one was smaller, with a sandy coat and he crouched beside her and mouthed her on the neck and jaw. The two wolves looked at me steadily for a moment, then they turned and trotted across the meadow and vanished into the trees.

When they were gone I saw there were wolf tracks on the ground around the rocks. Wolves. I thought they had been hunted from these mountains long ago, but they had been here in the night while I was sleeping. They must have followed me. And they'd come back, they'd attack me in the night... I thought of jaws clamped around my limbs, tearing flesh from bone, and shook like someone with a sudden fever.

I grabbed my pack to run and the leather pouch I'd tucked inside fell out and tumbled to the ground. As I picked it up, I paused. For the first time in many years I seemed to feel the touch of my grandmother's hands again, that way she had of holding everything as though it were alive, delicate as a bird in the palm. I felt as though she had touched me inwardly with peace and the first raw intensity of my fear began to ease. What had the wolves done to threaten me after all? I thought of the female's yellow gaze on me again. No – there had been nothing threatening in her eyes. She had simply looked as though she saw something in me that I myself was not aware of.

In the morning the meadow filled like a cup with light. The sunlight tingled on my bare skin as I poured water from the stream over my face and body and washed until I was flushed with cold. I felt I was washing the past away from me with every handful of the cold running water. Little currents of cool fire licked through my veins and bones and the white snowfields on the mountains came almost close enough to touch.

I was making a small fire when I looked up and saw the wolves again, trotting towards me across the meadow. The female came first, beside a larger male with thickly ruffled, gray-white fur. The sandy one I'd seen with her the day before was close behind with two others and a black female trotting at their side.

How easily they moved, lightly springing through every stride. I felt the life in them filling the small meadow, pressing against my chest so that it was an effort to take a breath. I stood up with my back to the rocks, thinking I should protect myself as they came near. But the wolves paid no attention to me at all. They lay down together, the female at the center, with her head on the gray-white male's back and the others curled around them and after a while I realized that they were sleeping. Then I lay down too, in a small hollow by the fire and listened to the liquid song of the birds until my eyes grew heavy and like the wolves on the meadow, I fell asleep.

After that, the wolves came every day to the meadow to rest and play and I sat on the rocks, absorbed in watched them. The three younger ones were always playing. They pounced and wrestled and pinned one another to the ground. Quarrels flared – low growls, raised lips, a threat made with bared front teeth – and were quickly forgotten as they pushed and tumbled together on the grass.

I was so happy in their company, in the days of silence without the restless need for speaking, that I felt that I could have stayed forever on the mountain. But it wasn't long before my little food was almost gone and I had to leave. I was climbing along the ridge, looking for a path back down the mountain when I heard a raven call and saw two ravens circling over the wolves on the meadow below. They were gathered around a stag they had backed against a tree. His flanks were stained with blood and sweat but still he had the strength to swing his quarters around, kick out and send them scattering.

The gray-white male came back and paced around him. Suddenly the stag was bounding away and the gray-white male was tugging at his flank; then the black female caught him by the throat and he staggered and collapsed.

I felt a noiseless shudder when the beautiful creature died, something that crackled and blazed like lightening in daylight as his spirit passed. The ravens croaked as they settled on his body and the wolves allowed them to remain and eat beside them.

When I saw that the wolves had eaten their fill, I approached. The male lifted his head and looked at me and I saw every detail of that masterful animal face as though something had washed my eyesight clean – the blue-gray shading of the fur around his eyes, the fawn streaks along his nose, the white ruffled fur on his throat. In his steadfast gaze I met a presence that held knowledge of life renewing itself through what appeared as death. As I recognized his dignity, he answered me with his eyes and I knew that I could take the meat I needed from the carcass.

I remembered the shining passage of the deer's spirit as I cooked the meat on a stick above the fire. The life in its body had come down, single and simple, from the sun, and taken form in the deer and the wolves and the birds and now it would find another form in me.

Now a time began that is hard for me to speak about. My tongue thickened and forgot the motions of human speech. I forgot my people and the shape and smell of the man I'd left behind. I forgot the strange torment of love that has twined with anger and with jealousy and grief. The ground blossomed with ferns and mosses but I had no longing for human touch and when I lay down in the cavern each night, on ragged piles of rough green plants tugged from the undergrowth, I breathed in the bruised green scents like another kind of speaking.

I cannot say how long I lived like this. I had no sense of past or future. I hollowed out from days of hunger with the wolves and when they killed, I shared the deer's warm flesh with them, with a passionate sense of belonging to the breathing animal earth.

Until the day came when I saw that the gray wolf mother was missing. The wolves had not killed for some days and when they gathered to hunt I held back and watched them lope away. I had understood – they had shared everything they could with me, but now they had a nursing mother and a litter of new cubs to feed.

The wolves did not return to the meadow again and for the first time since I'd come to the mountain, I felt alone. I ate bitter herbs and dried meat, and the fullness of the world faded from me and I lost the taste of its sap and ripeness.

Perhaps you think that solitude means to be alone? No – there are times when solitude is *peopled* – crowded with familiar ghosts, shapes woven from memory and the threads of every kind of feeling. In solitude you meet what lives in your own mind and heart. Alone as I had never been before, I walked back into the smoke-filled rooms that had closed around my life. The old resentments took powerful hold again and I repeated my bitter sense of wrong to him in ghostly conversations with his image on the air.

There were days when bitterness swallowed me entirely. At other times the love I'd felt for my husband once shone through again, like the red that streaks the sky at sunset. You must not think that I was always angry with him for his lies and his betrayals. No, there was always part of me that longed for him and craved his love and understanding. How harshly I blamed myself as a failure then. I felt ashamed of my own weakness. If I'd known how to love him better, he would have changed...

But through those days of solitude something in *me* began to change. The clear light and the stillness of the remote white peaks drew me up, out of these obsessions into the peace that lives in silence. For silence is not emptiness or absence, as you might think. No – silence is the very intensity and presence of undivided life. Before ever sound is heard there is the silence that allows all sound to be.

In silence I watched the exchanges in my mind as once I had watched the wolves out on the meadow. I was simply the open space through which the stream of thought and feeling moved, the clear awareness in which it rippled and divided. As I watched the stream it stilled; it returned again to peace, and the first touch of light on the grasses, the movements of the air and water were stirrings in the presence of the great silence and everywhere I looked, I saw reflections from its grace.

One evening, I heard one of the wolves howl in the distance. Another joined in a wavering call and the two voices merged and faded slowly into silence down a long, descending line.

How quickly, I thought, life takes flight from all its forms. How soon everything that takes shape in the world is undone. And these feelings that cry out in us – they dissolve and return again to silence. Who are we in that silence? My father and my mother, my dear grandmother, who have all passed out of this world, who are you, now that you no longer wear the faces of my father and my mother?

I took out my grandmother's sewing pouch again, opened up the drawstring mouth and ran the faded scraps of thread across my fingers. I remembered small things she'd made for me; the rents she'd mended in my clothes and the love in these memories spread warmth across my chest.

I closed my eyes and saw my grandmother's face again, scored with the lines of her patience and endurance. I watched my small bright swallow of a mother beat herself against the walls of life, like a bird trapped inside a room. I watched sadness darken around us like smoke as my father left and became nothing more to us than memory, a shadow passing along a wall, the sound of footsteps hurrying away.

And with even finer, inward sight, I became aware of these feelings and reactions as patterns – meeting, gathering and combining before the light that was glowing out within me now, stronger and stronger...

What can I tell you about that light? Subtler than sunlight, even more alive, spreading in warmth and radiance through my whole being from the very core until every breath within my body rose on the waves of light. Light was breathing through me, bringing waves of deepening peace, and when the figure of my husband came I saw him in the light. I saw past his outer appearance as the person who had brought me pain, into the places in his heart that were marked with rejection and despair and I realized where those places also were in me – patterns that had bound us to each other and found continuation in our life together.

As I saw our life together whole, these patterns shivered and dissolved. The cords of pain that had bound us to each other went from me completely, with a tremendous feeling of release. I let them go and found the freedom to simply be, in peace and the wholeness of the light within the heart.

My friends, you have come a long way with me. You have walked with me through my story and we are almost at the end, almost at the place where all stories and the words that make them return to the wordless, living stream.

The wolves lead me back to the living stream. They shared everything they could with me and when I met their eyes without fear I saw there is no division. No edge without a meeting, no boundary that does not open to another. Life is always flaring and dissolving on the immense breathing of creation and only the dreams and shadows in the mind separate us from the freedom of our being on its breath.

May you too know freedom. May you find it in every welling

up of breath within your body, flowing out through the space that allows all things to be, and returning again to the center, into the heart of peace.

The Book of Bear

Earth and Ice

Part 1 Earth

Brown Bear, Ursus arctos
Gold of the Wilderness,
Loved One,
Honey Paws.
Grandfather, Grandmother.
Names for the Brown Bear.

1 The Story of Valentine and Svetlana Pazhetnov

Bubonitsa, Tver, Western Russia
January 2002

When the woman lifts the lid from the wooden box the bear cubs stir blindly in the light and screech. Born a few weeks ago inside their mother's winter den, the three cubs are still blind and deaf and each one weighs little more than a couple of pounds. She lifts one cub from the box with her gloved hand and it squirms in her hold with a high-pitched mewl of protest, and extends feet that are tipped with small curved claws. The cub's soft downy fur is dark-brown all over, and it has a narrow white band around the neck that dips to a v at the chest.

Placing it down gently on a towel, she offers a bottle of warm milk formula which the cub eagerly accepts; at a kitchen unit on the other side of the room, the man checks the temperature of the milk he has just heated and takes the bottle over to a second wooden box where two more bear cubs are huddled.

The couple works together in complete silence, all their gestures smooth and practiced as they go through their familiar, domestic routine. They're in their sixties, handsome people, dark-eyed and still dark-haired, with strong cheekbones and wide faces; in the quiet suspension of these hours before dawn they might be a grandfather and grandmother, rising early and bringing a lifetime of experience to the care of small, demanding, helpless creatures. Their names are Valentine and Svetlana Pazhetnov, and they are two of the most remarkable people I have ever known.

After each cub has fed from the bottle, they massage it gently on the stomach and wipe it with a damp paper towel to help it defecate, as the bear mother would have done with her tongue. Then they close the cubs back inside their wooden boxes and leave the room as silently as they entered it. These orphan bear cubs should never hear a human voice, they say, while they are being fed like this by hand. They should not taste human skin or associate the smell of the human body with food or comfort. This is why the Pazhetnovs move so quietly and never speak around the cubs, why they always wear thick gloves and put on the same, unwashed set of old clothes. By autumn these orphans will have grown strong enough to be released into the forest and they will need all the integrity of their wild instincts if they are to survive.

The temperature outdoors is around minus 20° C and heavy snow loads the windowsills of the simple wooden house. We are deep inside the *taiga* forest of western Russia, among one of the densest populations of brown bears on Earth. All around us, brown bears lie sunk in their winter sleep, bedded down beneath the snow inside the dens they have hollowed beneath the roots of spruce or fir trees and lined with mosses and pine boughs. Many are females nursing newborn cubs, for the bear mother is unique among mammals in giving birth to her young near the midpoint of winter, at the time of deepest darkness, after she has submerged herself in sleep. All summer, the embryos that were fertilized during mating float suspended in her womb, their first surge of growth arrested until she has laid down the fat stores that will enable her to support them. When she curls her body into the den, after feeding intensively through the summer and autumn, the dormant life within her wakes and the embryos are implanted on the walls of her womb as the bear mother sinks into the depths of sleep.

Because she hibernates while pregnant, the bear mother cannot sustain the growth of these unborn cubs beyond a certain stage. When they slip from her body in January or early February, they are blind and deaf, toothless and almost hairless, and their legs cannot support them. The mother's nurturing and protective body and the earthen walls of the winter den are the second womb where they continue to develop.

These orphaned cubs lost their mothers to hunters not long after birth; the hunters used dogs to find the bear den and the drowsy mothers were roused by their barking and shot when they left the den. When they first arrived at the Pazhetnovs' bear sanctuary the cubs were so traumatized that they would not accept food from a bottle. But the Pazhetnovs have decades of experience in caring for orphaned bears, and they persisted until the cubs recovered the desire to live.

Very young bear cubs are like human babies, Svetlana tells me over tea in the kitchen: they need food and warmth and security and they can do nothing for themselves. The Pazhetnovs must wake every three hours in the night to give the cubs their feed of milk formula, or mix of milk, eggs and honey. While the cubs are very small, they keep them inside their house because the cubs need the warmth they would have received from lying on their mother's body in the den. By the time they are six weeks old, when their eyes have opened fully and they are strong enough to stand, the cubs can be moved to a colder room where the temperature is close to that on the floor of the den. In spring they are taken outside to a wooden hut at the edge of the forest where they live in semi-independence until autumn, when they are ready to leave the sanctuary.

While we sit talking in the kitchen, the sun rises over the crystalline expanse of the snow-covered forest – virgin stands of spruce and fir trees, mixed with aspen, mountain ash and birch among frozen lakes and muskeg bogs. This forest is a protected wilderness – remote, expansive, continuous, unmarked by large roads or other signs of intensive human use. Lynx and wolves live beside elk, moose and deer; there are otters and wild boar and more than 200 species of birds in summer – falcons and golden eagles, black storks, ptarmigan and cranes.

With one bear on average living in every square kilometer, this forest has the highest concentration of brown bears in Europe. This does not mean that each bear has that amount of territory to itself: bears move through home ranges that overlap with those of other bears, and the shape and size of their range reflects the seasonal rhythms of their lives. A home range includes sheltered places where the bear can bed down for a nap during the day, paths that lead him easily and safely between food sources, and den sites for the winter. It varies greatly in size according to the richness of its resources, and whether the bear is male or female. The adult male's range is always larger than the female's, because he is bigger, needs more food, and roams extensively in search of sexual partners.

The tiny hamlet of Bubonitsa at the edge of the reserve was almost deserted when the Pazhetnovs set up their sanctuary for orphaned bears cubs here in 1985. Over the years, other scientists have joined them and they live now within a unique scientific community whose members are all dedicated researchers into the lives of wolves and bears.

Understanding Bears from the Inside

The first time I met Valentine and Svetlana I was traveling around western Russia gathering information from scientists and conservationists about the killing of brown bears for their galls, the internal organ that secretes bile, which is tragically a prized ingredient in traditional Chinese medicine. Later I returned to them for a much longer stay, this time to write about their work with orphaned bear cubs. I went with a Swedish friend and colleague, the photographer Staffan Widstrand. It was a warm morning in late September when we arrived; after the long train journey overnight from Moscow, the Pazhetnovs' simple wooden house, with its carved and fretted window frames, had a potent quality of forest magic. A crow was perched on the gatepost and it pecked the latch and let the gate swing open as we approached.

"This is Kara," Valentine informed us, as the crow flew over and settled on his arm. "A very interesting bird," he added gravely, stroking Kara's raggedy black feathers and allowing her to climb onto his shoulder. I never saw Kara come indoors – she always perched outside the house – but she clearly considered herself to be part of the Pazhetnov family and whenever I sat down outside to talk to Valentine, she hovered around him or strutted bossily across the veranda table and scanned us with her sharp jet eyes.

The sense of having entered an enchanted world that was closer to myth and magic than the fabric of ordinary reality grew stronger in the afternoon when Valentine lead us away from the house into the damp green halls of the forest. He wore a long blue smock over his trousers with a hood that tipped forward to shield part of his face from view; as he moved fluidly between shadows and trees, his features masked, he appeared a timeless, anonymous guardian of the forest. He left us to wait for a short while; when he returned, three half-grown bear cubs were bounding along behind him, their dark-brown bodies barely two foot from the ground.

While he walked the bear cubs were drawn to follow, as though attached to him by some invisible cord, which his movements pulled taut. As soon as he halted, the connection slackened. The cubs plunged off the track and began rooting through the leaf litter, tossing the yellow aspen leaves around, and showing a lick of raspberry-colored tongue as they sifted through the rich humus of the forest floor. They used their long pointed claws to scrape away the mosses and lichens that crusted the fallen branches and raked through the soil in search of ants and other insects.

Mindful of Valentine's warning not to come too close to the cubs, we followed them from a distance as they moved deeper into the forest beneath the canopy of evergreen pine and spruce. They clambered with catlike ease over the fallen trunks of ancient spruces bracketed with fungi and overgrown with lichens, their chocolate-brown fur turning black beneath the pine-green light except where narrow shafts of brightness molded the curves of their shoulders, necks and haunches in paler hues of fawn and mushroom brown.

All the time the cubs' round ears and flexible black noses quivered in response to the stream of messages from the senses. A babble of different bear cries flowed back and forth between them and kept them connected along a network of sound. The base note was a deep, regular *chug, chug, chug* sound that reminded me of the throbbing of a small furred engine and conveyed a sense of deep absorption in the immediate sensations of smell and taste and touch. Sometimes grunts and hisses or longer, low-pitched rumbles interrupted that regular soft chugging. At other times I heard a high-pitched, plaintive-sounding *ummmh, ummh, ummmh* and, more rarely, a grating whine of irritation that suggested a quarrel might be near.

In the mossy overcast beneath the evergreens, the ripe berries burned redly on the rowan trees. One cub, the female Valentine called Dina, placed her front paws on a rowan trunk, and looked up, tempted by the berries bunched on the upper branches. Black nostrils flared around the satin-pink lining of her nose as she caught the scent of ripeness; then she was climbing, digging all four claws into the trunk and moving onto the slender upper branches as fluidly as if she were made of fur and flesh without a bone or a joint in her body. Prima – the other female – followed her and the two cubs clung like shaggy balls of dark-brown fur among the scarlet berries, and picked them off in bunches with supple movements of their claws.

I gazed up at them, so absorbed in watching that I didn't notice the other cub approach me until I heard snuffling near my feet. I looked down, straight into one of the most expressive and endearing animal faces I have ever seen. It was the male cub that Valentine called Box, and the look in his brown eyes eloquently conveyed deep interest in this human creature that had stepped into his world.

Remembering Valentine's warning not to come too close, I moved away. Valentine quickly stepped over and gave the cub a sharp tap on the nose with his stick. Box looked up at him with an expressive air of hurt and injured innocence, and then retreated. Valentine had not intended to hurt the cub – he was only discouraging him from approaching other people, for he knew from painful experience that one of most dangerous things that Box could do later was approach people out of curiosity or in search of food. Even here, where people are so few and bears so many, a curious bear is more likely to trigger fear than understanding.

When Valentine walked on, Prima and Dina flowed with boneless ease down the trunk of the rowan tree and the three cubs followed him, bunched together at his heels until we emerged into the warm sunshine on a clearing where wild oats grew.

At the sight and smell of the ripe grain the cubs almost danced onto the oat field, giving sharp cries expressive of their intense excitement. I sat down beside Valentine on the ground and we watched them settle down to feed in earnest on the grain.

I never could remember afterwards what Valentine and I spoke about while we sat together in that warm circle of yellow light. I took no notes of our conversation and Valentine's words have faded from my memory. What I remember is the way the cubs took hold of the oat stalks with their claws, and bent the grain heads to their mouths. The dry tearing sound they made with their teeth as they crushed the kernels open. The way the crisp September light reflected from the rows of ripe grain and burnished the tips of their dark fur to warmer tones of amber, wheat, earth, honey.

And Valentine's face, half-shaded beneath his blue hood and the light in his brown eyes while he was watching them.

"Maybe every zoologist has one animal to which they feel particularly attached," he told me later. "For me that is the bear. It is really a pleasure for me to be with them and to work with them. They are such beautiful, such intelligent creatures. I am always astonished by how gracefully bears move – they flow like a ball of mercury! And there is something else – something that is harder to explain. I have an inner relationship with these animals. I feel I understand them from the inside."

From time to time, Valentine called out to the cubs with a few soft clicks of his tongue on the roof of his mouth – the same sound the bear mother makes when she calls to her family in the wild. Each time they heard it the cubs looked to him for reassurance or stood upright on their hind paws like half-grown children, their paws dangling and their necks extended as they scanned the oat field for any sign of danger.

In the end Prima stopped eating and lay down like a child tired out from walking. She rested her head on her forepaws, gave a long, plaintive-sounding *uhmmmm* and began to suck noisily on one front paw, turning the brown fur black with her saliva.

"They are all tired now," Valentine whispered to me. "They want to sleep." He stood up; with a few soft clicks of his tongue on his palate, he called the cubs together and lead them back to their enclosure in the woods.

When the Pazhetnovs first began raising orphaned bear cubs, Valentine took them on daily walks through the forest as soon as they were old enough. With experience, he has reduced his direct contact with the cubs to a minimum. During the day the Pazhetnovs simply leave the gates of the bear enclosure open so that the cubs can wander freely through the forest without anybody to guide them. When the orphans return to the hut in the evening their food is already waiting for them – oat porridge with honey or a little meat, placed in individual bowls about which the cubs are stubbornly possessive. In this way the cubs never see the people who have brought them food, and when the gates to the enclosure are left open continually from September, most leave for the forest of their own accord. The two sisters Prima and Dina and the male cub Box – who had approached me in the forest – remained at the sanctuary after the other cubs had left because they had come into close contact with people and still depended on human care.

"Box is a solitary cub," Svetlana explained, as she sat on the steps of the porch sorting through the basket of wild mushrooms she had gathered, their rich loamy smell giving promise of the delectable soup to come. "This year, for the first time, a wolf attacked the sanctuary and killed his two brothers. Box didn't see the wolf but he smelled it and he was so frightened he ran to Valentine for protection. He's very attached to him."

A local woman had taken Prima and Dina from the hunters who had killed their mother. She had fed them by hand and kept them warm by keeping them in her own bed and the cubs had become accustomed to human touch and closeness. Prima, Dina and Box would remain at the sanctuary during the winter and hibernate together, she continued; during the long months of sleep, their attachment to Valentine would fade.

"We will make sure that they see no people when they wake in the spring and they should go straight to the forest. Of course I have protective feelings towards these cubs. In many ways, I feel like any mother with her children because I was with them when they were little and I took care of them. But at the same time I will part from them without any feelings of regret. As a biologist what truly matters to me is knowing that they can return home and live free in the forest without help from people."

"Bear cubs may appear similar but they are never the same," Valentine told me.

He was sat outdoors at the table on the veranda, with his shirtsleeves rolled up in the warm sunshine, showing the strength of his heavily tattooed forearms and callused hands. He might be in his mid-sixties, but he had the physique and the aura of vitality of a much younger man. With his son Sergei, he did all the building and maintenance work at the sanctuary himself, carried out the welding and metalwork, and repaired the vehicles while still keeping up the stream of research which has given him a worldwide reputation among zoologists.

Kara was perched beside him on the table and she kept

turning her sharp black gaze on the cameras and tape recorder – glittering metallic objects of desire, which she would clearly have liked to plunder.

"The orphaned cubs come to us at different ages – from a few days old to several months – so we must adapt the way we treat then. Just like the adult bears, cubs are individuals with their own personality and temperament. We notice very quickly that some are leaders and some are followers. While they are here with us they form families of two or three or four cubs. We release these cubs together so they can help each other."

"It is very important to remember that we are not their mother. All we can do is help them to grow up and become independent of us as quickly as possible. Even here, your must not think their life is easy. Some have died from eating poisonous plants. Several were killed by stray dogs. This year, for the first time, three were killed by a wolf. Normally wolves avoid bear cubs because they are afraid of the mother but this wolf realized that the cubs were here without a mother."

In the wild, young brown bears usually spend around two and a half years with their mother and siblings – although the period may shorten if their habitat is particularly rich in resources. These are the years of their childhood and early adolescence when they explore their world in safety and develop the skills and knowledge they need to survive in it.

The bond between the mother and her cubs is very strong during that first year. She watches over them constantly, frets and becomes visibly anxious if they move too far away, and responds immediately to their demands. The family moves according to the rhythm of the cubs' needs and the mother pauses often to let them nurse or sleep or to allow a tired cub to rest by riding on her back. The family dens together that first winter, and since bears rarely reuse den sites from year to year, the mother chooses a new site and the family prepares it together.

When they emerge from the den the following spring, the cubs are much stronger. They gather more of their own food; they nurse less frequently and they are confident enough to forage independently at some distance from their mother and siblings. But the family usually dens together through a second winter before breaking up the following spring or early summer. At the northern end of the brown bear's range you may even see some three-year-old juveniles still with their mother, although this is rare. The bear mother usually leaves the cubs or drives them away so that she is free to search for a new partner and breed again.

The siblings stay together for some time after the separation from their mother, but despite the support they give each other, that first year of independence is the most challenging time in their lives. Many newly independent juveniles die before they ever become sexually mature adults at around five to seven years of age.

For the Bubonitsa orphans, the protected time of childhood is drastically curtailed. When they leave the sanctuary at the age of nine or ten months, they must be able to fend for themselves entirely, avoid potentially aggressive male bears, find the most nutritious foods to carry them through their first winter hibernation, excavate a den site, line it with pine branches and leaves – all the essential tasks of survival which a wild bear will not face without the mother's help for almost two more years.

"These bear cubs are like the children of the Leningrad siege during the Second World War," Valentine said. "They must grow up quickly and they have to deal with harsh conditions at a young age."

As Valentine spoke, I sensed the care he took to choose the right words. He expressed himself with the precise intensity of a scientist; at the same time I was aware of another quality in his demeanor and his tone of voice, which I can only call lucid passion. He was deeply absorbed in his relationship with another creature and its well-being was intimately connected with his own.

When I asked him what it was like to see the bear cubs he had raised return to the wild, he broke into a smile. Open, generous, irresistible in its warmth.

"I have good feelings. I do not like to be sentimental, but those are good feelings. What man took from nature has been given back to nature."

Partnership with the Wild

Staffan and I told each other that we had fallen completely in love with Valentine and Svetlana. This wasn't just a joke: I have rarely met people who bring such grace to the difficult task of living in balance in this world. They were full of humor and vitality; being around them, walking with Valentine in the forest, or sitting in their kitchen talking, was an experience of pure happiness for me.

They clearly loved the bears they raised – Svetlana always spoke proudly about *our bears* – and they gave them the same dedicated care they must have given their own young children. But they never confused human needs with the needs of the bears; they honored its wild nature and did everything in their power to foster it. And they clearly loved each other, and the remarkable adventure of their life together.

"I never wanted to live anywhere except the forest," Valentine told me that evening while he prepared dinner in the kitchen and sliced the wild mushrooms Svetlana had collected to make soup. After leaving school, he had trained to be a welder and a metal-worker, but he couldn't bear to confine his life to workshops and factories. His dreams were all of space, freedom, and a living connection with the wild. Finally, inspired by his reading and long hours spent studying maps of the Russian wilderness, he decided to become a professional hunter in the Siberian *taiga*.

"The week before I was due to leave for Siberia I went to a dance in the village."

His dark eyes brightened as he glanced across the table at

Svetlana.

"That was the night I met Svetlana… "

"He was such a wonderful singer!" Svetlana broke in, laughing.

"I didn't know what to do. And then I thought – why not just ask her to come with me? So I did and the answer was yes!"

"We left for Siberia with one case between us," Svetlana added, indicating the size and shape of the small case with a few gestures of her hands.

They smiled, happy in the memory of their first meeting and the adventurous beginning to their life together, and the warmth of the feeling between them was as palpable as a touch.

They moved to the Siberian *taiga* near the Yenisei River, where they lived for much of the year in tents and hunting cabins among the reindeer-herding Evenk people. Valentine spent long periods alone in the forest hunting, carrying everything he needed and sleeping outdoors even during freezing winter nights – "on a bed of pine branches with a fire at my head and a fire at my feet," as he put it. Coming back from one of those expeditions one autumn evening, he met Svetlana out picking berries. Not far from her, feasting on another berry patch was a large brown bear.

"I was frightened for her. I didn't know what to do, whether I should shoot the bear or not."

"And I said to him, Valentine, whatever is the matter with you?" Svetlana added. "That bear is minding his business and I mind mine."

"Now you see what kind of a wife I have," Valentine said, and every line in his face became part of his smile.

The Courtship of Bears

It was not surprising that Valentine had feared for Svetlana's safety: a fully-grown brown bear, male or female, is a creature of formidable power. Although they are often remarkably tolerant of people, when the bears are stressed, suddenly startled or feel threatened for themselves or their cubs, they can certainly be dangerous. And the more that people encroach on their space, the more stressful their lives become.

Along the Pacific coast, where their diet is rich in protein from the salmon runs, mature male brown bears almost reach the size of the polar bear – their closest relative and the largest land carnivore of all. These males may weigh up to half a ton and stand five foot at the shoulder while the females are around two-thirds their size.

The brown bear's strength is combined with suppleness. Watch a fully-grown bear drop her body weight into the ground through her hind legs, straighten her spine and stand: her body rises in one fluid movement; her feet are planted, sole and heel, on the Earth and she stands with the groundedness that is the foundation of her grace. The muscled shoulders, which power her forelegs for digging, are released; her neck extends and she gazes straight ahead at whatever has captured her attention. She stands not to threaten but to see more clearly and to smell the different scent currents in the air.

Her long nose contains multiple scent receptors over which the air flows to be tasted in extraordinary depth and detail. A bear's sensitivity to the faintest diffusion of scent is something we humans can scarcely imagine; the range of our own physical senses is so limited. But the expansive motions of the air bring the bear messages across great distances – news of ripening berries, the carcass of a winterkilled deer. Or the scent of another bear that is searching for a mate.

It is not always easy for brown bears to find a partner at the right time and breed, especially as human pressure often forces them to live in small isolated populations or pushes them onto unproductive land. We humans rarely consider just how stressful this can be for bears – both physically in finding enough food, and emotionally, in finding sexual partners. There are always more males than fertile females, for each female bear only becomes receptive every third or even fourth year, after she has finished raising her previous family. So the male needs the freedom to roam in search of partners and this is restricted when the bears are confined to smaller reserves.

Maureen Enns, the Canadian artist and naturalist you will meet later in this book, spent several years among the brown bears of Kamchatka in Russia. Maureen saw four to five year old females playing with single males the year ahead of their first breeding season. One female, which Maureen called Biscuit, spent time with a single male of her own age the summer she was four years old. The following spring, that young male came around Biscuit's den when she emerged from hibernation. Another young male courted Biscuit that summer by staying near and crawling towards her on his belly. However, when Biscuit finally bred it was first with an older and more dominant male, and later with a younger one.

Male bears often compete with each other over fertile females and older males often show the scars of these battles on their noses and ears. The females are not always impressed by the most assertive males, though. While the big guys are busy swaggering in front of each other, roaring and urinating copiously over the nearest tree in ritual displays of sexual vigor, female bears in Alaska have been seen to slip quietly away and mate with some inoffensive (and probably astonished) juvenile.

There are places where bear courtship can be more relaxed. In rich, undisturbed bear habitat, such as the protected coastal flats of southern Alaska, where brown bears congregate around rich sedge meadows and abundant salmon runs, male and female have more opportunities to meet and court. With less competition for food, space and sexual partners, the males appear to be more tolerant towards each other. A female may take several partners during the four or five days when she is most fertile, and since each partner could potentially fertilize a separate egg, her two or three cubs may have different fathers.

When their breeding season is ended, the females aggressively chase males away with loud roars. The males make no contribution to their offspring's well-being and the bear mother becomes a self-sufficient and devoted single parent.

A New Family

The Pazhetnovs' son Sergei was born in Siberia – conceived in a tent by the Yenisei River, as Svetlana told me, with a gleam in her brown eyes.

Although their life in Siberia was happy, it was not long before Valentine realized he could not work as a hunter. He did not want to kill animals but to understand them and deepen his connection with the life of the forest. So he decided to radically change his life: he would study biology instead, and after six years at university, he and Svetlana came to work as researchers in the Central forest reserve where they have lived ever since.

One spring day he was watching a bear mother's den from a hide, waiting to see her emerge with the cubs. The mother came out to warm herself in the March sunshine and caught Valentine's scent; to protect her cubs she charged him, her fur erect, giving a hoarse cry. He yelled and waved his arms up and down and she halted and wheeled around, kicking up the snow beneath her paws. Then she charged again. This time he caught up a wood axe and swung it, sending her racing away into the trees. He waited to see if she would return and when she didn't, he reached into the den and drew out her three cubs – hissing at him, their fur on end – and tucked them away in his pack.

That night the cubs slept beside him in the tent, tucked into the corner of his sleeping bag. In the morning he walked away to fetch some snow to melt for tea. He had left the tent flat open and when he looked back, he was astonished to see that all three cubs had set out to follow him. They had never walked in the open before; they were unsteady on their short legs and they kept sinking through the snow crust – but they were determined not to let him out of their sight. They halted at his feet, breathing hard and trembling with the effort. And when he walked away again, they followed him.

Finally he understood that for the cubs sleeping beside his warm body in the tent was like sleeping beside their mother in the den; when he walked away, he had triggered the same instinctive urge to follow the cubs would have felt when their mother first lead them outside. Their bond with her had been transferred to Valentine; in the language of biology, the cubs had imprinted it onto him. For the next two years he spent long periods alone in the forest with his adopted bear family. At first he tried to guide them towards the plants which he knew were favorites with bears, because he believed that the bear mother taught her cubs by example how to find food – which plants to savor and which to avoid, where to look for insects, the best way to split open an ant's nest and extract the eggs and larvae. But as the cubs set about exploring their surroundings for themselves, he realized that there was no need to guide them. They naturally set about selecting the plants they liked best at different seasons – from the first tender shoots of young sorrel, wild angelica and cow parsnip, to rosehips and rowan berries, raspberries, cranberries and blueberries.

Womb of Earth

By early November, when they were around ten months old, Valentine's cubs had lost their enthusiasm for play and exploration and were becoming lethargic. Their bodies were getting ready for their winter sleep.

At first Valentine tried to teach how the cubs how to den. He built them a shelter from pine logs, lined it with branches and lay down inside it himself hoping they would join him. The cubs weren't interested. They sniffed around him and showed no desire to curl up for the winter with their human parent. But as soon as the first snow fell, they began to dig their own shelter under a dead spruce, biting through the roots to enlarge the cavity and laying pine branches across the floor. On the first night of hard frost, the cubs moved in and Valentine was woken in his tent by the sound of their snores. "They sounded just like those irritating men next door to you in a hotel," he wrote later, "the ones who keep you awake the whole night with the noise of their snoring!"

Brown bears hibernate because their food is scarce in the northern winter. During the cold dark months of the year, it would cost them more energy to search for food than they could gain by consuming it. Their solution is to slow themselves right down, excavate a shelter and sleep. Where winters are long and harsh, a brown bear may spend more than half the year asleep inside its den. (The longest recorded hibernation is that of a female in Alaska who slept in her den for eight months.)

The bear is not in a state of physical suspension like hibernating rodents whose body temperature drops almost to zero. The heartbeat and respiration slow but the bear's body remains warm; if disturbed, he can wake and defend himself if necessary. But throughout the long months of hibernation, the bear does not eat or drink or eliminate any bodily wastes. His body relies completely on its own resources; it burns its own fat as fuel and extracts all the water that it needs from the fat. At the same time, the metabolic wastes – which would be poisonous if they accumulated – are recycled by being turned into proteins. And through the long months of sleep, the bear keeps his muscle strength intact and retains the density of his bones.

It's an absolute marvel of bodily adaptation. If we humans lie immobile, even for quite short periods, our bones begin to weaken and our muscles waste away. And without external sources of food and water, we quickly die.

What the bear mother accomplishes during her hibernation is more extraordinary still. Like the male, she must metabolize her fat to fuel her own body and recycle the resulting wastes; in addition, she breaks down her muscle protein to feed the young in her womb. She must use muscle protein because her fat molecules are too large to be passed to her unborn cubs through the placenta. So that her muscles do not waste away completely and leave her too weak to walk when she emerges from the den in spring, her period of gestation is cut short, and this is why the cubs are born so helpless and dependent.

When the cubs slip from her body in January, they crawl blindly across her furred belly to reach the nipples for their first feed. She licks them clean and consumes the afterbirth and folds herself around them, enclosing them in the beating of her heart and the quiet rhythms of her breathing while they drink the high-fat milk that her sleeping body has prepared.

Walking in the woods again with Valentine, I find bear tracks sunk into the marshy ground where the cranberries grow. The hind prints show the sole of the bear's foot – bears stand and walk just as we do, on the soles of their feet – and the indentations made by the long claws. The bear has left a puddle of dark-red droppings, which are studded like frogspawn with the seeds of the cranberries it has eaten, on a bed of sphagnum moss as tartly green as unripe apples.

The plants will greatly benefit from the passage of their seeds through the bear's body. More seeds will germinate, stimulated by the bear's digestive acids and the workings of its gut, and they will be scattered more widely across the forest.

The forest has the complex life of a living creature whose organs are cranberry swamps and cloudberry patches, muskeg bogs and sphagnum moss beds. The green-gold layers of freshly fallen aspen leaves lie on rotting brown beds of older leaves. Broken branches crumble into dusty brown honeycombs beneath their fresh pelt of damp green mosses. The air is laced with the scents released by this marriage of fertility and decay. You catch the moldering echoes of fungus pushing to the surface from the cobweb of fine root filaments strung beneath the ground. The spicy balsam of the fir and spruce trees. The purple tartness of a patch of blueberries.

This is the forest – dense with potential, with opportunity – the bear cubs have come from and this is the forest to which they will return. In twenty or thirty years of life they will fertilize and transform it as they churn its seeds through their guts and disperse them in bright viscous puddles on the ground. Finally the forest will consume them; it will eat their flesh and take back their bones and bury them deep in its own dark breast.

Ahead of me Valentine crosses a small clearing; his head is bent, the hood of his blue smock is pulled forward to conceal his face. The three bear cubs follow him through the clearing, their dark fur lit by the hazy amber glow of the afternoon sun, until the tall trees close around them and they merge again with the shadows of the wood.

2 Following the Bear's Path:
Into the Sacred Cave

La Grotte de Pech Merle
The Lot Valley, Southwest France
April 2011

The flight of steps goes steeply down between stone walls and leads to a passage that slopes away further underground. I smell air laced with the damp cool tang of limestone and chalk and water, then the space around me swells to a great stone chamber, hollowed by the course of the underground river that once ran through these rocks.

The limestone billows in shadowy folds above my head. Molded pillars, some densely white, like quartzite, grow up from the floor and slender stone needles dart the roof. The way through the cave winds between the stone pinnacles and massive tumbled boulders and leads past small chambers that open like grottoes to the side. In places the limestone blooms into great circular disks along the walls, their surfaces repeatedly scored with runnels from the flow of water.

All these patterns of inorganic growth take shape from the darkness that the scattered lamplight on the floor cannot penetrate. How much darker it would have been twenty-five thousand years ago, how intense the blackness and the silence for the Paleolithic painters who entered these caves carrying the materials of their art – sharpened twigs for drawing in black charcoal, hollow bones for mouth-spraying pigments made from iron oxides, charcoal and white calcite and pads of mosses and lichens for blending and spreading color on the rocks.

The scored and molded surfaces of the limestone would have swelled in the weak light of their tallow lamps and pine torches and merged into the darkness when they passed on. The land above them was tundra and open steppe, with trees sparsely clustered along riverbanks, and it was filled with the most extraordinary variety of large animals. There were long-haired mammoths with sweeping tusks, aurochs, the extinct ancestors of cattle, reindeer and bison and horses; wooly rhinos and giant moose and cave bears, a larger relative of the brown bear, now extinct, that hibernated in these underground caves in winter.

The first animals appear on the cave walls – a frieze of long-haired mammoths, aurochs and bison drawn in black and red lines. The figures overlap or lie tilted sideways to each other in a way that suggests multiple dimensions opening within the surface field of stone. They are among the earliest paintings ever found, but there is nothing primitive or uncertain about the artists' work. The black charcoal lines are strong and sure, and the artists have worked with the contours, folds and hollows of the rock to give depth and relief to the animal's bodies.

The sway of a mammoth's shaggy hair as it moves is captured with a sweeping fall of black lines. The mammoth's shoulders thrust up, as though the massive, earth-bound body is rising on the wall. It has no face – the features are left blank above the dense fall of hair – but it has been imbued with such intensity of presence that when I look away the cavern walls seem to swell with other forms. I see a mammoth mother and her calf emerge from the rippling folds of stone. A bison thrusts its massive shoulders through the shadows. For a moment all these forms, in stone or paint, appear as manifestations of the one substance of life, and I feel the presence of mystery, as dense, as imminent as the rock.

In another chamber two dappled horses stand back to back, their hindquarters overlapping, on a smooth stone wall with a curving outcrop at one end. There is no ground line and the dappled bodies seem to float on the wall. They are surrounded by handprints made by mouth-spraying dark paint around hands placed flat against the stone. Such handprints are often found in the painted caves and they are intensely moving – the gestures of men, women and children reaching out to the other realities sensed within the stone.

The handprints on this wall were made by women and the horse are mares – they have longer bodies than stallions. Perhaps this artist too was a woman. I imagine her contemplating the rock face in her uncertain pool of lamplight. She belonged to a nomadic community of hunter-gatherers that followed the bison and the reindeer and other animals between their seasonal feeding grounds. She slept on bison skins, and dressed in reindeer skin clothes, like those of Siberian herders. She wore ornaments of fox teeth; she played simple, haunting melodies on a small flute carved from mammoth ivory. And she had the pleasure that every artist takes in the relationships of shape, color and line. She saw the horse's head appear in that curved outcropping of rock at the end of the wall and her painting grew from that moment of recognition. She painted a much smaller, stylized horse head inside the rock outcrop, then gave the second horse the same tapering neck and stylized small head, making an abstract play with different forms that is twenty-five thousand years old.

"The art of the light and the art of the dark coexisted for all the duration of the Paleolithic," wrote Dr. Jean Clottes, one of the world's leading specialists on cave art. The "art of the light" was engraved or painted in rock shelters on the surface and seen in daily life. The "art of the dark" was made deep underground and lit only by the flickering of tallow lamps and resin torches.

These deep caves were never inhabited. They were sacred space, the creative womb within the Earth, where the people came to commune with the powers sustaining physical reality, which were embodied for them in animal shapes. In the weak, flickering light, the solidity of the rock walls dissolved and the animals emerged out of the formless dark. They moved out of clefts and fissures in the rock, or floated suspended between dark and light, before merging again with the fertile void, the space of original unity beyond the reach of the daylight mind, from which all separate forms rise and dissolve.

The caves' only inhabitants were the cave bears that slept in them through the winter. One of these cave bears left marks along one wall – long furrows where it stood upright and ran its claws along the stone to sharpen them. From this point, the modern way through the cave has been widened, but for the painters it continued through a narrow passage where they crawled forward on their hands and knees. It was here, at the narrowest passage through the cave, that they placed the bear: the head and snout shown in profile, outlined in white, with one eye gazing directly at the viewer.

The image that follows the bear is human – a man's body, sketched on the sloping roof of a recess. Like almost all the rare human figures portrayed in Ice Age art, it is rudimentary. These artists put their powers of observation, and their sophisticated techniques of representation, into the depiction of animal and not human forms. I must crouch down to see it, which suggests that it was intended for a viewer lying on the stone beneath. A bird-like shape takes flight above the head and the body is pierced by radiating straight lines. Is the man wounded or receiving healing? Is he dying or radiating life?

The Wisest of Animals

This small drawing of a bear's head, placed inside the narrowest passage through the cave, near a figure who may be dying or radiating new life, is among the earliest expressions of the aura of great sacredness and healing power that has surrounded bears for thirty thousand years or more. The earliest bear images found were beautifully drawn in fluid, red lines on the walls of Chauvet, in southern France, which is the oldest of all the painted caves. Deep inside Chauvet, there is circular chamber where a fallen rock resembles an altar at the center. The massive skull of a cave bear, more than eighteen inches long, sits on the rock itself, with the canines hooked over the edge; thirty-six other bear skulls have been found inside the chamber. The bear skull has lain undisturbed on that rock for some thirty thousand years; it is no exaggeration to state that some of humanity's earliest sacred rituals were held in connection with the spirit of the bear.

In the bleak, bare time of winter, Paleolithic artists saw bears enter these caves and sink into a death-like sleep. While the Earth lies dormant, the bear remains still and takes in no food or water. The bear does not resist winter's cold and hunger, or fight to stay active and awake; it goes into the Earth and rests inside it. The bear mother gestates her cubs while sleeping, as though from the dream of shaping and making that she shares with the Earth. When life flowers in spring, the bear too is reborn, and she brings the new life in her cubs from the winter darkness and the depths of sleep. In the bear – particularly the mother – birth and death, sleeping and waking, rest and action are united in the creative fusion of opposites that brings renewal.

This mystery of renewal through alternating cycles of light and dark has made bears profoundly worthy of contemplation and respect in many different cultures. Throughout the circum-polar North, traditional hunters honored the bears they had slain as messengers, carrying their expressions of love and gratitude back to the spiritual guardians that watched over the lives of the animals. Similar rituals and ceremonies were practiced around the North from Lapland to Canada: the bear meat was eaten as part of a ceremony of thanksgiving and the bear's bones were treated with great respect, beautifully decorated and hung from a tree, or returned to the den where the bear was found. Bears also inspired the earliest known representations of a mother and child – small sculptures of a bear-headed woman cradling a child – or cub – in her arms, which were made around seven thousand years ago by the artists of the Vinca culture in what is now Romania.

As a mark of respect, traditional hunters never referred to the bear directly but gave it many beautiful and expressive names. In Northern Europe, the bear was the *Pride and Beauty of the Forest, Gold of the Wilderness, Loved One,* and *Honey Paws.*

Native Americans also called the bear by many names: it was Chief's Son, Dark Thing, Old One. But the most significant name of all was also the most intimate and respectful – *Grandfather, Grandmother.*

In the wisdom traditions of Native America, every created being has power according to the level of the spiritual reality that it reflects. The bear is greatly revered by Native Americans, and regarded as an ancestor and guide, because the bear's life reflects such a profound spiritual teaching: that life endures through continuous cycles of death and transformation. For this reason, bears are the guardians of many initiation rites – the ceremonies of symbolic death and rebirth which take the individual from one stage of life, or one level of knowledge and wisdom, to another. Through finding inner relationship with the bear, a man or woman facing a point of critical change is helped to die to the past – let go completely of old forms of thinking and acting – and move into new life.

On the day she started her first period, it was traditional for the young girl of the Ojibwa, a people of the Great Lakes region, to be taken to live alone for a time in a hut in the forest. *She is a bear,* her people said. Older women visited the girl and they spoke together about becoming a woman, making love, giving birth and raising children. Secluded in her den-like hut, the girl turned inward, just as the bear mother turns into the Earth to bring out new life. Her sexual power was potent as the mother bear was potent, and like her, it must be treated with respect. Through identifying with the bear at this critical point in her life, the girl could make her own inner connection with her feminine power before bringing it into a relationship in her external life.

On the Great Plains, the young Dakota boy also identified

with the bear as he made the crucial transition to adulthood. During the traditional initiation, the boy made a symbolic den where he remained alone, walking on all fours like the bear, growling and making bear-like sounds. After some days the boy was symbolically killed and his body was brought to the ceremonial lodge where an elder set all night with him to smoke and pray. When he crossed the threshold of the lodge the next morning he was greeted as an adult man.

The bear is also the guardian of adult initiations. Candidates for admission to the sacred Medicine Lodge Society of the Ojibwa would pass through successive degrees of initiation: the fourth, and final stage, which might not be achieved until old age, is traditionally associated with the bear.

In these powerful rituals of change and transformation, the bear is not some abstract symbol: the bear directly embodies the renewal that is inherent in the deep rhythms of life and through making inner connection with renewal *through* the bear, currents of healing flow that can restore the human mind and body to health and balance.

Among the Ojibwa, healers were said to *follow the bear's path*. Bears seek out the most nourishing plants in season and they also use them to clear parasites and prevent infection; traditional Ojibwa bear healers also studied the healing and nourishing qualities of plants, along with their subtle aspects that help bring emotional balance. Other healers worked directly with the bear's spirit, such as the bear doctors of the Hopi people of the American Southwest. Bear doctors wore necklaces made from bear claws; they placed bear paws over their own hands when they touched the bodies of the sick and dying, and they received guidance through the bear's spirit in a vision or a dream. In many Native cultures, those healers who worked directly with the bear's power were considered to be the most effective of all, although it was also said that the bear spirit was so powerful that only the strongest individuals could work with it safely.

Lakota healer John Lame Deer called the bear the "wisest of animals as far as medicines are concerned. The bear is the only animal that one can see in a dream acting like a medicine man, giving herbs to people. It digs up certain healing roots with its claws. Often it will show a man in a vision which medicines to use."

The bear's power as guide and healer has endured in so many different cultures over tens of thousands of years because it has helped people to find relationship with the truth that cannot be contained in mental concepts – life and death are not opposites but work together in renewal. Life springs new out of death, branching into a myriad of brilliant shapes that dissolve their separation and merge again with the Earth's dark ground –seedbed and grave, death chamber and birth chamber of the unpredictable renewal of life.

Here in these caves, among some of the earliest images made by human hands, I sense that power with an immediacy that brings my ordinary mind to silence. The bear's path leads down, below the flickering and distracted rush of thought, the flashes of memory, the current of words and images, to the deep ground of silence where the mind lets go of the attachment to continual thinking and finds rest. Trust, let go, and you drop into the presence of grace below the surface activity of the mind. In that sacred inner space of stillness and silence, we find sources of renewal: springs of inspiration, rising spontaneously from the fertile darkness of not-knowing and not-doing, and come home, where fear finds healing, into the heart of our being and the heart of all things.

In the last cavern before the exit at Pech Merle, there is a shallow depression in the ground. It shows where a bear once dug a bed from the sediments and lay down to sleep through the winter. This cave of painted images and visions was also the bears' winter den. The people would have passed among sleeping bears when they entered it in winter. They would have seen the bears nursing newborn cubs while half-asleep. The drowsing bears must have appeared to them like guardians at the threshold between physical reality and the spiritual dimensions beyond the cave walls.

Near that ancient bear bed, one of the oak trees growing on the limestone *causse* above sends a great tap root down through the cavern ceiling to the floor; the root has cracked open the way through the stone as it reaches for the springs of water that run further underground.

When I come out on the surface, the green fire burns so brightly in the oak leaves that it dazzles. The caves have taken me into the roots of things.

This story was inspired by an initiation tale from Hopi oral tradition, whose healers worked with the power of the bear. The original tells of a young hunter who goes to the wilderness alone, where he meets a woman and desires her and she shows him a vision of her skeleton beneath the flesh. That image of a young man who sees through the surface of a woman's body, into the very bones, spoke to me and it grew into this story.

3 The Story of the Young Man and Skeleton Woman

There was a young man once who thought he wanted to be a hunter. He tried so hard! But no matter how hard he tried things never came out right for him. He was always out of step with the other men. He'd forget something that he needed, or he'd be looking in the other direction when the deer appeared. His father would shout at him, his face red and mottled with anger while the other men laughed; his feet pointed one way, they joked, and his head another; he'd be better off staying at home with the women.

And they would have been glad to see him, too, for this young man was very beautiful. But he was too anxious to feel at ease with them, and he never noticed the way he drew the young women's gaze.

The truth is, it was the forest itself that gave him joy, with its rich smells and the bright whirring of the birds among the branches. He loved especially the icy stillness of certain mornings in winter, when the frozen world was stilled to many shades of white and even the sky was pale with cold; then he would gaze up at the clear winter light and sense a mysterious presence flowering in the bare white silence between the branches. In that presence there was peace, a profound stillness that eased his anxious and self-doubting mind. But he kept these feelings hidden for he knew they made him different to his father and all the other men and he yearned to be accepted and to win their respect.

In the end the young man resolved that he would prove himself as a man to them once and for all. He would go alone to the forest and he wouldn't come back to his village until he was carrying the meat from a deer.

He told nobody what he planned; he prepared everything he needed in secret, checked and cleaned his rifle and made sure his knife was sharp. There were many bears living in that forest and before he slept, he made a fervent prayer in his heart to the bear spirit. Grandfather, Grandmother, he prayed, allow me to hunt in your forest. Guide my steps. Be kind to me if we should meet and allow me to go on my way in peace.

He rose very early, while his father and his mother and his sister still lay sleeping, and crept down to the kitchen to dress by the iron stove, where his father's heavy boots sat drying, their thick tongues of dark brown leather curling in the heat. Looking at the familiar room, he was struck by a strange certainty that he would never see it in the same way again. Whatever the day might bring, he would not return to this house the same.

Outside the first light of morning was slanting through the groves of beech and hazel, which were filled like a bowl to overflowing with the piercing clarity of bird song. How fervently the birds welcomed the new day! He would have liked so much to simply wander and let their singing wash through him like water. But that wasn't what he'd come for... he belted up his resolve and walked on, checking the ground carefully for tracks and droppings, the way he'd seen his father do, and looking around him, front and back, left and right.

The morning lost its first clarity and nothing came; the forest seemed to have emptied at his approach and even the bird song was swallowed by the dense green silence.

He had been wandering for hours, getting more and more tired and frustrated, when he came upon fresh bear tracks pressed into the damp ground of a small clearing where the cranberries grew. He cocked his rifle and listened. The air was so still his labored breathing whistled in his ears. A yellow leaf broke off from a branch and rustled to the ground. And then – it was the strangest sensation – he felt the air around his body being ruffled by a breath.

His heart shuddered and restarted as he sensed the bear's presence behind him like weight upon the air, and turned –

The bear stood facing him, powerful shoulders and broad

furred face showing tawny-gold in the bright furrow of sunlight falling across the clearing. She – somehow he knew the bear was female – raised her head and circled it, nostrils twitching in her black muzzle as she stirred the air to draw his scent in deeper, and then she slipped noiselessly away and vanished into the darkness between the trees.

For a long time after the bear had left, he stood immobile, still feeling the power of her presence pulsing like a heartbeat through the clearing. Finally, when it seemed sure that the bear was really gone, he knelt down beside her prints and ran his hands around the marks of her soles and heels and the indentations of her claws. With that, a sudden impulse took him, and pulling off his heavy boots and socks, he placed his own bare feet inside her hind tracks, stood up and closed his eyes.

In the darkness a powerful weighty softness entered him. It drew his body down, into a meeting with the ground and waves of resilient power rose from the earth beneath his feet and spread throughout his muscles to his bones. His chest and heart expanded; his breathing deepened, as though the bear herself were breathing through him, and when he opened his eyes again, the clearing shone, as though a sudden shower had rinsed clean the air. He'd looked on each thing separately before, in a series of broken glances; now his eyes were lead along the subtle harmonies of connection that united the tree roots and the spreading branches, and the cranberries glowed so richly on the mosses he could almost taste them on his tongue.

That was when he caught a faint sweet smell of wood smoke drifting across the clearing. That smoke must have come from a camp or cabin, he thought with a sudden lifting of his heart at the thought of other people and putting on his shoes he set off to find it.

But it is hard to follow the smell of wood smoke through a forest; sometimes it seems to come from one direction, then another and the young man wandered about for hours and seemed to come no closer. It was evening, and the crows were making their tremendous racket roosting in the branches when he finally saw the smoke rising from the chimney of a little wooden cabin no larger than one room. The cabin had two small windows that almost touched the ground and the reed roof was all overgrown with a thick pelt of dark brown mosses.

Who can be living here alone, so deep in the forest? The young man wondered. And he wondered even more when the door opened and he saw the young woman who stood before him, straight and dark and shining, with the last light of day on her face.

She gazed at him, and never said a word. He muttered an awkward apology for having disturbed her, and he was about to turn away when she made one graceful gesture and invited him to come in.

The young man put down his rifle; he unlaced his muddy boots and bending his head beneath the lintel stepped down into the cabin. The one room was very simple; there was a wooden bench for sleeping, covered with a thick brown bear skin and a mat of woven reeds covered the earthen floor. A log fire burned brightly in the hearth and the air was scented with the herbs and wild mushrooms that hung drying from the ceiling.

He sat down before the fire and nodded shyly when the young woman asked if he were hungry; she brought him bread and honey and raspberries to eat, and sat before him at the other side of the fire. He said little at first, and he could scarcely touch the food; but there was such unassuming gentleness in her manner that he relaxed and allowed the warmth of the fire to enter his tired body.

He'd come to the forest to hunt, he told her; he'd looked hard all day, but he'd found no trace of deer. The frustration that he'd felt at his failure all that morning thickened in his throat as he spoke and he flushed and dropped his eyes to the ground, ashamed of his sudden uprush of emotion.

When he looked up, he met such openness in her dark gaze that his buried feelings of shame and failure rose in a burning tide and the words poured out, stammering and awkward. He'd always felt he was different to his father and the other men, he said; he was clumsy and forgetful, while they always seemed confident and sure of themselves. He described their mockery and rough humor; he told her how their taunts stung him and kept repeating in his mind. He told her about the anger that burned silently inside him while they joked about his clumsiness. In the end it didn't matter how hard he tried, he added bitterly; he'd never be accepted as a man.

He had never, in all his life, spoken like that to another person before, let alone a young and lovely woman. He was so shocked at his own daring that he fell silent, realizing how he'd exposed himself in that headlong rush of candor. When the young woman said nothing he burned inwardly with shame, certain that he had ripped the net of confidence between them away.

But she was simply considering what to say.

Why must you try so hard to change yourself and be like your father and all these other men? She asked him finally. Is theirs the only way to be a man?

The question came like an unexpected gift. He felt as though somebody had told him he was free to put a heavy burden down, and looking up at her again, he met her gaze openly and smiled.

The evening had grown dark while they were speaking; the fire lit up every corner of the cabin and the two young people looked at one other in silence. Each one was very beautiful to the other, and their awareness of the other's beauty was reflected back and forth between them in the firelight. Still neither said a word. But the silence was stronger than any words they could have spoken and as it continued it began to fill with power.

The young woman rose and put more wood on the fire so that it blazed up stronger than before. Standing in front of it, she shook her glossy black hair across her shoulders, took off her slippers and stood on slender feet. She unbuttoned her dress, slipped it from her shoulders and laid it down. And when only her slip was left she lifted up her arms and took that off as well and stood before him, naked and golden in the firelight.

Wrapped in a trance of wonder and desire, the young man did not dare to move. It was only one step more to reach out to her, fold his arms around her and merge their bodies into one.

Just as he was about to take it he noticed something strange. Backlit by the firelight that flickered on her body, the young woman's skin appeared to glow with the blood that ran through her arteries and veins. And then, something shifted in his sight and he was seeing through the rosy surface of her flesh to the bones beneath. Her bones shone so brightly through her lustrous skin they seemed to burn with their own white fire – her skull and shoulders and ribs, her spine and the narrow bowl of her hips. Then the vision faded and once again the warm, living woman stood before him naked, reaching out her hands to him.

If she ever touches me, he thought, I will surely die. The thought came with such a rush of cold fear that he rose to his feet and crossed to the door in a couple of strides. He didn't stop to pick up his rifle and shoes, he only ran out headlong out into the forested dark. But no matter how hard he ran, in his mind he seemed to hear the dry clicking of bones behind him and finally he halted, panting and shaking, and looked to see what followed him.

But the night was empty and utterly quiet.

He walked on. And heard it again – the same click of bone on bone. He plunged into the darkest place between the trees, tugging his way through the undergrowth until he tripped over some tree roots, and fell into a hollow full of fallen leaves. He lay there winded: all he heard was the pumping of his blood in his ears and the rustle of his body among the leaves.

If I stay hidden here until morning, he thought, I'll be safe.

With that, fear released its clutch and he knew that nothing had followed him through the dark; he had been running from the shadows moving through his mind.

A wave of misery washed through him and he wept. Perhaps you can imagine how he felt – how he reproached himself for his fear at that brief vision of the young woman's shining bones. Thoughts of shame and failure circled through his mind, carrion voices crowing harshly of accusation and condemnation. They rose to such a fierce pitch that he put one hand on the earth to steady himself and began to stroke the ground, the way you might stroke an animal for solace sometimes.

That was when he noticed the patch of hollow darkness underneath the torn-up roots of the fallen pine tree where he lay; he got to his knees and reached one hand inside the opening, and touched the earthen floor of a small chamber dug out between the roots. A bear must have slept in there; why shouldn't he do the same? He could hide this misery inside and try to sleep until day.

He wriggled his way through the narrow opening, first one shoulder, then the other, and curled up beneath the low roof of earth and roots, sheltered in a quiet darkness that his ragged breathing did not stir. The air smelled of the soil and the fading sweetness of the pine resin in the branches that the bear had laid across the floor.

He thought of the bear's slow breathing as she slept through the winter in this place. As the harsh voices in his mind were hushed, he began to sense a presence in the darkness, so accepting of him, in all his sense of weakness and failure, that his heart burned inside his chest to feel it. Hot tears sprung from his eyes again and ran into the ground beneath his head. But these tears came from the opening of the heart and they were washing his shame and failure away. He felt such relief as these feelings passed that he groaned out loud, from deep down in belly and groin, and then he let go even further and sank into a state of restful stillness that resembled sleep.

This was no ordinary sleep. While his body lay still, his subtle senses were lit up. The Earth was breathing as one conscious life through a multitude of changing forms and he was breathing with her, at one with that flow of molding and making, birthing and dying. He was being unraveled; he was being remade. His flesh was withering; it was shriveling to a handful of dust a breath of wind would blow from the bare white bones that gleamed like starlight through his sleep, the hidden structure of his own foundation.

And then he was rising on another pulse of life into the naked body of a man. In his dream he stood again with the young woman in the firelight and now he could recognize who she really was for him – his invisible other, the image of his more graceful, feminine self, who had come to offer him the knowledge of his own completion. And he accepted it: stepping forward, he took her hands, and as bare skin met skin, and bone met mortal bone, such a sense of consummation swelled that all his fear dissolved in bliss.

It was growing light inside the den when the young man stirred and woke. He heard the first bird sing – a flash of silver water through the dawn – and lay for a while remembering how he had come to that place and the dreams of the night. Then he crawled out through the den's narrow entrance and stood up. He stood barefoot on the damp ground and as his feet touched the earth he knew that he had never been alive before within his body; life was welling up within him and overflowing like a fountain on the breath into the space around.

He looked at the dark entrance to the bear den beneath the tree, the place where something in him had died, the place where something new had been brought to birth; then he brushed off the fallen leaves and, turning around, he began the walk back to the moss-covered hut in the forest and the living woman he had met.

4 Words and Bones

Around the world, from the Arctic to Mexico and the Kalahari, drawings of human and animal bodies showing the bones have been found. Visions of bones are found in almost all shamanic traditions and they always have profound significance. In the physical body, the bones give structure and support to the flesh. When you really feel the bones within the body, you are connected with your own core strength and the support of the ground beneath you. The bones will remain when the flesh has wasted away, so the vision of bones represents the experience of the underlying structure that gives support to physical reality.

To see through to the bones, or to be stripped back to the bones, indicate a powerful initiation – the death and rebirth that mark the transition to a new way of being. So the vision of the skeleton has a double aspect. It represents the death – the complete transformation – of old ways of thinking and acting. At the same time, it represents the deep structure that supports that transformation. Although the vision of the skeleton may appear frightening, it is extremely positive: it indicates that even when inner transformation seems chaotic and unpredictable, there is an deeper, underlying pattern that supports renewal.

In this story, the young man finds a more complete way of being a man as he accepts and integrates certain qualities that are usually associated with the feminine – emotional openness, sensitivity, deep intuition and connection to the subtle energies in the body.

At the beginning of the story he is ashamed of these qualities and he keeps them hidden from others. He wants to be a man just like his father and the others, so he tries to imitate them. But the effort of imitating others keeps him on the surface, a prey to anxiety and self-doubt and it prevents him from being fully present in his own body and conscious of the subtle energies that are flowing through him from the Earth. The stinging mockery of his father and the other men are the external voices of this inner insecurity.

However, he has a real, inner connection with the life of the forest, and this manifests itself when the bear shows herself to him in the clearing. The bear is not divided in herself. She has no self-concepts. She is not trying to imitate anybody or be other than she is – present in each moment on the Earth and directly connected with the intelligence of life.

Standing within the bear's power – in her footprints on the ground – the young man finds his own connection with the Earth; as his senses open he becomes aware of the subtle energies that continually pulse through his body from the connection with the ground.

That is the moment when he catches the faint smell of wood smoke that guides him to the door of the young woman's cabin – the magical space of acceptance in the forest where he can express himself freely. The young woman responds to his emotional openness by revealing herself to him – first her naked body, then the bones beneath the flesh.

The young man reacts first with fear – the fear of being naked with another person, beyond sexual roles and social masks and the fear of the uncompromising nature of real change. The personality and the will may work changes on the surface but authentic inner transformation is beyond the will. Although the young man runs from his vision of the bones, the experience is already working on him inwardly and it brings his inner conflict to the surface where it rages more painfully than before. However painful it may be, this emotional storm is the opportunity for real healing because it has brought the young man's inner conflicts and self-doubt more fully into his awareness.

Entering the Bear's Den
And the young man accepts this healing. He could have run

further through the forest and allowed the self-tormenting voices to rage unchecked. He could have analyzed the experience endlessly and become completely caught up in his mind. He could have taken refuge in resentment and blamed the young woman. But he does none of these things. He stops and he turns inward. He connects more deeply with the bear's power by entering the den where she gestates and brings out new life.

The den is the place of complete safety inside the Earth where the bear rests, supported by the rhythms of rest and renewal. The bear den is also an image for the sanctuary within each person, that inner space where there is complete acceptance, safety and peace. This is also the space of deep healing, where pain and limitation may be dissolved, leaving no residue of guilt or recrimination.

Such healing is beyond the ego-driven mind, which cannot simply accept freedom and allow the past to be the past. As I have begun to see some of my own habitual emotional patterns more clearly, I have realized that the mind always resists freedom. When painful emotions that have been suppressed in the past rise to the surface, the mind tries to keep them going, beyond their first, necessary release. The mind gets caught up in analysis and the apportioning of blame. It clings to any activity, even the most painful kind, which will maintain its hold on awareness. Instead of simply releasing and letting go, the mind tightens the knots in Sedna's hair and makes more tangles of guilt and resentment and self-reproach.

When the young man lies down inside the bear den and lets go into the support of the Earth, he enters a deeper level of consciousness in which these inner voices of blame and self-judgment are hushed. As his thinking stills, he experiences the unconditional acceptance and peace of his true nature and he opens to powers of renewal deep within.

These are feminine powers of gestating and birthing new life but they do not belong to women alone: they are part of the inner being of both women and men. When he recognizes the dream image of the young woman as the feminine aspect of his own, larger self, the young man finds wholeness. In accepting the feminine aspect of his being, he also accepts the larger self that holds both masculine and feminine aspects in dynamic balance.

When he wakes, he brings the night's experience of expansion into his waking life. He stands in balance and connection on the Earth, trusting the support of the ground, sensing the continual renewal of life within his body and strong enough in himself to turn back to the real, living woman in the forest and be open to whatever might await him there.

Part II Ice

Ursus maritimus, the sea bear.
Nanuq, the white bear.
Kokogiaq, the many-legged bear, the traveller.
Tornarssuq, the one who gives power.
The one that always wanders
The bear that flew down from the stars
Names for the Polar Bear
Arktikos. Greek. The Country of the Great Bear

5 In the Circle of the Sun

In the pack ice off the northwest coast of Spitsbergen
On board the Aleksey Maryshev
June 2008

The first pale band of pack ice appears no more substantial than a line of thin cold cloud. As it nears, it becomes perceptible as weight, slowing the open water's blue-gray slide, then chills to a narrow frieze of floating stone, chalk white, buoyant as pumice – cold's polished artistry, the sculpting of water, salt, light.

The ship enters the outer edges of the pack through a jumbled tide of ice boulders that tip and jostle before the ice-strengthened bow. Flat planes of ice shear off to the side and spin like frozen leaves on the water. Their surfaces are pocked with shallow pools of turquoise melt-water, and the gold-brown fuzz of algae spreads into their crevices and corners, the earthy colors as unexpected as a dusting of cinnamon across the compacted, blue white ice.

On the right the glaciers pour in gleaming frozen falls between the turrets and scalloped cirques of West Spitsbergen's coastal mountains. The geographic North Pole is scarcely 600 miles and ten degrees of latitude from here across the frozen Arctic sea. On this journey, we will see no night. At these latitudes, almost 14 degrees above the Arctic Circle, the sun does not leave the sky from late April to late August. The North is inclined towards the sun on the spinning axis of the Earth, and turns through a tilted circle of continuous light.

The Arctic sea ice is the floating roof that cold has made over Sedna's sea-home. Sunlight's shining mirror, reflecting back white light to space. A corolla of white cold that opens its petals to the winter dark and folds them back in summer. The floating bed on which the walruses and the ringed and bearded seals take their rest, give birth, converse and sleep. And the turning floor on which the polar bears walk across a thousand trackless miles of ice.

Spitsbergen and the other islands of the Svalbard archipelago are set within the Arctic Ring of Life – the richly productive circle of coastal waters around Arctic islands and archipelagoes where the wind and currents and warm upwellings break the ice apart and allow seawater and nutrients to meet in the presence of light. This ring of life around the edges of the polar ice cap is where the walruses and most other Arctic seals find their food, breed and give birth, and with them their hunter, the polar bear. Around 3,000 bears roam between Svalbard and the Russian islands of

Franz Joseph Land and Novaya Zemlya. Some bears travel widely along the southern edges of the pack ice; others, particularly females, remain closer to the Svalbard coast and their denning areas on land – one of which, Kongsøya Island, has more polar bear birth dens than almost anywhere else.

Womb of Ice

We find the first signs of polar bear by Smeerenburg at Spitsbergen's northeastern tip. The day is very clear; the temperature is just above freezing. A bright cold wind is stirring the open water into choppy blue-green waves as we come through the fjord by inflatable and land on the narrow band of exposed brown sand and rock which rims the shore; the gleaming snow plain beyond it stretches away inland and blooms with shallow hyacinth pools of melt-water.

There are several links from a walrus spine lying on the snow, still hung with tatters of the red-brown flesh and a line of polar bear tracks heads away from the bones towards two exposed rock domes. The tracks are some days old: the outlines have blurred and softened as the tracks melted and refroze but they still show the ridges of the bear mother's thickly furred front paws, flanked by the lighter paw prints of her two small cubs.

Something of the animal's presence, a faint trace like an elusive scent, always lingers in its tracks. You run your hands around the edges, you examine the spaces between the steps and wonder what came before they made these marks and what comes after.

Did the mother scavenge that walrus carcass on the shore and drag the broken vertebrae onto the snow? It is unlikely that she killed it herself. Although polar bears do attack and sometimes even kill walruses when they are hauled out on the shore, the hunt is dangerous for them, unless they can manage to separate a calf from the rest of the herd. Adult walruses defend themselves very ably with their tusks and their thick skin can resist even a polar bear's sharp teeth and claws.

Although she would scavenge a walrus carcass, this mother would not risk her life and that of her small cubs by attacking a healthy adult. It looks as though she may be leading her cubs inland, along a path across the mountains to the shore-fast ice on the other side of the fjord where ringed seals are found. Polar bears often make use of mountain passes and ravines to move between coasts or take a short cut between hunting areas on the ice – one sign of their remarkable intelligence and their ability to make mental maps and use them to navigate the landscape.

Like the polar bear mother, the ringed seal shelters her newborn in a snow cave. The mother builds her lair above her breathing hole on the ice and feeds her single pup until more than half its body weight consists of fat. This is the prey the bear mother needs to replace the flesh that she has lost in more than half a year of fasting while she gestated her cubs, gave birth to them and suckled them inside the den.

The mother would have conceived the cubs on the pack ice, late last spring. She lived and hunted with the father for a while, played with him and slept next to him on the ice and when she left, the embryos were dormant in her womb. All summer she searched for young seals on the ice and when she was fat from seal hunting, she came on land and excavated a snow cave from a deep inland drift – a crystal chamber protected from the wind which she raised above a narrow entrance tunnel to keep the air inside warm. She scraped part of the roof away until it was thin enough to allow fresh air to enter and circulate, and where the snow ceiling melted from her body heat and refroze, it shone like thick glass.

Inside this cocoon of ice and compacted snow, the bear rested and slept, while the embryos implanted on the wall of her womb and began to grow. The cubs came from her body as two small scraps of helpless and dependent life – almost naked, unable to see or hear, to stand or smell. They were so tiny she could fold one easily inside a thickly furred front paw. She fed them and she sheltered them in the warm crevices of her body until they were strong enough to leave the den and follow her onto the sea ice where she could hunt and break her long fast.

Nikita Ovsyanikov: The Story of the Man Who Walks among Bears

Even at the height of summer, conditions in Smeerenburg are too harsh for the hardy Arctic flowering plants. But there is one sign of human occupation – the walls of an old brick oven lie collapsing on the shore. The oven was built almost four hundred years ago, for rendering whale blubber into oil, by Dutch whalers who came to hunt the bowheads, which once crowded the waters around the Svalbard archipelago in great numbers.

In 1633 seven Dutch sailors overwintered here at Smeerenburg as they waited for the whaling fleet to return in spring. From late October until February, the men did not see the sun rise above the horizon, but they saw polar bears often. The bears showed no fear and they came almost daily around the camp. They must have been more numerous than they are now, for the sailors described them as "going in troops like the cattle."

Spitsbergen had never been inhabited before, and the bears – which included many mothers with cubs – were certainly curious about these strange new arrivals on their territory. The great white bears must have appeared ominous as pale ghosts to the men, looming through the freezing darkness or the gray twilight, which briefly lightened the sky at noon. The sailors reacted to them fearfully and with intense aggression. They shot them on sight and finished them off with lances, killing many mothers with cubs and leaving others injured.

The men were certainly frightened and it is not difficult to understand the sense of threat they must have felt in this remote and alien place, in the lightless, bone-chilling cold. Yet what strikes me most forcibly about these accounts is the way the men never questioned the need to kill, never once thought of the bears as anything other than savage, mute and dangerous beasts.

Of course, polar bears are powerful predators; as an inexperienced stranger in their territory, you must go very carefully, with sensitive awareness and take all possible precautions against coming anywhere near them. Especially as the bears are increasingly under pressure: the retreat of the sea ice in recent summers is forcing them to spend more time on land, where they cannot easily find food and come more often into contact with people. But when I read the sailors' accounts of that relentless killing, I thought of one man who has learned how to relate to polar bears on their own territory – he knows how to communicate with the bears directly and he walks among them freely and without fear.

I got to know the Russian biologist Dr. Nikita Ovsyanikov at the Pazhetnovs' research center, where he often visits, accompanied by his beautiful Samoyed dog, Nanuq, who has pure white, bear-like fur. A barrel-chested man with red-blonde hair and beard, Dr. Ovsyanikov is one of the world's most experienced polar bear researchers; since 1990 he has spent many summers among the bears on the High Arctic islands of Wrangel and Herald, north of the Siberian coast, often accompanied by his faithful Nanuq.

Many polar bears come together on Wrangel during the summer melt season, when the pack ice withdraws to the north. They mill around his observation cabin and gather in large groups along the shore. Nikita Ovsyanikov has developed such a sensitive awareness of the bears' sense of space and body language, such an ability to communicate his own intentions, that he walks among them freely, dressed in white and carrying only a stick. He is "an animal among other animals," as he puts it. When I met him first, he showed me some of the body language and gestures that he uses to communicate with the bears – stepping forward and making a sharp feint to command the bear's attention if necessary, and ask for acknowledgement and respect.

His body language and his attitude works. Nikita never carries a rifle on Wrangel, because to do so would mean relying on the weapon rather than his own inner strength and his understanding of the bears. The bears are nearly always calm and quietly accepting of his presence; in thousands of encounters, only a few have ever turned threatening, and he believes that he himself was largely responsible for those because he had misread the bear's intentions.

In *Living with the White Bear*, an account of his time on Wrangel, which is one of the most fascinating and engaging of all books on polar bears, Nikita Ovsyanikov dispels many myths about them. Curiosity is natural to the polar bear, he insists, and it is wrong to assume that their interest must be aggressive. While they hunt alone, the bears are not necessarily solitary loners; they can form strong social bonds, be very playful and companionable, and they willingly share food when it is available.

Ringed seals are the polar bear's habitual prey, along with bearded seals and harp seals. The ringed seals are the smallest and the most numerous of the Arctic seals. They make long dives beneath the ice to feed and when they return to the surface they use the strong claws of their front flippers to scrape their breathing holes clear of encrusted ice. The bear waits by the edge of a lead or breathing hole for the seal to return, and remains completely still, focused and quiet. When still-hunting like this, the bear shows extraordinary patience: she may wait an hour or more for the seal to surface if she judges it worthwhile. In spring, polar bears also search out the snow-covered birth lairs which shelter young seal pups. When the bear hears or smells a seal beneath the surface, it rises on its hind legs and plunges with front paws through the snow roof to catch the seal pup inside.

The bear's concentration, precision and intense quiet may suddenly snap with the release of pressure if the seal eludes her.

After an unsuccessful hunt, polar bears have been seen to discharge their accumulated tension by roaring loudly, swatting the snow or even flinging blocks of ice about. Ian Stirling, a Canadian polar bear researcher who has spent thousands of hours watching them, once saw a bear spend half an hour stalking an oil drum on the ice that he had mistaken for a seal. When the bear finally saw what he had caught, he was so outraged he gave the drum an angry cuff and sent it spinning away across the ice.

Accounts like these fascinate me because they reveal something of the intense emotions that are concealed behind the impassive white planes of the polar bear's face, emotions that we can easily recognize from our own lives. The strength of the devotion between the polar bear mother and her cubs is also powerfully revealed in another story, this one recorded by the nineteenth-century British explorer, William Scoresby.

A group of walrus hunters set fire to a pile of blubber to attract bears. When a mother with two cubs approached, they threw bits of blubber at her, which she picked up and took to her cubs. As she approached her cubs with the last piece of blubber, the men shot them both dead. For half an hour and more the distraught mother pawed her cubs' dead bodies and tried to raise them up; she called to them, she licked their wounds and "stood for some time moaning... pawing them with signs of inexpressible fondness."

Eventually, the men shot her too.

The Life of Ice

Several days later, moving through thick pack ice off Spitsbergen's east coast, we see a bear resting on a great wheel of ice, his rump turned into the wind. The floe drifts before a range of coastal mountains, which are banded with snow, and exposed slopes of charcoal-gray scree. Along the outer edges, where it turns to formless slush, the ice heaves and sinks with the swell;

at the compacted center where the bear lies resting, it is piled into roughly hewn, unpolished geometries.

The sleety overcast is rigged with the taut passage of glaucous gulls, blue-phase fulmars and black guillemots. Against the cold gray sky, the gritty charcoal slopes and the blue-white platform of the ice, the bear's fur is luxuriant, like thickly folded cream. He rises and presses his heavily furred front paws against an ice boulder, stretches out his back and shoulders and climbs fluidly across the tilted rods and cones of ice. He halts by a blue translucent pyramid and turns his head, staring at the ship, which is some hundred yards away on the ice edge.

According to the ship's biologist, the bear is young – four, maybe five years old, in his first or second year of independence from his mother. His narrow head and long Roman nose are clear and smooth, with none of the battle scars that often mark out older males, and his eyes and nostrils are black cores through the white planes of his face, passages that lead inward to the mind, the intelligence that lives inside this cloak of thick, lustrous fur.

The bear extends a sinuous neck and raises his nose to the wind. His sense of smell is so refined that he could catch the warm exhalations of a ringed seal beneath a snow hummock from a mile or more away, or follow the scent of sex hormones from a fertile female across fifty miles of ice without ever hesitating or deviating for a moment from the assurance of his course. What wind does he receive from us... this collective animal swaddled in Gore-Tex, housed in a clanking metal carapace smelling of diesel fumes and heated pipes?

He stares at the ship again, at the people hanging on the deck rails, then dismisses it. He pads over to a blue-white wall and lies down again behind his rampart of ice.

Until I saw him for myself on the ice, I had not fully realized what an extraordinary creature the polar bear is. That young male was utterly at home on the drifting ice. He had never hibernated in winter. Since he followed his mother from the den as a young cub he had remained active through the months of polar night, lashed by freezing winds and blinding snowstorms or submerged in drifted snow during a blizzard. The hairs of his coat have hollow cores that trap warm air against his black skin; along with his padding of fat, which can be four inches thick, they insulate him completely from the freezing air and water. (The hairs are not white: they have no color of their own. The hollow cores scatter visible light in the same way that ice and snow does, and the bears' coats can reflect many subtle shades and tones from pure white when they are very young, to ivory and cream, darkening to warmer tones of yellow straw.)

The bear is so well wrapped in his mantle of fur and fat that if I were to reach out my hands and touch him, I would sense no radiation of body heat at all. In thermal images taken with infrared equipment, polar bears quite literally disappear – the only detectable heat they give off surrounds their nose and head and it comes from the exhalations of the breath.

Their thick insulation allows polar bears to stay comfortably warm through long periods sitting or lying on the ice but it has one disadvantage – the bears easily overheat. As a result they rarely do things quickly; although they are capable of a powerful rush of speed over short distances, they usually keep a steady, unhurried pace as they walk across the ice. "The Farmer" the nineteenth-century whalers used to call the polar bear, because of his "agricultural appearance as he stalks leisurely across the furrowed fields of ice." This reluctance to hurry is why the bear often relies more on the intensity of his concentration and his perfect timing when he hunts than he does on speed.

I had not realized either how extraordinary it is that bears should have learned how to live on the sea ice. Brown bears are the polar bears' direct ancestors and their closest living relation: the rhythms of the brown bear's year, its sense of space and security are attuned to the seasonal growth of green plants, berries and herbs which return in regular patterns from year to year.

The inorganic surface of the Arctic sea ice is an utterly different world. The polar ice cap is a floating world of temporary forms, whose edges are always cracking, dissolving and being remade with the turning of the North to and away from the sun. When the ice takes form in winter it shelters the plankton and other microorganisms, which are the foundation of the ocean's food web by shielding them from contact with the freezing air. As it cracks with the movement of wind and currents, the ice opens the way for the seals to dive to feed beneath the water. And when it melts in summer, it allows the ingress of undivided light in which the ocean blooms.

Sea ice is pressure: it takes form against the resistance which the dissolved salts in seawater make to the process of freezing by lowering the temperature at which it can take place. As sea ice ages, it undergoes a process of crystalline refinement in which these salts are gradually squeezed from suspension and compacted into small pockets of dense brine. When it is young, the ice is brittle, honeycombed with channels in which the brine accumulates and concentrates, becoming heavier and more densely saline until it drops through and sinks to the lower levels of the water. As it endures through several summers the ice hardens until the drinking water it provides when melted is completely free of salt.

Pressure builds the sea ice and pressure breaks it open. The roof, the floor, the bed of ice is never still but moves continually on tides of air and water. Pulled apart by wind and currents, it shatters into long cracks or leads and closes again in grinding heaves that weld it into tumbled hummocks and pressure ridges. Warmer waters well up from below and make open pools, known as *polynyas*, which may be many miles across. On the greater scale, the sea ice flows in a sliding current from east to west across the Arctic basin and spins through an immense circle in the Beaufort Sea, north of Alaska, known as the Beaufort Gyre.

And the sea ice is life – the shelter and support, the habitat and home for the polar bears and the marvelous array of other Arctic wildlife.

Standing on deck, I watch a group of harp seals – dark-bodied and sleek as dolphins – flash like the running edge of a wave along the slushy edges of the pack ice. The wings of a rare ivory gull describe arcs of pure dense white across the heavy gray overcast.

A dark-eyed fulmar hefts beside me on the wind – a sturdy, barrel-necked bird with a tubenose bill. This far north its plumage is pale blue, the color of shallow seawater under a clear winter sky.

Puffins whir past on stubby wings; they have plump white cheeks and their wedge-shaped beaks are enameled in primary bands of red, yellow and blue.

Some Brünnich's guillemots, elegantly patterned in black and white, settle onto a wedge of drift ice. A pair of black guillemots – their sister species – have a single white patch on the middle of each matt black wing, while their legs and feet are booted and shod in the high-polished red of supple leather.

Two walruses stir sleepily on a bed of drifting ice. Their tusks – one roughly broken – are stained yellow-white and the blood vessels show rosy-pink between the ridges of their gray-brown hide. One rolls over; eyes closed, he folds both flippers comfortably across his rounded belly. His companion rises on one flipper and scratches himself with an air of solemn concentration along the flank with the edge of his tail.

A bearded seal rests on a raft of drift ice, floating on indigo water crazed with chunks of freshwater glacier ice. The seal's rolls of heavy flesh are wrapped in a coat of russet and dun-brown suede. Long whiskers stiffen and the eyes, with their look of mild inquiry, reflect in liquid darkness some ancient, unsayable simplicity.

At the seal's back, the glacier's broken crenellations mark the borders of two worlds – as the weight of inland ice thrusts forward to the sea, it falls, gashes, and opens onto interior halls where a cold blue fire is burning.

The Great Silence

We cannot separate polar bears from the sea ice. It is their hunting platform and without it they cannot hunt effectively for seals. When the ice edge contracts north in summer, some bears will travel great distances to remain within their floating world, which is founded on the pressures of constant change. As the pack ice drifts across the Arctic Ocean, it breaks jaggedly apart and reforms in irregular patterns from year to year. The abundance and the distribution of seals may change with it, and so the bears must be able to adapt and follow them. As the ice spins and slides away beneath them, drifting now one way, now the other, the bears have no fixed marks to navigate by – none, at least, that would be perceptible to human senses.

These shifting, seemingly unpredictable motions of the ice were dangerous and frustrating for the early Arctic explorers.

"It is astonishing we have not got further. We seem to toil all we can but without much progress. Beginning to doubt seriously of the advisability of continuing northwards much longer," the Norwegian explorer Fridtjof Nansen wrote in his journal in 1894 as he traveled with dogs, sleds and ski toward the North Pole, with one companion, Helmar Johannson. Only 240 miles separated the two men from the pole, but the ice had begun to shift beneath them and it was now bearing them south again.

Several weeks earlier, Nansen had left his ship *Fram* and its crew deliberately frozen into the ice, just above 84 degrees North. *Fram* was a unique vessel: Nansen had designed it to ride up on the ice rather than sit within it and be crushed, then sailed it to the pack ice and deliberately allowed it to be frozen in. A scientist as well as Arctic explorer, Nansen was aware that the ice drifted and he hoped to use the ice currents to bring *Fram* as close as possible to the North Pole at 90 degrees, which no explorer had yet reached.

But the ice did not move in the way that Nansen had hoped; for two years *Fram* was kept continuously circling and the ice brought them no further north. Finally Nansen could wait no longer. He left the ship with Johannson and a team of sled dogs, laden with enough food and supplies for 100 days, resolved to reach the North Pole on foot. Their journey was continually frustrated by the drifting of the ice to the south; to save their lives, the explorers were forced to abandon the attempt to reach the pole and began heading south again, hoping to reach Franz Joseph Land, off the Siberian coast. After turning back, they travelled swiftly for five days over smooth ice that was free of pressure ridges, yet when Nansen next took a sighting of their position, he found they had scarcely come five miles further south in the entire five days. The ice had reversed its direction; it was bearing them north again.

Nansen called the ice "the great silence". The vast white silence of the ice also powerfully affected his companion Johannson. "Never had I felt anything so still," Johannson wrote of this point on their journey, as he sat alone for some hours on the ice. "It was so frighteningly still I had to remain where I sat. I dared not move a limb; I hardly dared to breathe."

Yet the polar bear is utterly at home in the great white silence, on the trackless, moving ice. The bears have a sureness of inner direction that carries them across it. The ice in the Beaufort Sea, for example, turns slowly through the great circle, the Beaufort Gyre – clockwise usually, but sometimes reversing its direction. Polar bear biologist Ian Stirling has regularly found the same bears at the same location on the turning ice – the same latitude and longitude – year after year. The bears, he suggests, have powers of orientation that enable them to compensate for the moving of the ice, but how they do this remains unknown.

It is a vivid illustration of the difference between human and animal intelligence: the men relying on calculation and analysis while the bear moves within the unreflecting intelligence of life.

Nanuq is also known as *the one who always wanders.* The bear is also called *Kokogiaq* – the many-legged bear or the traveller – because of these great journeys across the ice, as it moves with wind and water and forms anew each year. Polar bear tracks have even been found far to the north, on the ice cap near the pole – which suggests that *Nanuq* may be the only creature other than the human one that has ever walked or stood on the ice at the North Pole itself.

Late one sunlit evening, with the sun high in the sky, I watch a bear swim between the ice floes. Chunks of broken drift ice float in lavender pools of evening light and overhang their violet shadows on the water; among the rippling reflections of translucent ice, the bear's damply ruffled neck fur deepens to the mottled shade of old ivory.

A few more strokes of effortless power and the bear climbs out, pads across the sea ice and slides smoothly back into the water with scarcely a ripple. The still water between the ice floes is shot through with threads of turquoise; in the evening sunlight, the bear's wet fur is warmly gold.

The Light Wanderers

As the ship leaves the edges of the pack ice and moves south along Spitsbergen's west coast, the tundra blooms in warm colors – russet and ocher, primrose-yellow and rose. Landing from the inflatable on shore, I find small round cushions of pink moss campion and yellow tufted saxifrages growing on the shingle; inland, the tundra is covered with soft beds of saffron-colored mosses and the cream-white heads of the Arctic poppies nod on delicate stems.

I hear a stream of clear notes, sweet as fresh water, catch a flash like the dart of a silver needle from the corner of one eye –

and see a snow bunting settling on a stone brocaded with orange lichen. The little gray-black and white bird with the plump white stomach and patches of mottled gray around the eyes is the only songbird to nest in the High Arctic. I could hold it easily in the palm of one hand, yet it has flown hundreds of turbulent miles from northwest Europe to be here during the brief summer flowering of the tundra plants and feed on their seeds.

Snow buntings conceal their eggs inside nests woven from mosses, lichens and reindeer hair. The eggs of some other tundra birds are more exposed and vulnerable. A purple sandpiper staggers before me across the tundra; it is feigning injury by dragging one wing to lead me away from the eggs, which lie in a shallow depression on the ground.

I can feel the intensity of the bird's agitation jangling in my gut and I follow it obediently, stepping as carefully as I can on the firm places on the tundra; when it judges that it has drawn me far enough away, the sandpiper drops the pretense of injury and flies back to its nest. The cord of tension that was strung between us slackens, but the bird's naked resolve to protect the life inside that fragile casing is utterly humbling.

I stay well away from the pair of nesting Arctic terns. They are much easier to see on the open tundra than the sandpipers – the plumage on their bodies and wings is brilliantly white and they have a black cap on the head. Scarlet beaks burn like a visible sign of the inner fire that animates them. If I came near the nest, one of the terns would attack and it might slash me across the head and shoulders with its beak.

These small fierce terns travel further, and experience more daylight than any other bird on Earth. They live entirely between the northern and southern edges of the polar ice caps. During the southern summer they feed off the coast of Antarctica; when the southern winter approaches, they fly north to their breeding grounds in Spitsbergen and other parts of the High Arctic, only to return again to Antarctica when the Arctic summer ends – an immense arc of flight, north and south between the ice edges of the Earth, which takes them from day into day and from light into light.

Bones and Light

On a tundra ridge above the fjord I meet a reindeer stag with several hinds and their small calves. The reindeer examine me with mild and fearless interest; when I stand still, they approach, step by hesitant step until they are only a few yards away, then stop and look again. The most northerly wild reindeer on Earth, they are short-legged with mottled light-gray coats and dark patches around their eyes, much smaller than the reindeer I have seen in Siberia.

Further on, I find some polar bear bones lying on a ruddy bed of mosses – the bones of one paw, with the wrist and forearm still attached. I touch the bones gently, without disturbing them. They are lime-white and patched with rosettes of gray lichen. How long have they lain here, these enduring bones? It is rare to find polar bear remains on land. The bears usually die out on the sea ice before the age of thirty and the ice bears their bones away and drops them to the sea floor when it melts.

As a result there are few fossils to show exactly how polar bears evolved from their brown bear ancestors. The earliest found so far was here on Spitsbergen – part of a polar bear jaw that is estimated to be around 130,000 years old.

Based on the latest analysis of polar bear DNA in 2012, scientists suggest that polar bears began to diverge from brown bears around 600,000 years ago, during a period of intense cooling. It may be that one population of brown bears became isolated within the glacial walls of a frozen world. It would have been a period of intense pressure for the bears, as the land around them grew increasingly barren and became thickly swathed in ice. But it was also a time of great opportunity: before them lay the Arctic sea ice, with its fertile areas of open water and abundant seals, where no other land animal had ever learned to hunt before. That was a great advantage, as the bears had no other hunters to compete with.

As the bears took to the sea ice, their bodies began to change. Already powerful swimmers the bears became more streamlined to enable them to swim easily across leads and *polynyas* – the areas of open water in the ice. Webbing grew between their toes and gave them added power in the water; their fur became oily, neither retaining water nor allowing ice to form. Their paws grew huge and thickly furred, spreading out their weight like snowshoes and keeping them from breaking through the brittle ice of spring. The soles of their feet developed a nubbed texture that allows them grip on icy slopes and pressure ridges and the fur itself turned white, reflecting light and allowing their bodies to blend with snow and ice.

Despite these remarkable changes, brown bears and polar bears have not separated completely. They can be attracted to one another: they have mated and given birth in captivity and – very rarely – in the wild and the female offspring from these unions are fertile. What separates the two bear species is less their body shape than their choice of habitat and way of life, which makes encounters between them rare in the wild and probably alters some of the subtle signals that draw male and female together.

There is one very significant, inner difference between brown bears and polar bears – polar bears have greatly refined the ability to hibernate. Except for pregnant and nursing mothers which make a den to gestate and shelter their newborn cubs, polar bears have no need to hibernate in winter: they are fully insulated from the cold and they easily find food on the sea ice. It is summer, and the withdrawal of the sea ice that marks their season of scarcity and potential famine. In the more southerly parts of their range, where the ice edge retreats far to the north in summer, the bears are often marooned on land, where for long months they find no food. While they wait on land for the winter ice to form, they slow their metabolism down – in other words, they hibernate with open eyes.

Biologists call this state *walking hibernation* and polar bears have the ability to enter and leave it at will, according to the availability of food, which the brown bears cannot do. Brown bears are tied to seasonal rhythms and they cannot hibernate in summer. But the polar bear can deliberately switch its body state to walking hibernation while it waits for winter and the ice to form.

I find them magical, these stories of evolutionary transformation. They teach you to regard the animal differently – you begin to see it as a traveller moving through time, the way a river branches and changes direction through the landscape, and each individual becomes one point of temporary equilibrium within a continuous process of transformation.

We limit ourselves, I think, when we rely exclusively on the metaphors of struggle and competition to explore the idea of evolution. These metaphors have their own value, but when metaphors become fixed and rigid they limit the exploration of other ways of understanding.

Think of evolution *through* the bear and a different range of metaphors emerges.

Evolution can be understood as the bringing out of a new form from the reservoir of potential the creature holds within itself, encoded in the mutable language of its genes.

As the drawing out of the animal's powers of transformation in response to the intense pressures of earthly change.

As the relationship between birth and death, in which the bear dies to one form of itself and allows another to be born.

The polar bear bones on the tundra remind me of the polar bear sculpture that was carved from walrus ivory by the peoples of the Eastern Arctic some fifteen hundred years ago. Archaeologists call it the flying bear because it seems to be flying or gliding through the air – the forelegs sweep back along the sides and the legs are extended out behind. Even in a photo, the carving conveys a sense of weightlessness, as though the bear has been transformed into a creature of the air, and taken on the power of flight. The other remarkable thing about this small carving is that the artist has incised the outline of the bear's skeleton – the ribs, the spine, and the joints – onto the surface of the body. Like the young man's vision of the woman's bones in the story of Skeleton Woman, the artist is looking *through* the bear's flesh to the bones, which give the physical body structure and support.

Arctic peoples have always treated the bones of the animals they hunted with deep respect. I remember the sacred site made entirely of bowhead whalebones where I camped on Yttygran Island, off the coast of the Chukotka Peninsula. I think of how the traditional Yupik and coastal Chukchi peoples would never remove whalebones to the inland tundra, but gathered them together on the shore, so that they remained close to the sight and sound and smell of the sea. The bones represented the animal's enduring essence, the pattern and structure from which it would be reborn.

Across the Arctic, bones and light came together in powerful visions of transformation. The Arctic shaman's enlightenment came through an inner experience of death – the dissolution of their previous, limited identity and their contracted sense of self. In visionary experiences of death and rebirth, a powerful spirit came and devoured them, stripping their flesh away until all that remained of them was bone.

In the Arctic the guardian spirit of these profound visions of death and rebirth was the polar bear. *Tornarssuq* – meaning, the master of the helping spirits, the one who gives power.

The bear of the lake or the inland glacier will come out, he will devour all your flesh and make you a skeleton, and you will die. But you will recover your flesh, you will awaken, and your clothes will come rushing to you.

The experience may sound extreme and terrifying, yet it took the shaman beyond the ordinary fear of death. He or she came to know from deep inner experience that death is not life's end, but the pole through which it is continually renewed. They experienced their own disintegration, the stripping away of their flesh in a state of lucid awareness, and when all that remained was bone, they named the bones, one by one, watched as they were clothed again in new flesh, and knew the power of resurrection through the bones.

Such intense experiences might not happen only once. A shaman grew in wisdom and consciousness along a spiral of transformation, on which experiences of death and rebirth were repeated, taking him or her ever deeper into the core of their being.

"It is said that the really good shamans are cut up three times in their life, the poor only once," a Yakut of northern Siberia said. "They say that great shamans are reborn three times."

The Death of Ice

These experiences may come from a distant time and culture, but they remain very powerful because they touch on the deepest levels of human experience. They tell us that life renews itself through change and transformation, through letting go of previous forms. To resist change is a form of death – stagnation and decay come in resisting the pulses of renewal. Through consciously facing the fear of death, we may come to know within ourselves the undying essence that sustains life through all its changes of physical form.

Every single one of us will know death. Each one of us loses some person that we love; we all know grief and taste the bitterness of loss. And death is absolute. You cannot grasp it with your mind. You cannot make it better. The person you knew and loved is gone and they will not come again in the form in which you knew them.

And each one of us will come to our own death in the end. Not one thing that we have accumulated, no possession, no external achievement, no wealth or fame or physical beauty can endure. On that sacred threshold, all that is real is essence, the light within the soul.

To grieve for somebody you have loved, to contemplate the certainty of your own death, is one of the most profound experiences of life. But who is willing to contemplate the death of an entire ecosystem? Who is willing to face and truly feel the possible loss of the light-wandering terns, the deep-eyed bearded seals or the great ice bear itself?

The Arctic icescape is the most vulnerable habitat on Earth, fragile in ways that were scarcely imaginable until recently. The sea ice is showing a pattern of inexorable, long-term decline. In September 2007 the ice reached the lowest extent ever recorded – more than one-third below the average summer minimum between 1979 and 2000. On Wrangel, during that year of extreme summer melt, Nikita Ovsyanikov watched the pack ice around the island retreat far to the north; exhausted polar bears fell through rotting ice and swam long distances through turbulent open water to reach land. Starving and disoriented, walruses collapsed and died in hundreds on the Wrangel shore. Nikita has suggested that the walruses were carried away from the fertile coastal waters into parts of the Arctic Ocean where it was too deep for them to feed; by the time they swam back to coastal waters, they were so weak, they quickly died. That year was the harbinger of the disintegration of their world.

Paradoxically, the presence of many weak and dying walruses allowed the polar bears on Wrangel to survive: the bears were able to feed on their carcasses. Nevertheless polar bear numbers in the region have declined steeply, to around 1500 – a third, perhaps, of what they were twenty years ago. (So far, the population around Spitsbergen, which lies further north than Wrangel, appears stable.)

Although such extreme losses have not repeated yet, the ice has never really recovered. It is losing thickness and volume as well. The older, more resilient ice that has endured through many Arctic summers has almost vanished. Much of the ice cover that remains is scarcely one or two winters old, frail leaves of cold floating on the warming sea. One more melt season like 2007 and much of the summer ice cover could dissolve completely.

Long-term Arctic ice loss is not part of any natural climatic cycle. It is the consequence of human actions and our unwillingness to change. Our breathing is out of balance on the Earth, the emissions from the massive combustion of fossil fuels are fatal exhalations of warmth, tipping the Earth into a much hotter state.

The ice does not deliberate about a changing climate. It does not argue facts or statistics; it does not look for some other force to blame. The ice simply melts.

Few people understand how great the loss will be, if it disappears. The sea ice is not only the shelter and support for the ocean's food web on which the walruses and other seals and ultimately the bears themselves depend. It is our shield too, our shelter and support. The Arctic ice is intricately coupled with the great planetary forces that keep the climate in the dynamic balance that supports our life. By reflecting some of the sun's heat away from the Earth, all ice and snow, both on land and sea, act as powerful cooling agents. Without the white shield of the ice, open water around the pole in summer would absorb vastly more heat and could trigger even more feverish temperature increases.

I would keep the ice and protect it if I had the power. I would fold myself around it and shelter it in the white purity of cold. But all I have are words to bear witness to its life. Before we lose what we have not the power to restore, what will not come again within any time that has meaning for human life, can we not find it in ourselves to change? To become not consumers, but guardians and protectors, lovers of what is most precious on the Earth? The tremendous power of transformation that *Nanuq* shows is not abstract or external. It is not confined to the realms of biology or shamanic ritual and myth. It is the power that is inherent in the very nature of life and it exists within each person in potential.

The need to transform and find a deeper connection with life could not be made clearer. Not only for the sake of the Earth herself, and all the intricate and uncounted marvels of the natural world, but for *ourselves*.

Without that connection, what are we humans becoming? Creatures increasingly hollowed out, emptied of true life, trapped in a mind-made realm in which fears of destruction are being made increasingly real. Insensible to the light and beauty of the spirit, cut off from the living energy that constantly flows from the Earth.

I have always believed that we would save only what we love; it has taken me a long time to understand that we ourselves are saved by what we love. That love is what can save us from our own destructiveness, from the emptiness, the loneliness and fear which haunt our hollowed lives.

The White Heart of the Circle of Light

In these days, which are one day in the continuous circle of the sun, the Arctic is showing me the essence of everything I have ever loved on Earth in reality or dream, a formless simplicity like light shining through the marvelous shapes of the visible landscape.

In the timeless evenings, I stand on deck for hours and watch the different textures and tones of white that are reflected from the snow pack and the freshwater ice of the glaciers. Exposed banks of sedimentary rock, rich with iron oxides, cast their tawny reflections across the back of a glacier. Set against the reddish sandstone, the glacier's broken face burns even more intensely, more vibrantly blue.

On this journey there is no night. The sun never sets; the circle of light drawn across the sky tilts and dips but never comes near the horizon. The distinctions of twilight and midnight and dawn, the changing shades of night and half-light have disappeared. The sun alone is starlight and moonlight, the evening star and the Milky Way. If I were to go north from here, if I walked across the ice as *Nanuq* does, north and still further north until I reached the pole itself and stood on the ice cap on midsummer day, the sun would turn around me in a circle. It would neither rise nor fall in the sky but circle above the horizon and for that one day I would stand at the white heart of the circle of light.

As panes of white ice float on the lacquered black surface of the water, I think also of the night I cannot see, of the worlds and stars that turn through the dark sea of space. In the invisible night, the stars pulsate; the constellation of the Great Bear revolves around the Pole Star, at the center of the turning wheel of the heavens. And I remember another traditional name for *Nanuq – the bear that flew down from the stars.*

The water stills in the presence of ice; it becomes a liquid mirror. Icebound mountains meet their pellucid reflections, their other selves, in the clarity of still blue depths at the boundary between one world and the next. Low streaks of cirrus cloud soften the great coastal turrets, the cirques and the spires of rock – some slate-gray, others gleaming darkly like obsidian. Great rivers of ice, whose weight and motion are not perceptible to my eyes, pour down whitely from clouded, invisible heights and melt into water that is itself dissolving, losing itself in a formless merging with the light.

On these evenings, the power of the formless essence pressing through the substance and the manifold shapes of this world become so near and real that the very intensity of this side-piercing beauty shivers at the edge of dissolution. It becomes a marvelous dance of light, flaring and dissolving like the wings of the aurora, beating soundlessly across the night.

These are the borders of the country of silence, the country of union where no words are needed to know and be known.

I say them one last time: *Earth, ice, light,* then I put the words away and lay them like bones among the white flowers of the ice.

One of the most moving of traditional stories about polar bears comes from West Greenland. The original version tells of a woman grieving for the death of her child who leaves her home and walks alone into the snow. She finds refuge with a polar bear mother and her two cubs. Inside their house, the bears appear exactly like humans. When they leave, they put on their cloaks of white fur and appear as bears in the outer world. The mother bear is very kind to the woman, and when she is ready to go back to her husband the bear mother asks one thing: she should not tell anyone that she has been with bears, for the hunters would come to kill them.

Of course the woman breaks the prohibition, as people always do in stories. The hunters come with dogs and they surround the bear's home. But the bear has heard them speaking and she knows their intention. She kills her cubs so that they do not fall into human hands, and she strikes out at the dogs that surround her. In that moment, the bear shows her full power: shining brightly, she rises into the sky and takes the dogs with her in the shape of stars.

Although the woman has betrayed her, the bear shows that the hunters cannot touch the essence that is beyond physical form and the mind-made duality of life and death. I found this aspect of the story very poignant, as polar bears confront the warming of the Arctic and the loss of the summer ice, which threaten their very survival as a species.

6 The Story of the Woman Who Spoke with a Bear

Once there was a woman whose only child fell sick when he was less than one year old. It was late in winter when the child grew sick and the day was made of shades of darkness. All through the weary weeks of sickness she held her child and rocked him in her arms while he sweated and convulsed. She stroked his head and tried to cool him and sang to him under her breath. When he shuddered and died she held him and called out to him with every tender word she knew, and searched his shuttered face for any sign of breath and life.

So sure she was the child could not be gone from her forever…

Her husband stroked her matted hair; he put his arms around her and spoke her name, but she scarcely noticed he was there. When he could no longer bear to see her rocking the baby in her arms he took the little waxen body away from her and buried it. The woman felt the emptiness where her baby's weight had been and she sank onto the earthen floor and turned her face to the wall. The room grew dim, shapes and colors thinned to cold gray mist. All vanishing, she thought dully, all slipping away and she closed her eyes and leaned her head against the wall.

Her husband's voice was calling from a distance, begging her to come back, but she could not lift her lids or move. It seemed she sat before a lake whose dense black waters never stirred. In all the worlds nothing existed but that weight of water, and she dared not look away because all around was empty and void. As long as she kept her eyes fixed on the dense black water, emptiness would not invade her utterly and she sat before it for a long time and knew no change of light or time.

When she opened her eyes at last, the room was dust and shadows and she was alone. She stood up and went to the door and let the daylight in. The air of early spring spun around her and with a soundless tearing in her heart, she knew she was in pain. She ran out from the house, down to the shore where the shining panes of ice were still held fast and looked across the blank white plain. She could walk away, she could leave everything she'd ever loved and hoped for behind and walk across the ice until it fell away beneath her and she sank into the dark water that would end this pain. How merciful the touch of cold would be. How kind. It would send white tendrils through her blood and bones, lay frozen hands upon her heart and fasten her body into a casket of ice. Such white cold stillness would be hers at last, the peace of complete forgetting, perfect rest.

She took one step onto the ice, then another. Clouds came down and mist encircled her until she was walking through a muffled overcast with nothing to mark what came before from what came after. The ice burned beneath her feet with a sensation of intense cold. With every step it seemed to bend and flex and she heard it creak and groan as though it were speaking in its own inhuman tongue to her of cold kept in crystalline alignments and rare white blooms of frost. Then she stopped, struck motionless, listening.

It seemed she stood within an arching presence, sheltered between great wings of cold. A heartbeat like the pulsing of a star. Intelligence clear and pure as light. That presence was space, arching into dimensions far beyond the reaching of her mind and it was warmth and light within, touching her very core. Within these wings, she thought, the ice is dissolving and dying, falling away and forming again like white flowers on the water... and she began to weep, helplessly like a child, for in this guardian presence there was love, in purity and stillness, as she had never known it in her life before.

The still pure presence held her human heart, as her grief and loss were raw again, the helplessness, the terrible sense of failure as she struggled to keep her child alive while he was slipping away.

She began to speak aloud to him, as though he were there beside her, at the other side of the mist and ice. She spoke to him of love in broken words, tears hot on her frozen cheeks, and when she had told him everything that was in her heart, she no longer wished to die.

She gathered herself together and turned around again, facing the direction where she thought the shore should be, and began her long walk home, carefully testing every step.

The ice held. It supported her steps.

Something moved in the mist, a cloudy stirring that took on solid form – two powerful shoulders and front paws, a narrow head... short round ears... and her heart swooped like a startled bird as she met the bear's black gaze.

The bear's fur showed with living warmth, as if the bloodless ice had been churned by sunlight until it thickened into yellow cream. It padded towards her, head held low, with a rolling swing through the shoulders and haunches, and then it swung off to the side and paced around her.

The bear's feet brushed across the ice; white hairs swished as it came closer, and she turned around the spot where she was standing to try to keep the bear in sight.

Again it turned, with such powerful, slow, deliberate intent that she felt sure it meant to kill her. A burst of heat flared from her chest into her throat, the cry of her own life rising up, then a wave of weakness took her and she fainted.

She woke in a cavern inside the ice. She lay beneath a dome of ice blue cold and the light poured down in indigo and violet waves that rippled around her like seaweed tendrils in a wash of water. There was a fire glowing at the cavern's center – not the flickering, yellow flames that she knew with her daylight eyes, but a sun of rosy gold that burned inside the crystal lattices of the ice without consuming them. In all her days, the woman had never seen anything as beautiful as the light that burned inside the ice; as she gazed, the light kindled warmth inside her that left no corner of her being untouched and took her deeper and deeper into stillness and unbounded peace.

Sometime, without time, she looked up and saw – what did she see? A being incorporeal as ice, that shivered between the planes of sight like the mist of breath before a frozen wall.

"Am I dead?" the woman asked.

"What is death?" the bear spirit answered.

That was a strange thing! A voice not made by flesh and breath, that rang inside her like the remembered stars.

The pure cold sound rang on after the words had ended and the thousand blues in which the light was veiled broke out more brilliantly than before and shivered across the cavern's walls and ceiling. In the ringing space the singing made, she knew that the baby she had lost was not her child alone. He was another being, beyond time and changes, who had briefly touched the earth in that small body, known mortal love through her and withdrawn.

"Then who is dead?" the woman asked, in some bewilderment.

With that the drumming started. At first it was no stronger than the quiet beating of the heart inside her breast. It slowly deepened to the resonant throb of the skin drum and the rhythm quickened as other drums came in. The ice walls dissolved and she saw the ancestors that had gathered all around her, the guardians whose subtle presence she had sensed but never seen as they drummed on for her and chanted.

Die, they chanted, to the dream of fear
Die to the anguish, the loneliness, the grief,
Die to the dream that has kept you small.

Die to the hatred, the jealousy, the greed.
The emptiness that would eat the earth away
And never know rest or peace.
Die to everything that has kept you small.

205

Die to the death-maker, the dreamer of fear,
The one that has kept you
Alone and afraid in the dark.
Die to the one that has kept you small.

The drums throbbed inside her skull. They beat inside her eyes and ears; inside her tongue and throat; inside her heart and the very marrow of her bones. And then she was expanding on the drumbeat, out beyond the edges of her separate self, into the formless light that has no end and no beginning, and love itself held her and dissolved the seeds of the grief she bore.

Sometime, without time, she woke again outside the ice. The sun was a great gold-orange disk, glowing above the frozen horizon and she was leaning against her husband's body while he held her against his chest.

I thought I'd lost you, he said. I followed your footprints until I found you like dead on the ice with the bear's prints all around you.

What is ever truly lost? She said.

He took her hand and held it for a moment to his heart, then he helped her to rise to her feet and they went home together, walking through the long rays of red-gold light falling over the fields of ice.

7 Ice and Light

While I was writing about the polar bear, one of my close relations was dying. I'd lived with her for a time as a child, when my parents had separated, and become close to her as an adult, and it was very hard to see her body waste and know that I had to let her go. The realization that her death was approaching also brought up deep-rooted feelings of loss and abandonment from the time when I had lived with her; these rose each time I went to see her and added to the grief I felt at losing her. At the same time I became aware that she was ready to leave her physical existence. I saw the essence that is deeper than the physical body stirring, ready to take flight and realized again what grace there is in dying. As she passed away, she released many of the constraints that had limited her in this life, and this helped me to release a layer of pain that I was still holding from the past and allow it to be dissolved by the grace of letting go.

"What is death?" the bear spirit asks the woman in the story. That question is also rising from the depths of the woman's own being, under the intense pressure of her grief and feelings of powerlessness before physical death. She has come to the point where she must face the question with her whole being or be unable to continue living.

In the story, the pressure of grief leads the woman inwards, towards the light within her at the center, the radiant, undying essence that gives rise to, and sustains, physical form. She comes to know, with the unshakable truth of inner experience, that death is not the final extinction of what she loves but the portal to another dimension, the threshold between the worlds of Spirit and the flesh.

Birth and death are the most sacred of thresholds. You can only feel intense humility and reverence before the mystery of these transitions that transcend the ordinary personality and the mind. As mystery presses close, there is a profound opening to grace. You begin to realize the truth of what all the mystical traditions teach – death is not the loss of the physical body but the mind-made separation from the Spirit. The only death we ever know is to become unconscious of the true immensity of life.

As I have worked with the polar bear, I have come to regard it with reverent respect. Not simply as one of the most beautiful creatures of the Earth, but as a being with its own connection to the life that sustains physical form. Moving through the shifting and temporary icescape, which is always forming, cracking and dissolving, the bear has become for me a living meditation on the mystery of physical change and the impermanence of all forms. The bear incarnates the knowledge that there is nothing, ultimately, to grasp and hold. All separate forms rise and dissolve; essence remains, rooted in the stillness of Eternal Presence. And so there is nothing to fear in letting go: trust, release your hold and you drop into grace and the life that is beyond the pain of separation and all the forms of time.

The Book of Horse

Wild

❧❧❧❧❧❧❧❧❧❧

1 White Horses from the Sea

In the beginning the horses rolled in on the waves of the sea and tossed to the shore in the foam of white flanks and haunches: wind-driven, liquid curves of muscle and strong bone.

Those were the white horses of my imagination. I watched them gallop alongside the bus I took every day to school, flowing over the fields and clearing the ditches and the hawthorn hedges with ease, and part of me became horse and raced with them, as powerful as they were, and free. I drew them endlessly in my copybooks when I got to school, trying to capture the lovely arch of the neck and the driving power in their shoulders and haunches. I drew, I think, to work a kind of magic, to make a bond with their fluid strength and grace and bring some part of it inside.

Horses were more beautiful to me than any other animal; their presence touched the commonest field with magic. I have never lost the memory of the princely gray Arab stallion I saw when I was maybe eight or nine years old. I was standing by his stable and I could not look away from the beauty of his finely molded head and the expressive gentleness in his large dark eyes.

The love of horses ran through my family. On my father's side my ancestors had been farmers for generations and my father used to ride his own horse twelve miles and back again to the nearest town as a boy. I had one great-uncle, Bernie, who was well-known for his skill as a breeder and trainer and his love for the horses that he raised. "Bernie would cry every time he took one of his horses to market," my father always used to say of him.

My own pony was a stocky palomino, with a golden-brown coat and a white mane and tail. He grazed in the field outside my bedroom and his long pale face outside the window, looking in, was often the last thing I saw at night. I usually took a carrot or a few lumps of sugar with me when I went to bed so that I could open the window and give it to him when he appeared. This was probably what gave him the bad habit of wandering into the kitchen in the morning when the table was laid for breakfast to see what else he might find to eat. That is another early memory of horses – walking into the kitchen to find my pony at the table, knocking the crockery over and eating cornflakes from the bowls.

He had a very sociable nature. He liked to wander off and visit other horses on the neighboring farms and I sometimes woke early on a summer morning to find him gone, with a gap in the hedge where he had pushed his way through, leaving the other horses still quietly grazing. I would take his bridle from the stable and walk out to find him, then ride him home bareback through the lanes, or set him jumping across the ditches of tea-brown water in the bog.

I liked to race him against my brother's pony in the big field opposite the farmhouse, shortening my stirrups and crouching low over his neck like the racing jockeys we both admired. The best ride of all, though, went through the lanes to the seashore to gallop through the shallow waves and send the sea-spray splashing all around.

I loved the wild exhilaration of those gallops, the feeling of growing into the body of this other creature and being carried effortlessly on his power. I sense it now, even as I write: that fluid merging with the horse's motion, carried on a mutual impulse of delight in movement – a wind moving through the ocean, blowing me awake, bearing some of the essence of what I feel as *wild*.

We lived in an old farmhouse then. It was long, low and thatched, and it looked across the wheat fields and the purple-brown bog to the North Kerry hills. On a clear day, you could see the mountains of the Dingle Peninsula swelling in the distance, their granite masses made insubstantial by the expanse of intervening air. When I was a child those mountains also pointed the way to wildness – the rocky edges of the precipitous world, plunging between the windy curtains of rain-drenched light. I have vivid memories of taking the narrow roads of the Dingle Peninsula that wound high above the rolling of the sea. Look west, and you see the Blasket Islands turning through the Atlantic; to the south, two stark rock pinnacles known as the Skelligs, rise steeply, almost eight miles out to sea.

In the Irish stories that I loved as a child, horses had magical powers to cross that ocean and carry the rider into another world beyond the mist and waves.

Once, the story says, the hero Oisín was walking alone along the seashore. It was one of those days that you often get at the edge of the Atlantic when six different kinds of weather are moving through the sky and the pillars of dark cloud are pierced by brilliant shafts of sunlight. On such a day you might glimpse a distant country rising out of the ocean to the west. It was called Hy-Brasil or Tír na nÓg, and it was said to be a place out of time, where there was no sickness or sorrow, age or death.

Walking by the sea, Oisín saw a shaft of sunlight pierce the clouds and fall on one cresting wave, making it shine more whitely than all the others. As the wave rolled to the shore it became a white horse, carrying a fair-haired woman on his back.

Oisín had never seen a man or woman sit so lightly on a horse before, with such ease and perfect balance that even as the horse moved over the water the woman was still. Horse and rider halted before him in the shallows and the woman said she had come to take him to that timeless country in the ocean. How could Oisín have refused? He leapt up behind her and the horse carried them to the timeless land, where they lived in great happiness until Oisín was struck with the desire to see his father again and the friends he had left.

When she heard this, the woman was silent.

Go, she said at last. Although I fear in my heart that you will never return. My horse will carry you across the sea and he can bring you safely back, but Oisín, promise me one thing – do not set foot on the ground of Ireland while you are there.

Oisín promised her faithfully that he would stay on the horse's back and he rode across the water, eager to see the people and the places he had left. But when he reached Ireland, he saw nobody that he recognized and the people looked worn and shrunken, with no light in their eyes.

He came to a group of men at work on a stone building. They were struggling to take a large rock out of the ground, and knowing that he himself could lift it easily, he leaned down and grasped it with one hand. But the movement brought him tumbling to the ground, and his body immediately began to crumble under the weight of all the time that had passed in Ireland since he left.

As a child, the story told me that horses have magical power to protect the rider. The horse had carried Oisín to the freedom of the timeless land and while he stayed on the horse's back, he had not really left. It was only when he fell to the ground that he became subject to time and loss and all the coils of human sorrow.

Thinking of the story as an adult, I realize how much depth it contains. The horse that moves so lightly over the water evokes something essential within – the freedom from the psychological weight of time, which becomes such a burden when it freighted with past pain and future fears. There is a flowing vitality that is new in every moment, welling up within all things from the formless. The connection with that vitality, both within the body and the elemental life of nature, lifts you out of the ordinary, conditioned mind, with its habits of regret and fear, and carries you into the immediacy of presence that is new in every moment.

That sense of presence is intimately related to the unthinking awareness you know as a child. I still remember seeing formless radiance shining through the physical world when I was very young: welling up from within, pouring through the thickets of leaf and branch and filling every wild bloom in the hedgerows. The forms of this world were not completely solid: they were the filling and the overflowing of that intangible essence of light, and the light-filled blossoming was in me also, so natural that it needed no thought or consideration.

Many young children have this immediate awareness of life flowing out of the formless until education and the expectations of adults close it down. Although I can't remember exactly when this happened, I still remember the sense of loss I felt as forms solidified and surfaces became opaque to me, instead of fluid and open to measureless dimensions. I did not find that openness again until I was an adult, and watched a tree dancing rooted in the light.

I think I was around ten or eleven years old when I first saw the film that expressed this childhood fascination with the freedom of white horses and the sea. It was a black and white childrens' film called *Crin Blanc*, or *White Mane*, and it had been made among the reed beds and lagoons of the Rhône Delta, where the white Camargue horses roam semi-wild.

Crin Blanc is a wild stallion that refuses to be tamed by the horse herders of the Camargue. He breaks out of the paddock where the herders have confined him and he easily outruns the tamed horses that they ride. A young boy becomes so entranced by this powerful, determined animal that he grabs the trailing rope around his neck and holds on while the horse drags him on his belly through marshes and reeds beds. At last the stallion halts on the salt flats by the shore and allows the shaken boy to approach and put one hand on his shoulder.

The boy is the only person the stallion will accept on his back.

When the herders see this, they give chase and pursue them through the sand dunes to the shore. Horse and boy evade capture by plunging into the sea and swimming to the land beyond the ocean, the timeless country of Celtic legend where both horses and men are free.

That film was more real to me than anything I had ever seen. It haunted my imagination. Although it was a fairy tale for children, there was nothing ethereal about it. The shadeless southern light poured over the lagoons and salt flats, heightening the different tones of white in the horse's coat, and Crin Blanc himself was a powerful, physical presence, whose dignity was inseparable from his will to be free.

The Wild Horses of the Caves

This bond between humans and wild horses dates back to the very beginnings of art. Thirty-three thousand years ago, the first known painters depicted wild horses with dazzling artistry on the walls of Chauvet cave, in southern France. The discovery of Chauvet, in 1994, revolutionized the understanding of prehistoric art. These are the oldest paintings ever found. They are also fully realized masterpieces, the equal of what came later in world art.

We cannot draw like this now, Picasso said, when he first saw the images from Altamira, a prehistoric cave in Spain. He would have walked spellbound among the great panels of horses, bison, rhinos, lions and other animals that decorate Chauvet. Some of the horses grouped on its walls have such distinctive features, postures and facial expressions, that the artists must have known them as individuals, interacted with them and walked among the herds without causing them any disturbance or fear. You can sense that they found the same pleasure in watching horses move as we do today – one engraved horse moves along the cave wall with the fluid grace that delights anybody who has ever watched a riderless horse trot across a field.

Others float weightlessly across the rock. One horse emerges from a deep fissure in the cave wall. The horse seems to be passing through the veil between dimensions, a creature in physical form that is radiating numinous power. The painting is thirty-three thousand years old; even in reproduction, it is hauntingly beautiful.

The bond with wild horses endured almost unchanged for fifteen thousand years or more. Wild horses leap with extraordinary grace across the walls of Lascaux, the cave in the French Dordogne that is so richly decorated it has been called the Sistine Chapel of prehistory. At Lascaux, horses appear more often than any other animal: they make up an extraordinary *sixty percent* of all recognizable creatures, appearing far more often than stags, aurochs and bison.

According to the leading authority on European cave art, Dr. Jean Clottes, the preponderance of horses in the art of the Upper Paleolithic is so remarkable that: "We might say that the theme of the horse is at the basis of Paleolithic rock art. This is all the more remarkable as that animal... was often less plentifully killed and eaten than reindeer and bison."

If horses were neither ridden nor vital for food, what was the source of their enduring power for the peoples of the Paleolithic? How are we to understand the intensity of relationship with wild horses that is so evident in these early expressions of human creativity? After visiting one of the deep caves, and looking at the paintings, I can only suggest that these people were not divided from the consciousness of Earth. They lived within an extended community, which included the wild horses and the other animals, as well as their fellow humans. The horses they painted are shown moving freely between the different worlds, or dimensions of reality, and they shared that freedom of movement with those who found inner connection to their power. Horses were companions in the spirit long before they became companions in the flesh. They helped to carry us into further dimensions of consciousness before they ever carried us physically on their backs.

Nobody knows when a man or woman first sat on a horse's back. Until recently, it was believed that horses were tamed and used for milk and meat around five thousand years ago, among the Botal people on the vast steppes of what is now Kazakhstan. However, several horse sculptures discovered at al-Maqar in Saudi Arabia in the summer of 2011 have pushed the point of domestication back much further. The stone horses of al-Maqar show signs of selective breeding and traces of a simple bridle, suggesting that horses may have been used for riding or hauling nine thousand years ago in the Arabian Peninsula.

It is humbling to consider how much horses have given humanity since we first captured and restrained them. Horses have labored and carried for us. They have worked to build settlements and cities, borne our burdens and been wounded and killed in the terrors of war. They have become so integrated with human needs that it is claimed there are no truly wild horses any more, as all free-roaming horses have passed through domestication and selective breeding. Even the wild *takhi* of Mongolia, which closely resemble the horses of prehistory depicted on the walls of Chauvet, and were never domesticated, only survived extinction because they were kept in zoos before being reintroduced to the Mongolian steppes in the 1980s.

The bands of horses that live freely in parts of North America and Europe today are usually described as "feral" because they are the descendants of domesticated horses that escaped and went back to the wild. But the word *feral* carries negative connotations and suggests a nuisance animal, which is not truly part of the landscape. Although many free-roaming horse herds have been living independently for more than a century, they are not recognized as being truly wild animals. Their societies are frequently disrupted and their close family ties are broken when the horses are rounded up and sold for domesticity or slaughter.

2 The Wild Horses are Our Sacred Places: The Story of Maureen Enns

Few contemporary biologists have observed the lives of these free-roaming horse herds or studied their behavior in any depth. I searched for some time before I came into contact with a most remarkable woman, a leading Canadian artist who is also a naturalist, Maureen Enns. The powers of bear and horse meet in Maureen's own life and art just as they do on the walls of Pech Merle and Chauvet caves. Her art is inspired by wild relation-ships and the power and beauty of her paintings and her photog-raphy come from her experience of living among the brown bears of Kamchatka in Russia, and riding among the wild horses of the Ghost Forest, north of Calgary, in the Canadian Rockies.

In her paintings, Maureen captures the wild horses' poised alertness, the sensitive quickness of perception that is evident in their posture and bearing. Their black and bay coats gleam darkly through the broken shadows of the aspen, pine and spruce forest where they have lived for over a hundred years, avoiding all human contact.

In our conversations, Maureen and I discussed what that word "wild" evoked for each of us. I told her that I wanted to take the word back to its roots in Old English, when the *wildeor* – the wild creatures – were associated with self-will and self-deter-mination. To call these free-roaming horses *wild* would be a way to acknowledge that they have their own authentic life, which they have the right to determine for themselves away from human interference.

"Yes, that idea of self-determination resonates for me," she agreed. "A wild horse is one that can determine its own movements through the landscape and this is the freedom that we humans take away from them. I often think that the wild horses I see on the land look like a proud Indian chief and his wife. They have that pride and that assurance that they can travel the land and be fully independent on it, and survive winter and drought – everything but the white man rounding them up."

It was Maureen's own horse, her mare Hope, which revealed the horses' silent presence among the trees.

"Hope is my partner. I just think and she responds. One day she suddenly froze on the trail. This was very unlike her because she is very forward going. I couldn't see anything, but I trusted her, so I froze with her. I sensed that she had picked up on something. I was looking into the forest when I saw some hairs from a horse's tail, way deep down in the shadows, just flick out into the light and back again. Then I realized that the wild horses were right there. They were standing very still in the shadows and Hope had picked up on the signal that told the herd to freeze. Then I heard a blow – that's the sound the lead stallions make to tell the herd to move – and they all fled."

The wild horses have learned to protect themselves from wolves and other predators by remaining still in the deep shadows, just as the deer do, and breaking up their outline between the trees. Although horses evolved on steppe and open grasslands where safety usually lies in taking flight, these horses have adapted to an environment where safety lies in stillness and silence. Their coats have darkened to aid concealment, as pale colors would make their presence more apparent in the forest. The process of natural selection for darker colors means that they are all blacks and bays.

The wild horses have rich social lives, with strong emotional bonds that are based on loyalty, empathy and respect for one another. They live in families, usually a single stallion with several mares, new foals and older colts and fillies that remain with the family until they are around two or three years old. The stallion and the senior mares educate the young ones in the ways of survival and right behavior. They insist on respect towards others in the group and they will scold a young colt or filly if it shows carelessness or disrespect.

The lead mare and the stallion make critical choices about the herd's movements as they feed and rest and take responsibility for their safety from the wolves that also live in the Ghost. When the colts reach sexual maturity, they are driven away by the stallion, for inbreeding must be prevented for the well-being of the entire herd. These young males join together in 'bachelor bands' until they are ready to form their own family – either challenging an older band stallion and defeating him in combat, or bonding with a young filly who is ready to leave her first family.

Maureen's connection with the wild horses of the Ghost forest began as she was *following the bear's path* – the Native American expression from the Ojibwa people for consciously working with the wisdom of the bear.

"I'd always been terrified of grizzlies; I'd been told they were dangerous and I believed it all. I grew up on a cattle ranch and the first time I saw a black bear I turned my horse around and galloped away. My father was a hunter and he'd hung a bearskin on the wall. That dark bearskin seemed huge to me as a child. It took on mythic proportions. It was a symbol of fear. So when I first went into the Banff National Park to watch the grizzlies I studied them from a truck. Later I went in on horseback. One day I was riding through the park on my horse, Spud, really wanting to see the bears, but at the same time not wanting to get too close because I still had this fear of them, when Spud walked right up beside a mother grizzly and her two cubs. And the mother bear stayed completely calm, and so did her two cubs.

I had a packhorse with me and the two horses stood there and had a snooze while one of the cubs got under their feet. The mother grizzly went on eating; she was completely unconcerned. Then the cub scampered off to the mother and she walked in front of me and her presence... her presence was so profound that I felt I had transferred into another dimension. I called her the Queen of the Rockies.

And that's where it all began for me, the unraveling of the old negative mythologies about grizzlies. It was the horse that took me down that trail. And the horse is still taking me down that trail today because I've learned that I can trust my horse and I've learned that animals have the ability to communicate in ways that people don't. The horse and the grizzly bear were communicating, and they understood each other perfectly.

Another time I rode Spud over a saddle back pass and came right between a mother grizzly and her two cubs. The mother had just killed an elk; now if there's one thing that will get a mother grizzly upset it's somebody who might take away the food that she's had a hard time killing or threaten her cubs. Again my horse did not panic as riders are warned will always happen in such situations. He stood there in a completely relaxed way while the cubs wandered around. Then the mother got her cubs by her side and I left so as not to disturb them further."

Maureen began to envisage a different relationship with grizzly bears – one closer to the calm understanding that she had witnessed between the bears and her own horse. Her quest took her to the remote interior of Kamchatka in Russia, to live for several years among some of the largest brown bears on Earth, with her research partner Charlie Russell.

"I wanted to know if it is possible to live peacefully with such a big animal, potentially able to kill you with one swipe of the paw. So I left my horse behind and went to live in Kamchatka with Charlie. For the first year, we had no communication with the outside world. Even afterwards, when we got a satellite phone, the storms that blew in for weeks at a time would have made getting help from outside impossible. One of the things that you do in such a place is accept your own death – while doing everything you can to stay alive, just as a wild animal does. Many years later, I realized that this is the first step in entering a truly wild landscape – you accept the responsibility for your own life, while realizing that it could terminate."

Charlie and Maureen took three orphaned female cubs from the local zoo; they named them Chico, Biscuit and Rosie, and raised them by a remote lake, among a dense population of wild brown bears. Like Valentine Pazhetnov, Maureen was astonished by the cubs' early strength and independence.

"I had imagined that I would be like a mother feeding them from a bottle, but they were so independent from the beginning – in fact, they were the ones looking after me! When these cubs were two years old, I had a profound experience with them that really influenced how I viewed the wild horses later. I used to take them for walks and they always went in the same order. Chico went first, then Biscuit and Rosie."

Maureen had her own place on the trail – she walked last behind Rosie. She thought of the little bear as the artist of the group, because she went slowly, paying great attention to the texture, shapes and colors of her surroundings while they walked. Finally, she realized that Rosie walked last not because she was slower than the others, but to guard their rear on the trail.

"The next time we went for a walk, I slid between Biscuit and Rosie and all three bears – you could feel it – let out a sigh of relief that this human had finally caught on. There was a palpable feeling that I was within an aura of protection and it was profound."

Walking within that protective aura, among the bears, not behind them, she realized the intensity of their focus and attention. "I became aware of how closely they were listening to every change in the footfall on the ground, paying attention to every little sound, always gathering scents from the air."

Without the need for words or thinking, the bears had become her teachers: they were guiding her into a state of intense presence, undistracted by needless thinking.

This may well have saved her life, when she was stalked by a predatory male bear, which was tracking her with what she sensed was the intent to kill.

Certain males predate on cubs and this behavior occurs among those males that have not been disciplined by adult females to leave cubs alone. Maureen had already witnessed how females stand up to these predatory males: she had watched one dominant female trash a young male who had tried to sneak up on her cubs. On this particular day, she had been watching as another female defended her cubs from the large male that was determined to feed on one of them. This male disappeared from view, only to reappear across the marshland, this time crawling on his belly in Maureen's direction. As she observed the movement of the grass Maureen realized that she had now become this male's target.

Maureen knew how to talk bears out of aggression with the tones of her voice and the appropriate body language. She had perfected this ability in hundreds of surprise encounters. She also knew that the stinging pepper spray she always carried would only deflect the bear's attack when he was already in full charge towards her. So with adrenalin pumping, she decided to incite the male bear to charge in order to use her pepper spray effectively. Using the language of bear aggression, she stood face on to the male, yelling loud obscenities and was intensely relieved when he slowly backed off and retreated.

These experiences developed the acute sensitivity that Maureen now brings to her observations of the wild horses of the Ghost.

"When I first entered the country of the wild horses, I had this gateway open in my brain because of living for so long in extreme wilderness with the bears. At the same time I had this preconception of horses as being purely domestic animals. As I've been watching the wild herds, I keep seeing things that completely shatter these preconceptions. One day I came across around thirty horses all together. I thought – no, this can't possibly be, there's no herd that big in here. Then I realized what I was seeing – three of the herds had come together in a rough circle with the stallions outside. I heard a wolf howl and realized that a wolf pack was passing through. I understood that the stallions were standing on the edge for protection and collectively guarding the others just as the male buffalo do. Yet I've also watched a wolf walk right through the whole herd, with a foal lying on the ground beside its mother, and the horses showed no concern at all."

I told Maureen about Jason Badridze, who also lived for several years in remote wilderness and bonded with a family of wolves. Jason had observed the same behavior among desert gazelles. He watched a wolf pass among the gazelles without disturbing or frightening them because the gazelles knew immediately that the wolf wasn't hunting.

"Yes. When the wolves are really hunting, the wild horses know it. When they're not, the horses don't waste energy worrying about it.

People believe so many things about horses that are based solely on their experience with domestic horses. For example, the young stallions that run in these bachelor herds – six or eight together – are so respectful and polite. People are often surprised that I ride alone among the wild horses on my mare, but I always say that I couldn't be safer because these wild stallions have been taught to respect the mares. I can ride among them on my mare, even when she's in heat and she wants to be with a stallion, and they'll circle or stop but there is absolutely nothing rude or aggressive about them. They won't infringe her space, because that's how they've been brought up to behave.

These horses really have returned to nature. I've learned from them what immense value there is in allowing some horses to live free, because what they can teach us about how horses are when they're away from humans is so important for how we relate to our domestic horses. But their landscape is threatened by logging, and their freedom is threatened by people who want to remove them from the land unless I can do something to prevent it."

The others who recognize and honor the horses' freedom are the people of the Stoney Nakoda First Nations, whose lands are adjacent to the government forest reserve where the wild horses live.

"The Ghost forest is right beside the Stoney Nakoda First Nations' land. When I started to make friends among the community I kept asking them about the sacred places within the landscape. Finally my friend Hank Snow, who is a respected member of that community, said to me, "You know you have already found what is sacred in that landscape. The wild horses are our sacred places."

The Love of Horses

These words – *the wild horses are our sacred places* – are a beautiful expression of the Native American understanding of sacred relationship. Sacredness cannot be confined in buildings or tamed by the structures of religious dogma because sacredness is in *life*, and all the authentic relationships of life.

It is often believed that the imminence of the sacred within the natural world, which is so integral to Native America, is absent from the Western traditions, but this is not entirely true. The Celtic traditions of Britain and Ireland express the same kinship with the life in nature. Like the Native American image of the cross within the circle, which represents the sacred unity of all things, the Celtic cross is equal-armed and placed within a circle. The center of the cross unites the four divisions of the circle, and the four cardinal directions with the Earth and Heavens. At the heart of the six directions is the place of unity, the sacred center within each person and within all things.

There are many places in Britain and Ireland where the land

itself is still imbued with that spirit of connection. I feel it most strongly on the Skelligs, the two rock pinnacles that rise steeply from the Atlantic, off the Southwest coast of Ireland where I grew up. To this day the Skelligs are among the places I love best in the world. Twenty thousand pairs of gannets congregate around their waters; puffins make their nests in small hollows on the slopes in summer and the seals haul out on the lower ledges. The larger of the two is called Skellig Michael, or *Sceilg Mhichíl* in Irish, from the word *sceilg*, meaning rock and it is considered sacred to the Archangel Michael, the guardian of the element of fire. In the Scottish Celtic tradition Michael is also the guardian of horses and the sea, and he is depicted riding a white horse in the midst of a great wind. Horse and rider are borne up as one and carried on the wind of the Divine Breath – *Ruach*, in Hebrew, the breath of creation moving over the waters.

Even today the sea journey to reach the Skelligs can be difficult. Like the timeless country of Irish legend, the rocks appear and disappear between the mist and sea and you may wait days for the fog to clear and the Atlantic swell to calm so that a small boat can be safely moored under the high peak of Skellig Michael. When you land, you still face a steep climb over hundreds of hand-carved stone steps until you reach the narrow summit and a small group of dry-stone "beehive" huts.

The huts were built by Celtic Christian monks and scarcely a stone has moved in more than twelve hundred years of Atlantic wind and storm. But the monks of Skellig built no church. Like their druid ancestors, they prayed always in the open air, saying mass and taking communion with the sunlight and wind and swelling ocean, the gannets and the nesting puffins, the seals and whales and dolphins as their companions. In the Celtic Christian tradition, the presence of the Christ is not confined to some church or distant heaven. It is imminent now, in the wonder of this world's life and the love of animals and the wild leads directly towards the Divine.

Early Irish folklore is full of stories about eccentric hermit saints who shared their lives with animals. Saint Kevin of Glendalough allowed a blackbird to nest in his outstretched hand while he was praying. Saint Ciarán of Saighir lived and prayed in a monastic animal community – his fellow monks were a fox, a badger and a wolf. The wolves that lived in the dense Irish forests until the 1700s were neither fearful nor demonic: in the folklore they helped people in trouble and they would always reward a kindness.

The best-loved sacred text in the entire Celtic Christian tradition was the Gospel of John and it was common for people to learn the whole text by heart, inwardly repeating favorite passages, such as the sublime opening lines which recall the first words of the creation story in the Book of Genesis. "In the beginning was the Word" or *Logos* in the original text, which was written in Greek.

The Logos of John's Gospel means far more than word. Before it was ever written down within the Gospel, the term had been used by Heraclitus and other pre-Socratic Greek philosophers to signify the very essence and indwelling spirit of all that manifests as physical existence, the Eternal Presence that brings forth, and sustains, what appears in time and space.

Everything has come into existence through the Logos and is sustained by it, in the mystery of the unity of being. Like the Great Mystery of Native America, the Logos is present in all the forms of nature as the essence, the spiritual power, which inhabits all beings and natural forces. The creative Word is speaking *now* – in the elemental powers of thunder, wind and rain, in the formless outpouring of sunlight, in the slow unrolling of the Earth's crust over molten, roiling rock. The power of the first creation is not in the past; it is welling up in this very moment from the timeless, formless source, as life is continually renewed throughout the Earth and cosmos.

This awareness of one sustaining presence through all

separate-seeming forms flowed through Celtic Christianity and allowed people the freedom to find spiritual connection with the entire natural world and relate to it as the manifestation of Divine Presence.

"Look at the animals roaming the forest: God's spirit dwells within them. Look at the birds flying across the skies: God's spirit dwells within them. So when our love is directed towards an animal or even a tree we are participating in the fullness of God's love," wrote Pelagius, a Celtic Christian teacher of the fourth century.

Whenever I stand before the *léacht* or the bed of small stones around which the Skellig monks said mass, I remember that ceremony of communion which was always held in the open air – the bread and the consecrated wine cup shared with the wild cries of the circling birds and the wind-swept furrows of sunlight moving over the Atlantic swell. Then it fills with universal meaning. It becomes the recognition of Divine Consciousness welling up from the untold source and pouring into this world, to give freely to all creatures, according to their capacity to receive, "grace upon grace."

As Christianity became more centralized and hierarchical, that freedom to live in spiritual relationship with the body, the animals and the Earth was curbed. The Pagan and Celtic traditions of the Christian communities of Britain and Ireland were suppressed and believers were taught to be fearful and suspicious of their sexual energies, the body and the life of the wild.

This change, which also separated the masculine from the feminine, finds a very poignant expression in a late medieval version of Oisín's story, the Pagan hero who was taken to the timeless land by the rider on her white horse, but drawn back to Ireland by the desire to see his father and his friends again. As Oisín reaches for the great stone, which the men are digging from the ground, he falls from his horse's back and his body shrivels. Before he dies, he is brought before Patrick, the

Christian saint who converted Ireland to Christianity. It was Patrick's church the men had been working to build and it was the stone for the church walls that had pulled Oisín to the ground.

Patrick tries to convince Oisín of the truth of the Christian faith; but Oisín has no interest in the abstractions of belief. Instead he speaks to him with lyrical intensity of his great love for the natural world – the piercing song of the blackbird in the hedge and the lowing of the stag coming clear across lake water are sweeter sounds by far, he says, than the ringing of Patrick's church bells.

In this version, the story becomes a vivid expression of how mental structures close around the experience of inner freedom. We find love and beauty in the depths of the heart and enter the timeless country of union but do not remain present because the mind pulls away and builds the walls of isolation using abstractions and the dogmatic forms of belief. Leaving the life that is always welling up within the body and the Earth, the egocentric mind seeks to control the freedom of the formless Spirit and makes an ultimate reality of aging, loss and death.

3 The Friend of the Soul

The love of horses is also an integral part of the mystical teachings within John's Gospel, although this is usually overlooked because the references to Greek philosophy in the text's symbolism and language, which would have been evident to readers of the time, have become obscured. Like the wisdom traditions of shamanic Siberia and the spiritual teachings of Native America, John's Gospel uses the symbol of the point within the circle. The figure of the Christ holds the consciousness of the center, in unity with Divine Being, and the twelve disciples represent the twelve aspects of humanity and the twelve divisions of the zodiac turning around the constant light of the Pole Star at the center of the night sky. The Pole Star is also evoked in one of the names given to the Virgin Mary: she is the "star of the sea" the light that gives a sure direction to all those who travel on the sea.

The names given to some of the disciples in John's Gospel are not historical. They relate to this deliberate, symbolic order, which places the consciousness of the Christ at the center of the circle of life. One of the first disciples called by Jesus in John's Gospel is Philip, a Greek name meaning the "love of horses".

In classical Greece, the love of horses represented the conscious relationship with the vital energies that flow through the physical body and the Earth. We might also call them the energies of the wild, which are continually renewing the life of the body and the entire natural world. Eastern practices such as yoga and Tai Chi recognize the importance of living in conscious connection with the body's inner life, that dancing vitality on the breath that is continually renewed. "Energy is eternal delight" wrote William Blake, a phrase which captures the joy that is inherent in the flow of life through the body. Giving full attention to that subtle aliveness within the body and allowing its energy to flow in harmony with the natural rhythms of the breath bring you into the freedom that is beyond the thinking mind. You are lifted up, out of the anxious preoccupations of the mind, and brought into the abundant grace that is always welling up within the present.

Greek philosophy drew on the imagery of horse and rider to express this conscious connection with the vital energies of life. The rider is the man or woman who lives and moves in dynamic equilibrium with these energies, not fearing and suppressing them or seeking to control them through force of will, but bringing them into unforced union with spiritual consciousness, the light within the heart. So when Jesus calls to Philip in John's Gospel, the text is indicating that the vitality of the body and all the world's wild life are being called into the dance of union with Divine Presence.

The Irish Celtic tradition has a beautiful term for the relationship that lifts you into this abundance of grace: the *anam chara* or the friend of the soul. The *anam chara* is any person whose company helps to reawaken what is most authentic within, renewing your faith in yourself and kindling the desire to be more fully alive. It need not be another human person – the *anam chara* might be a mountain peak or running stream or any living creature that touches you with the immediacy of presence.

The horse that came to me as an adult became my *anam chara*. He was nothing like the flowing white horses of my childhood imagination: he was muscular and compact, with a strong back, a deep chest and a red-gold coat. Bred from a German Hanoverian sire and an Irish Draught mother, he had great physical power but it was the strength of his personality that struck me the first time I saw him. As I walked towards his stable, he swung his head around and the moment I met his dark gaze I knew that this horse was for me. I had not intended to buy him, but, strange as this may sound, I felt that he had resolved to come with me and all I had to do was accept this. His previous owner had simply called him Joe, and since it is considered bad luck to change a horse's name, Joe he always remained for me.

The relationship got off to a very fiery start. The first time I rode Joe out of the yard alone he bolted into a flat out gallop along a narrow trail, which was stony, slippery with autumn leaves and wound tightly through the trees. I clung to his back with no control as he careered around the blind narrow corners and only brought him to a halt by riding him towards some railings that were too tall for him to jump. I was shaking and he was plunging restlessly around, a muscular ball of coiled-up energy, ready to release another uncontrolled burst of power and speed.

I'd been badly frightened yet I knew instinctively that he hadn't intended to hurt or frighten me: anxious and insecure in a new environment, he was full of abundant energy that was being too tightly constrained to suit the human way of doing things. And he had sensed immediately that I wasn't really present on his back. I hadn't begun to make the inner bond of energy and intention that brings horse and rider together into one.

That free-flowing harmony and grace cannot be feigned. Horses cannot lie and the rider cannot fool them. Unless their senses have been dulled by drudgery or abuse, horses are aware of our emotional states. They can be far more sensitive than many riders because they have not disassociated their awareness from the body. They do not live through mental images and self-concepts and they do not suppress authentic feelings. What a horse knows and trusts is the immediacy of emotional truth *in the present*, for as Maureen has learned, their wellbeing in the wild is based on their trust in one other and the clarity of their relationships.

Horses immediately sense the tensions and insecurities that are knotted into the vital energies of the body and they reflect this back in the way they respond and carry the rider. So working with horses gives you a choice: you can try to relate to them as consciously as possible and make relationships where there is mutual trust and understanding, which is the kind of relationship that comes so naturally to them in the wild. Or you can fall back on the ego's desire for dominance and struggle for control.

That is what I did at first. I used a stronger bit and held Joe tightly when I rode him on the trail. He no longer tried to run away with me but he often resisted the rigid way I held him by bracing against me and dancing on the spot. My own body tensed against him in turn and riding became more about proving that I could control this powerful animal and make him obey me than the spontaneous freedom that I'd found with horses as a child.

Yet for all his strong-willed fire, there was a bond between us. He would call to me if he saw me walking through the yard and follow me along the fence when I walked beside the field where he was grazing. And I loved his company. I began to ride him alone through the fields to a quiet spot where I could dismount and sit beside him on the grass while he grazed. There should be a special word for the peace of horses. Their company brings release from the whirring anxiety of the ordinary mind. Their beauty is a continual wonder, which is free from the human taints of self-consciousness and vanity. Their strength is without arrogance or the craving for power for its own sake. Without any expectations or pressure to achieve, we were simply two related beings inhabiting the same quiet space, and I found a bond with him by doing nothing that had eluded me completely while I fought with him for control.

As I relaxed, I became less rigid in the saddle. He immediately responded. His own resistance softened and he moved more lightly. Then, one gusty spring day, when I was riding through the woods I felt that wind of speed begin to build in him again. I sensed that he was about to spring away into another uncontrolled gallop, but this time my body knew far better than my mind. Instead of tensing and tightening the reins, my body spontaneously softened and connected with his back. Our vital energies met – body to body, spine to spine, breath to breath – and he immediately sensed their connection. For a few seconds longer he danced on the spot, snorting vigorously... then he moved forward calmly with a wonderfully fluid, springing stride.

That moment of meeting was his great gift to me. I have never forgotten it. He had shown that what he needed was not my clumsy effort to control him, but authentic connectedness – a calm centering to which he gladly joined his energy and will. Without the need for words or mental abstractions, simply through being what he was, this powerful, beautiful animal became my teacher: he was my guide along the path to becoming more real.

He was a friend to the truth in me and – like all real friend-ships – this could be very challenging to live with. The first time I saw my father again after more then sixteen years without contact I took him to the stables to see Joe. I was working hard to control my emotions and appear outwardly calm, but inside there was a mass of confused and turbulent feeling – a sickness of the heart made of loneliness and sorrow mingled with the tentative hope that we might find a relationship with each other again.

Determined to do everything as usual, I saddled Joe and took him for a short ride through the woods. But he knew better: he stopped and for the first and only time he reared up and almost sent me tumbling off his back. And for the first and only time I dismounted and lead him back to the yard on foot.

Later, when I was trying to understand what could have upset him so much, I realized that he had reacted to the emotional turbulence that I was trying so hard to keep under control. The attempt to master my feelings through the will and keep a social mask in place might appear to work around other humans but it was utterly meaningless to him. The tension of withheld feeling was constricting the flow of life through my body; this constriction was immediately perceptible to him because the body – like the horse – does not lie.

By rearing up and refusing to carry that burden of unresolved pain, he was challenging me to be more real. I could not make an authentic relationship with him, and ride with the ease and freedom that brought so much joy and still keep suppressing so much of what I really felt. And he became my faithful companion as I began to work with yoga and breathing and other methods of awareness to become more present and release some of the trauma from the past that was knotted into my vital body.

Old pain that is carried in the body cannot be released all at once. It takes time to trust the reality of healing, for habits of inner repression are tenacious and it often seems safer to stay contracted and keep volatile feelings locked away with the will. But my horse supported me. As I began to slowly release some of the layers of suppressed emotion, I found more ease and vitality and he responded. He moved more fluidly. He carried me more happily. He helped me to trust my own body's subtle, indwelling aliveness and the growing sense of connection between us, rather than the effort of control. He seemed to sense every small shift I made towards greater freedom, and he supported it by sharing his own abundant vitality with me.

Airs above the Ground

After some time, I found a sensitive and gifted riding teacher who taught in the tradition of classical horsemanship, which aims to develop the connection between horse and rider to the highest degree of refinement. "Ideally you need only think," she told me, "and the horse responds."

The practice helps the horse and rider to attune their energy and will through the practice of gymnastic sequences with a dancer's attention to the music of movement. As the energy of attention builds and flows between horse and rider, it brings them together in a heightened state – separate minds and bodies, hearts and wills gathering into unity and working together in dynamic, ever-changing balance. In finding balance the horse's power grows in such lightness that horse and rider almost take on flight. At the very highest level, they make great flying leaps through the air that are known as *airs above the ground*; yet even through these most dynamic of all steps, there is intense stillness. Movement and stillness meet as one: horse and rider find their connection in the quietness of profound concentration and they move together from the unity of consciousness they have found.

Practiced like this, riding can become a way to greater awareness. The harmony that is sought cannot be hurried or forced. The rider must give up the ego's drive to dominate through force, master their own impatience and desire for external achievement and work always from inner quietness.

Of course, this takes years of dedication. I was a very unskilled beginner yet even the attempt took me into another dimension of relationship with my horse. As I began to practice with frequent changes of pace and rhythm through circles, spirals and other figures, first on one rein, then the other, there was no time for fruitless thinking or distractions. I had to bring my attention fully into the moment, be present with the seamless flow of movement and sense the small shifts in the horse's pace and carriage. I had to become aware of the imbalances in my own body that were causing him to stiffen or lean to one side, and make the subtle corrections of posture and breathing that helped him to move in balance beneath my weight.

The practice was one of the most challenging things I had ever attempted and there were times when my own clumsiness and lack of coordination almost brought me to despair. Mostly, I tried too hard, and that sense of strain and effort raised a barrier between us. Yet there were also times when something magical happened. I found the natural ease of connection to his movement through my body – spine to spine, breath to breath – and he responded. His movements filled with buoyant energy. His carriage shifted into such balance and lightness that I felt I was being lifted up on waves of effortless power as he moved. I was set free from the effort of control and brought into a mutual dance of movement, heartbeat and breathing, experiencing motion with the intensity of attention that creates a sense of inner stillness.

This affected me so deeply that I brought him to a halt before my teacher in the school one day because I could not continue: I was on the edge of tears. She stroked his neck and smiled at me. Then she said, "Now you know how it's meant to feel."

It is little wonder that horses are associated with flight; that the Greek heroes ride on winged horses and the Archangel Michael is carried on a white horse on the wind of creation moving over the waters. Horses not only lift and carry us physically: if we work with them in consciousness, they will take us out of the brittle ego and the domineering will and carry us into the experience of flowing unity that belongs to the life within the soul.

The Book of Whale

The Circle Closes

1 The Story of Francisco "Pachico" Mayoral

Laguna San Ignacio
Baja California Sur
March 2010

Where the lagoon opens to the wind-driven Pacific, the gray whales are rising all around us. The green water roils over the slow serpent-turning of their spines and the pulsating mist of their breathing. A barnacled head rises straight from the water as the whale thrusts upright and stands balanced on its tail, "spy-hopping" for a moment above the surface before it sinks again as smoothly as it rose.

A mother breaches with a gusty exhalation, her calf's head resting on her side. The calf slides beneath the surface and swims towards our boat, a dark shadow undulating through the gray-green swell. I dip my hand in the water, waiting for the calf to come near, when the mother herself breaks through the surface beside me, rising beyond all expectation and soaking my skin with the spray of her breath. She brushes my hand with her back and the sudden contact with the sea-washed smoothness of her skin unleashes a powerful burst of inner warmth that is still pulsing like sunlight through my heart as she sinks back.

Behind me the boatman has bent down to touch her calf. He is murmuring to it in Spanish, caressing it with the tones of his voice and the movements of his hand. A slight man in his late sixties, with sun-darkened skin and luminous black eyes, his full name is Francisco Mayoral, but to his family and his friends he is known simply as Pachico.

Forty years ago, in February 1972, Pachico Mayoral was fishing for grouper near the mouth of the lagoon, with his neighbor, Luis Perez. That day the gray whales were particularly numerous; they were spy-hopping and breaching all around his *panga* and he was anxious to avoid coming near them. Like the other fishermen on the lagoon, Pachico was wary of the grays, which could overturn a *panga* with one slap of the tail and fling the men into the water. A few years before, several San Ignacio fishermen had died in such an accidental encounter with a gray whale.

That day something entirely new happened. A gray whale deliberately approached them and lingered alongside for more than an hour. It swam under and around them and made the *panga* rock by rubbing the underside with its back while the two men sat immobile, unable to pull up their fishing lines and start the engine for fear of causing a dangerous collision. Until, finally, Pachico reached out his hand and touched the whale on the side.

As soon as he touched it, his fear vanished. "I began to stroke the whale. And I could feel that the whale liked it, so I kept on stroking it."

He's sitting next to me in the dining tent that evening after dinner, still in his salt-stained jeans and drinking a beer, while the canvas walls crack and rattle in the strong wind that sweeps across this side of the lagoon each evening. As I speak no Spanish, camp manager Ruby is translating, her dark eyes bright with intelligence, at the other side of the trestle table.

"We went back and we told the others but they did not believe us at first. They all thought we were crazy. Even Carmen, my wife, at first she did not believe me either, and I thought, but she's supposed to love me!"

Pachico tells the story simply, with warmth and humor, as he has told it to others before me, but there is a stillness and clarity behind his words that give them power.

"After that, I changed inside. I saw everything differently – even the plants, even the stones. The only thing that I can compare this to is the feeling that I had when my first child was born."

What are the whales seeking to communicate when they approach the boats? I ask.

"I believe that the whales come to share peace with us. They are bringing us peace and showing how we can live together in harmony."

"I also have these things also from my father," he adds, after a short pause. "My father always told me that it is more important to be honest and truthful than to have money. I am poor but I have peace and happiness. I have a vision of being able to share these things with the people who come to the lagoon to see the whales with me. I know when they feel connected to the whales. I know when they feel touched by them inside. Without the need for speaking, I sense this. For me it is no longer so important to touch the whales physically because I always feel the connection with them in my heart."

I feel the same way, I tell Pachico. When I first came to the lagoon, the experience of being approached by the whales and invited to touch them physically was so overwhelming that it changed forever the way I relate to my fellow creatures. Three years later, I feel connected to the gray whales inwardly even when I'm no longer near them physically and cannot touch them.

In 1978 biologist Dr. Steven Swartz arrived in San Ignacio Lagoon to study the grays with a colleague, Mary Lou Jones. With Pachico as their guide and friend, the two scientists soon began to experience their own astonishing encounters with the grays.

Between 1978 and 1983, they documented more than five hundred friendly interactions with the whales. One female was so playful and free with them that they called her "Amazing Grace".

"She would roll under the boat, turn belly up with her flippers sticking three to four feet out of the water on either side of the craft, then lift us clear off the surface of the lagoon, perched high and dry on her chest between her massive flippers." Steven Swartz wrote. "When she tired of the bench press technique, Grace would do the same thing with her head, lifting us out of the water and letting us slide off to swirl around her in circles, like a big rubber duck in the bathtub with a ten-ton playmate."

"Pachico is like my *abuelo*, like my grandfather," Abby, the young biology student who is the camp's naturalist guide tells me, as we get ready to meet the whales with him again. There is a lightness of spirit in Abby that is a delight to be around and on this particular day the grays move around us with the grace of dancers. The wind is tossing the light through fluid alterations of sunlight and shadow as one whale glides slowly towards us. She rolls belly-up with her pectoral fins spread wide and keeps turning in one continuous smooth motion as she sinks down beneath the boat.

"That's the OM whale!" Abby calls out delightedly, for the way the whale opened out her pectoral fins on the water. Two others approach the boat from behind. They separate and slide close past on either side, then come together at the bow and submerge in a single dive, which is so perfectly timed we seem to be lifted and carried on the turning roll of their backs.

I gasp in astonishment and look around to see Pachico smiling. "In forty years I never saw the whales do that before," he tells me afterwards, when we have left the whale watching area and landed on the beach by the white sand dunes that rim the Pacific shore. It is a place of clear immensities and windy light, where the shallow water shows pale turquoise over the white sand and the sleek-sided dolphins surface with short puffs of misty breath. Caspian terns swoop among the brown pelicans overhead, scattering arcs of white light with their wings and a gray whale moves past offshore, so close it must almost brush the sandy bottom with its belly.

While we eat on the beach, Pachico tells me about the young male gray whale he knew which never went north with the others. He remained alone by the lagoon after they left for the Arctic, and he found enough food to sustain himself. "He never grew big. He stayed like a calf, and he was very, very friendly. When I went fishing, I called to him and he always came to meet me."

This reminds me of the story Afanassi told me once about the hunter on the Bering Strait who had such a close friendship with one orca that it would always come to his skin boat if he whistled or called. When the hunter's boat was foundering in heavy seas, the orca came to help, bringing the others in the pod, and brought the boat safely back to shore. I thought that story had a mythical ring when I heard it first, but hearing Pachico speak of his own friendships with the grays, I realize again how little we really know about the connection we could have with the whales and other cetaceans.

In forty years of watching the grays mate, give birth and care for their calves, Pachico has seen more of their lives than even the most experienced scientist. After dinner in the tent that evening, I ask him to tell me about their relationships with each other and that immediately launches him into an animated account of their sexual behavior.

Sex is a communal experience for the whales, he explains; in human terms, he would describe them as bisexual. The grays gather in large groups for sexual play, and the male and female unite surrounded by others that are supporting their bodies in the water and jostling to join in.

Ruby demonstrates the structure of a gray whale mating group with her fingers and hands. "So here you have the female," she explains briskly, extending her index finger. "There is the male alongside her, with another male below. Then another female at the side here and a male here..."

Soon Ruby has run out of fingers, and we're all laughing. Pachico has brought us seamlessly from the peace that he experiences among the gray whales to their abundant sexuality, which flows without borders between the mating pair and the other whales that surround them.

According to Steven Swartz, gray whale mating groups are "herculean... males and females copulating with an assortment of partners. This promiscuous activity sometimes blossoms into a giant free for all, involving as many as eighteen to twenty individuals at a time." The encounters may last for several hours; the males take turns, bumping and nudging each other, but never seeming aggressive. On occasions, even the lagoon's bottlenose dolphins have been seen to join in.

The older and more experienced males help the younger ones through their first sexual experiences, Pachico continues, and they show them how to direct the flexible penis, which can be six foot or more in length when fully extended. The playful and relaxed relationship between young males is evident in the observation made by one biologist who was watching the grays migrate off Alaska. He saw three adolescent males close together on the surface. The flexible penises, which are usually kept tucked away inside a slit in the belly, were fully extended, and they had wrapped them around each other in a companionable way.

The female grays also give each other help and support, Pachico adds. When a young female is about to mate for the first time, her mother, aunt or older friend is there to reassure her. When the birth is near, the pregnant females enter the mangrove channels, where the water is shallow and calm. An older female may be with her during the birth and help the calf to emerge by massaging the mother's belly with her head. These older females are very protective of the new mothers with calves and they fend off amorous and impatient males by lunging at them and slashing with their tails.

"Pachico is always very careful to speak only of what he has observed for himself," Ruby clarifies at this point. "He is like a scientist in this way. He has great respect for the scientist Steve Swartz. The two of them have been friends for nearly thirty years and they have shared their knowledge with each other."

I had been fortunate to see a small group of mating grays for myself once, inside San Ignacio Lagoon. Two males and a female were rolling together in a churning maelstrom of white water and tall pulsations of misty breath. The males uncoiled their pink penises above the surface. They rolled onto their backs and slapped the water with their pectoral fins and tails as they jostled and turned around the female. The whales' fervor, the intensity of their energy and their engagement with each other staggered me. After that experience, the word "mating" came to seem bare and clinical, giving no sense of the immensity of the life flowing through them as they unite.

Whales move through a world without borders. There are no fixed structures in the ocean to confine them. Direction, height, depth are sensed through the pressure of the currents and upwellings and the swell of the tides. Imagine, for a moment, how different their sense of space must be – for whales do not see space, they *hear* it. The three dimensions of the ocean are structured for them through their perceptions of sound, shaped by resonant beams and echoes crossing the immense darkness of the sea.

The whales never stop moving. They have no territories to defend. What they have is each other, the mobile community of their relatives, partners and friends. There are entire whale societies in the ocean: extended families, friendships and partnerships. For a long time, Western observers were unable or unwilling to acknowledge the strong community life of the whales and other cetaceans. Commercial whalers had no interest in whale cultures and kinship bonds. They saw the whales as purely material objects, mere containers of meat and oil. But when industrial whaling reduced entire whale populations to remnant bands, it was not simply killing individuals in great numbers. It was also breaking up extended families, killing the grandparents and elders who had kept the long-term memories of families and clans and reducing the complex richness of their cultures.

Whales are intensely cultural species – they innovate and learn from one another and they pass on their knowledge and information. Their social relationships and their culture have driven the evolution of their large and complex brains. Of all creatures on Earth, the sperm whale is the one with the largest brain. And sperm whales live in close and supportive communities. Female sperm whales raise their offspring within extended families, with the support of grandmothers, other mothers and female friends. The sperm whale baby can swim within a few hours of birth, but it cannot remain long below the surface. The mother must leave to forage at great depths and she remains below for thirty to forty minutes. So the females stagger their dives and they take care of one another's babies near the surface, watched over by the long-lived family matriarch, the grandmother or great-grandmother. In one sperm whale community, the mothers even share feeding – the babies have been seen going between different females to nurse while the birth mother has gone deep underwater.

These sperm whale females also do something that was once thought to be unique to humans – they stop reproducing and live for another thirty to forty years. These older females are the matriarchs that hold the memories and the life experience of the community. They know the longer cycles that affect the life of the oceans, and they guide others through the changing patterns of climate and currents and the shifting movements of their prey.

Although it is not known for certain whether the female grays also stop reproducing when they reach middle age, it seems likely. The grays can live to be seventy or eighty years old and these elder females are surely the ones that Pachico has seen helping the young mothers to give birth, and moving protectively around a mother with her newborn calf.

Whales also cooperate and work together in teams to catch their prey. Humpbacks, the master musicians of the whale world, use air bubbles as tools to fish for herring and other schools of small fish. Diving below the surface, one humpback releases a controlled stream of air through its blowhole and allows it to slowly expand until it forms a large air bubble in the water. Meanwhile, the other humpbacks are spiraling around the fish and producing a high-pitched sound that herds them towards the air bubble. Once the fish are inside, the air bubble acts as a net that keeps them from escaping until the humpbacks surge through them and feed with their great mouths agape.

This is highly skilled work. It demands close timing, trust and intricate co-operation between team members. Individual whales specialize in different tasks. One whale concentrates on making the air bubble grow to the optimum size for capturing the school of fish. Others direct the fish towards the bubble net. A group of humpbacks that work well together will meet on the same fishing grounds year after year. The whales are collaborating in ways that were once considered to be purely human – using their bubble nets as fishing tools and building relationships and trust through a series of shared tasks.

"My father raised us to think of the gray whales as our family," Pachico's son, Jesus, tells me. He runs the small camp by the lagoon between February and April, opposite a small island where the ospreys build their nests in ragged towers along the shore. In the evenings, burnished by the slow incandescence of the sunset, the desert mountains on the other side of the lagoon turn copper-colored, and their sides are hollowed with purple shadows. The shore beneath them is fringed with mangroves, long corridors of glossy green silence where the whales go to give birth.

Jesus generates the electricity for the camp's simple cabins with wind and solar power and he recycles rubber tires and old tin cans for use as construction material. His mother, Carmen, is a *curandera*, a traditional healer who works with the local plants; his brothers are also naturalist guides, with intimate knowledge of the life of the lagoon. During the whale season, Pachico guides visitors into the whale watching area, although he will not take people on the lagoon in January, when the whales have recently arrived from their long migration, and should, he believes, be left in peace.

"A few years ago we thought it was time my father stopped spending these long days out on the lagoon," Jesus continues. "When he heard this, he went very quiet for a while. Then he said if you take away my *panga* you take away my life. We've never dared to suggest it since."

"I love this community," Ruby says fervently, driving me along the graded dirt road that connects the network of small fishing villages that runs inland from the lagoon. Each wooden house sits within a small ecosystem of recycled materials: old rubber tires have been used to build fences; the salt-battered jeeps that were rifled for spare parts have been set on bricks and used for storage. It is easy to see where Jesus got his enthusiasm for building with used tires and empty soda cans filled with sand.

Ruby has a remarkable flair for bringing people together. As well as running the whale camp in season with Pachico's family, she oversees the protection of endangered sea turtles in the lagoon and takes care of community liaison with the Vizcaino Biosphere Reserve, a major UNESCO World Heritage site that protects desert habitats and coastal areas around San Ignacio and the southern Baja California peninsula.

She takes me first to see the medical clinic and community center that she has helped to build, with the assistance of some Californian doctors, then to the nursery where the young mangrove plants grow in glossy lines. They will be replanted to regenerate the areas where the mangroves were stripped from the shore.

Talking to Ruby and Jesus in the evenings after the long days on the water among the whales, I realize that Pachico's modest camp is a powerful nexus of connection, drawing many different people together through their shared love of the gray whales. And the same is true of the entire San Ignacio Lagoon. Ten years ago, this remote desert, which is several hours by dirt track road from the small oasis town of San Ignacio, was the focus for a remarkable international campaign that united people from around the world to protect the gray whales and their birthing grounds.

San Ignacio is the only one of the gray whale birthing areas along the Pacific coast of Baja California whose pristine fertility is undisturbed by human activity, a protected circle of birth and breathing. But in 1998, the Japanese company Mitsubishi, which had been heavily involved in commercial whaling, announced plans to construct a massive industrial salt works at the edge of the lagoon. The project would have built a mile-long concrete pier across the whales' migratory path. A huge network of saltwater concentration ponds would have replaced the natural salt flats and great volumes of toxic byproducts from the industrial salt production would have been released into the ocean.

It never happened. Pachico and his family, the local community and the fishing cooperatives of San Ignacio joined over a hundred Mexican groups and international conservation organizations to oppose the salt works. Around the world, more then a million people wrote letters and cards of protest. Along the gray whales' migratory route, city councils passed resolutions to condemn it. After several years of this sustained opposition, Mitsubishi, and its Mexican partner, abandoned the salt works for good.

Most of the people who joined the campaign to protect the gray whale's birthing lagoon had never seen its beauty. They had never heard the plosive exhalations of the gray whales' breath or felt their touch. It didn't matter. They had gained a sense of shared community with the whales.

Writing this book I have come to know – not as theory but as living experience – that I am part of the great community of Earth, a community as much of the heart and soul as of ecology. At the same time, I have become more aware than ever before of the destructive urge that now rages through human actions. There is nothing abstract about this knowledge: the effects are visible among the gray whales in the lagoon.

Spending every day among the whales with Pachico, I have realized how few females have had calves in the winter of 2010. On average, there are only twenty to thirty new mothers with calves inside the lagoon, the lowest numbers since scientific research began in San Ignacio. Thirty years ago, three and four hundred adult grays thronged the lagoon in the birthing season; at the peak, it was not unusual to have two hundred or more new mothers with calves, resting and playing before their journey into Arctic waters.

Like all baleen whales, the grays are powerful and very wide-ranging. Their movements vary with changing weather patterns and ocean currents in the Pacific and they move easily between the different lagoons and coastal areas of the Baja California coast. Some whales may simply be frequenting other lagoons or spending more time in the open ocean. But there is no doubt that the gray whales are coming under increasing stress because it has become more difficult for them to find food. The once abundant amphipod colonies that fed them on the Arctic seabed are disappearing.

When I first saw the gray whales feeding in the Bering Strait in the late 1990s, these amphipod colonies were considered to be the most densely fertile seabed communities on Earth. But amphipods need cold water and thick sea ice through the winter to thrive, and as the Arctic waters warm and the ice cover withdraws, these colonies are failing. The grays must swim further in search of food and some are strikingly thin, with the clavicle bones protruding through the skin when there should be a healthy wrapping of blubber around flesh and bones. In recent years, around 13% of the gray whales seen in San Ignacio are showing these visible signs of starvation. As the females swim further, they have less energy and resources for pregnancy and lactation and so have fewer calves: instead of a calf every two years they have one every three or even four years, and their calves are smaller. Overall, gray whale numbers have declined by at least a third since 1994, when they were taken off the endangered species list.

Even as the whales are being forced to swim further in search of food, areas to the north of the Bering Strait, in the Arctic Ocean, are being leased for offshore oil exploration, which will expose them to extremely traumatic increases in underwater noise as well as the continual threat of a lethal oil spill, gushing uncontrolled from the seabed into some of the coldest and most turbulent waters on Earth.

I know the emptiness of waters where there are no longer any whales. Three hundred years ago, tens of thousands of Arctic bowheads were slaughtered by British and Dutch whalers operating around the High Arctic Svalbard archipelago. Even today, the bowheads remain rare. They have never really recovered from the onslaught and you seldom hear the plosive warmth of their breathing rising from the openings in the ice off Spitsbergen. Something inexpressibly beautiful and vital and alive has not returned to that coast.

When I visited the ancient whaling sites on Spitsbergen and

saw the remains of the brick blubber ovens that had rendered the bodies into oil, I felt the darkness lingering where so many whales had died. Standing there, I thought also of the many other creatures whose lives are being extinguished as the wasteland spreads across the Earth. The oceans are being stripped of life and clogged with waste and poisons. The richest tropical forests are felled, leaving barren ground where life once bloomed in staggering diversity. As the shining cap of polar ice dissolves, it opens the dark surface of open water that absorbs more light, and accelerates the warming of the world.

We humans are sleepwalking towards desolation. The impoverishment of the Earth's life is accelerating to such a pitch, that in this very century, within the lifetime of children now being born, unchecked population growth, destruction of tropical forests and the effects of climate change on all wild habitats could send up to *one half* of all species now living into extinction. Such extreme losses have been unknown on Earth for sixty-five million years, since the extinction of the non-avian dinosaurs. They have never before occurred with such relentless speed. Most people do not even realize that this is happening; those who do find it difficult to take in.

Diversity is holy. The dazzling play of relationship within the diversity of form is the expression of the inherent sacredness of life. This wanton destruction of the creative flowering from sixty-five million years of earthly evolution is a tragedy that beggars art, language and all the forms of human expression. It is, says the renowned American biologist, Edward O. Wilson, a crime for which our descendants will hardly be able to forgive us.

I do not believe that the way out of this tragedy can be found through new technologies alone, or by giving wild ecosystems some arbitrary financial value. The transformation that is needed can only come from the depths of our being, in the creative unfolding of new relationship as each person awakens to the light of love and beauty in the heart. And life will support that transformation. It will respond, in the most unexpected and astonishing ways, just as the gray whales have graced us with their presence and their touch.

I began this book by asking how the gray whales could approach us in such peace, as though they had never known suffering and death at our hands. I have come to feel that they come in peace because that is what is most natural for them. They share peace as simply as they share touch and the warmth of their breathing. When I met the gray whales first, that experience of shared peace was so rare and extraordinary that it seemed far beyond everyday experience. Since then, I have come to feel differently. I believe that the experience of shared peace the gray whales bring is what is most natural for us humans also. This is what the shamans and the mystics know, what the poets and the storytellers and the painters of the caves have expressed in their different ways – life itself is sacrament, a continual making holy that unfolds within each person, and in countless new expressions through the diversity of life.

For millions of years the voices of the great whales have interlaced through the dark of the sea as they move with the Earth's great cycles of change, breathing in the continuous power of the present, moving with the pulses of wind and light. The whales have never lost their connection to the unity of Being. They are coming to touch us now using only the ways of grace – acceptance, openness, play, peace – reaching out to help us to awaken from the dream that we live alone on Earth.

Before leaving San Ignacio Lagoon, I give Pachico the book I brought along as a gift for him. *The Cape Alitak Petroglyphs: From the Old Ones* documents the rock carvings on the coastal rocks of Kodiak Island in Alaska, which is along the gray whales' migration route. The petroglyphs were made by the ancestors of the Alitak people who live on Kodiak Island today and there is one that seems to express the very spirit of their ancestral relationship with the whales: two great whales swim side by side, with their pectoral fins outstretched to the small human figure that swims between them.

"That is like Pachico!" Abby exclaims, looking at the page over his shoulder. "Very interesting," he agrees quietly. He continues to leaf slowly through the book, pausing when he comes to the image of a shaman, standing with a drum in one hand. The shaman's other arm is raised, captured in the moment before the downbeat on the drum, and the upraised hand is marked with a star.

In that moment, it becomes an image of human connection: the pulse of the Earth meeting the drumbeat of the human heart, and the voices of stars, expressions of the pure consciousness of light, traveling like whale songs across the great sea of space.

2 Epilogue The Community of Sound

With the Blue Whale, Balaena musculus
Loreto Bay, the Gulf of California, Baja California Sur
March 2010

The desert ridges that rim Loreto bay are purple-red in the clear morning light. The indigo water is pure pigment, unmixed with tones of gray or green, and it darkens further where the seabed plunges steeply just offshore, to a canyon several thousand feet below.

A long current of pale turquoise ripples through the water, like a wave breaking across one section of submerged reef. A pressurized jet of misty air pulses skywards and the whale's sleek blue back appears, revolving in one continuous fluid motion through the surface. The polished skin on the side is pale blue-gray, silk-smooth and gleaming in the sunlight as it turns, and a strange, deep-toned humming resonates across the water as it slides again below the surface.

It sounds like a note made at the edge of music. A wind moving through great organ pipes, cavernous, echoing, carrying the suggestion of enormous spaces. It takes a moment before I recognize what I have just heard – the audible vibration of the air being drawn through the blowholes to the lungs as the blue whale breathes in.

That resonant shaking of the air on the power of the blue whale's in-breath carries the sense of its immensity into my heart. You see so little of the blue whale's body on the surface. There is the massive sleekness of the side, like polished blue-gray marble, as it breaches. The fountain of the out-breath, rising twenty or thirty feet into the air. The flexible coiling at the end of the spine at it prepares to dive.

But these are only surface glimpses of the blue whale's remote and fabulous immensity. This is the largest creature that has ever inhabited the Earth. People reach for surreal comparisons to evoke the dimensions of the blue whale's body – a full-grown elephant could stand on its tongue. Or a child could swim on the tides of arterial blood that are pumped from the heart. These whales reach ninety or one hundred feet in length and they weigh well over one hundred tons. The largest blue ever known was measured after her death on a whaling vessel in Antarctica: she was estimated to be one hundred and ten feet long.

But facts and numbers are poor things before the reality of the blue whale's presence in the water as it cleaves smoothly through the surface, breaching and submerging five times in quick succession. Again I hear that long, resonant hum bouncing off the water as the whale breathes in, rolling to the end of the spine as it dives to feed.

This largest of all animals lives on one of the smallest – the small shrimp-like crustaceans known as krill that swarm in fantastic abundance at certain times and places in the oceans. And the krill are swarming here, in the clear indigo waters of the Gulf of California, where the winter winds and the pull of tides are drawing the nutrients that feed their growth up from the depths.

Krill swarms resemble alchemical transmutations of the seawater. They are so densely concentrated that if you were to dive among them, you would not see your hand before your face. The blue whale dives, turns and lunges straight upwards through the very thickest krill patches with its jaw wide open at ninety degrees. Ventral grooves on the underside expand into a massive pouch that holds several tons of krill and seawater to be filtered through the whale's thick baleen.

These fast upward lunges against the weight of water combust such great quantities of energy that only the very richest krill patches make the intense effort worthwhile. But these dense krill swarms do not always occur at predictable times and locations: they are dynamic events, driven by the changing patterns of the storm winds that bring the nutrients welling from below. How, then, do the whales locate the krill in the vast expanses of the oceans?

They listen. Blue whales find food by listening, as they travel with global tides of nutrients and light, sending their voices across a thousand miles of ocean. The whales hear the turbulence of the great ocean currents that wash around the roots of islands and they listen for subtle alterations in the sound quality of the water that indicate where a dense krill patch is forming. They may even hear the distant thunder of the oncoming storm that will scour nutrients from the seabed and feed the krill's explosive growth.

And the whales listen for each other as they move within the great community of sound. A blue whale in the North Atlantic can hear another singing off Bermuda. Blue whales feeding off the Grand Banks move within a net of conversation and song that stretches from the coast of Nantucket to the Labrador Sea.

Every thing in the world has a voice, the shamans say. The animals, the insects, the plants and all beings sing their shaman songs within the single, continuous song of the turning Earth. The blue whale's song is the most expansive of all, strung across a thousand miles of open ocean.

If we ourselves are to make the next, and most critical step in our own evolution, we must, I think, begin by turning inwards, and listening, from the pure stillness and silence of our own deepest reality, to all these other voices of the Earth.

I leave you now with the pure presence of the real in the deep-toned hum of the blue whale's breathing: with the living community, buoyant on the breath, moving on waves of song through the fertile, incandescent, borderless sea.

Author's Thanks

I did not write this book alone. I owe so much to others that I could not name them all. I would like to thank especially the following people:

My dear friend Afanassi Makovnev, who has been my companion on so many journeys. Pat O'Hara, the wonderful photographer who taught me to see the landscape with new eyes. Staffan Widstrand, a great photographer who inspired me with his clarity and his passionate dedication to the natural world. Dr. Jason Badridze, my great friend who was my guide among wolves. Professor Valentine Pazhetnov and his wife Svetlana who allowed me the privilege of walking with bears. Dr. Nikita Ovsyanikov, Viktor and Volodya Bologov and Maureen Enns for sharing their knowledge and living experience of brown bears, polar bears, wolves and horses in the wild so generously.

In Russia, Masha Vorontsova helped me over many years. I also warmly remember Nikolai N. Vorontsov for the way he inspired me with his great love and knowledge of the natural world.

I thank Natasha Hoffman for her encouragement and the beautiful drawings that illustrate this book. I thank Woody Knebel and artist Alixe Wallis for kind permission to reproduce the rock carving of whales and humans swimming together. In Baja California, I remember Francisco "Pachico" Mayoral for the gift of meeting the gray whales in his company, along with his son Jesus Mayoral, Ruby and Abby; Cuco and Maldo Fisher at Campo Cortez, and Debora and Geraldo for the warmth of their welcome in Loreto.

My thanks to Dame Jane Goodall, who reminded me of the magic of storytelling around the fire one night at Schumacher College in Devon and to Rosamund Kidman Cox, who read some of this manuscript in draft.

I remember my wonderful yoga teachers, Heather Marlow, Carrie Tuke and Marc Woolford. I have been truly blessed to meet you.

I thank especially Heather, without whom the journey might never have begun, and Steve for love, laughter and all our wonderful conversations.

Finally I remember the storytellers whose names I will never know, the anonymous ones from so many cultures who received and passed on the magical patterns of meaning that inspired me in this book.

Some of the royalties from this book will be donated to the World Land Trust, which works with local partners to purchase and directly protect areas of tropical forest, and the Tairona Heritage Trust, which supports the Kogi people of Columbia.

Selected Bibliography

The Book of Whale

Watching Giants. The Secret Lives of Whales. Elin Kelsey. University of California Press 2009

Wild Blue. A Natural History of the World's Largest Animal. Dan Bortolotti. Thomas Dunne Books 2008

Eye of the Whale. Epic Passage from Baja to Siberia. Dick Russell. Island Press/Shearwater Books 2004

Whales. Touching the Mystery. Doug Thompson. New Sage Press 2006

Among Whales. Roger Payne. Delta 1995

Thousand Mile Song. Whale Music in a Sea of Sound. David Rothenberg. Basic Books 2008

The Shaman. Voyages of the Soul. Trance, Ecstasy and Healing from Siberia to the Amazon. Piers Vitebsky. DBP Macmillan 1995

Arctic Adaptations. Native Whalers and Reindeer Herders of Northern Eurasia. Igor Krupnik. University Press of New England 1993

Crossroads of Continents. Cultures of Siberia and Alaska. William W. Fitzhugh and Aron Crowell. Smithsonian Institution Press 1988

Native Cultures of Alaska and Siberia. Valerie Chaussonnet. Smithsonian Institution Press 1995

The Cape Alitak Petroglyphs. From the Old People Woody Knebel Alaska Donning Company 2007

The Book of Wolf

Of Wolves and Men. Barry Lopez. Simon and Shuster 1978

Wolves. Behavior, Ecology and Conservation. Edited by L.David Mech and Luigi Boitani. University of Chicago Press 2003.

Decade of the Wolf. Returning the Wolf to Yellowstone. Douglas W. Smith and Gary Ferguson. Lyons Press 2005

The Company of Wolves. Peter Steinhart. Vintage Books 1996

Mind of the Raven. Investigations and Adventures with Wolf-Birds. Bernd Heinrich. HarperCollins 2002

Yellowstone. Land of Fire and Ice. Gretel Ehrlich. HarperCollins West 1995

Touch the Earth. A Self-Portrait of Indian Existence. T.C. McLuhan. Abacus 1986

Wisdomkeepers. Meetings with Native American Spiritual Elders. Steve Wall and Harvey Arden. Beyond Words Publishing 1990

The Sioux. Royal B. Hassrick. University of Oklahoma Press 1962

The Spirit of Native America. Beauty and Mysticism in American Indian Art. Anna Lee Walters. Chronicle Books, San Francisco 1989

Lame Deer, Seeker of Visions. John (Fire) Lame Dear with Richard Erdoes. Simon and Shuster 1994

Black Elk Speaks: Being the Life Story of a Holy Man of the Oglala Sioux. John G Neihardt. State University of New York Press 2008

The Sacred Pipe. Black Elk's Account of the Seven Rites of the Oglala Sioux. Joseph Epes Brown. University of Oklahoma Press 1989

Blackfoot Physics. F. David Peat. Red Wheel/Weiser 2005

The Book of Bear

Bears. A Year in the Life. Matthias Breiter. A&C Black, London 2008

Grizzly Years. In Search of the American Wilderness. Doug Peacock. Henry Holt and Company 1990

Avec les Ours. Valentin Pajetnov. Terres d'Aventures 1997

Grizzly Heart. Living Without Fear Among the Brown Bears of Kamchatka. Charlie Russell and Maureen Enns. Vintage Canada 2003

Cave Art Jean Clottes Phaidon Press 2008

The Mind in the Cave David Lewis-Williams Thames and Hudson 2004

The World of the Polar Bear. Norbert Rosing. A&C Black, London

2007

Polar Bears. Ian Stirling. Photographs, Dan Guravich. University of Michigan Press 1998

On Thin Ice. The Changing World of the Polar Bear. Richard Ellis. Alfred A. Knopf 2009

Polar Bear. Living with the White Bear. Nikita Ovsyanikov. Voyageur Press 1996

A Naturalist's Guide to the Arctic. E.C. Pielou. The University of Chicago Press 1994

Arctic Dreams. Imagination and Desire in a Northern Landscape. Barry Lopez. Harvill Press 1998

Ninety Degrees North. Fergus Fleming. Granta Books 2001

This Cold Heaven. Seven Seasons in Greenland. Gretel Ehrlich. Fourth Estate 2003

A World Without Ice. Henry Pollack. Penguin 2010

The Future of Ice. A Journey into Cold. Gretel Ehrlich. Vintage Books 2004

The Weather Makers. The History and Future Impact of Climate Change. Tim Flannery. Allen Lane 2003

Giving Voice to Bear North American Indian Myths, Rituals, and Images of the Bear. David Rockwell. Roberts Rinehart 2003

The Book of Horse

The Nature of Horses. Stephen Budiansky. Orion Books 1997

The Complete Training of Horse and Rider. Alois Podhajsky. Wilshire Books 1979

Saint Patrick's World. The Christian Culture of Ireland's Apostolic Age. Liam De Paor. Four Courts Press 1996

Horses and the Mystical Path The Celtic Way of Expanding the Human Soul. Adele McCormick, et al. New World Library 2004

The Tao of Equus. Linda Kohanov. New World Library 2007

Horses Never Lie. Mark Rashid. Skyhorse Publishing 2010

General Mythology and Natural History

The Hero with a Thousand Faces. Joseph Campbell

The Masks of God, Vol. 1: Primitive Mythology. Joseph Campbell. Penguin 1968

The Masks of God, Vol. 3: Occidental Mythology. Joseph Campbell. Penguin 1968

The Masks of God, Vol. 4: Creative Mythology. Joseph Campbell. Penguin 1968

The Encyclopedia of Mammals. Dr. David Macdonald (Editor). Andromeda 1999

The Diversity of Life. Edward O. Wilson. Penguin 1994

The Creation. An Appeal to Save Life on Earth. Edward O. Wilson. W.W. Norton 2006

The Future of Life. Edward O. Wilson. Little, Brown 2002

Other Resources

For the most current information on the ecology and conservation of gray whales consult the following websites and groups:

The California Gray Whale Coalition www.californiagraywhalecoalition.org/

The International Fund for Animal Welfare www.ifaw.org/

For the most current information on the ecology and conservation of wolves in Europe and North America consult the following website and organizations:

The International Wolf Center www.wolf.org/

Wild Wonders of Europe

http://www.wild-wonders.com/

Defenders of Wildlife www.defenders.org/

For the most current information on the ecology and conservation of brown bears and polar bears consult:

The International Fund for Animal Welfare www.ifaw.org/

WWF www.worldwildlife.org/

Polar Bears International www.polarbearsinternational.org

For the most current information on the wild horses of the Ghost Forest consult Wild and Free at:

http://galileonetwork.ca/wildandfree/content/home

EARTH

BOOKS

Earth Books are practical, scientific and philosophical publications about our relationship with the environment. Earth Books explore sustainable ways of living; including green parenting, gardening, cooking and natural building. They also look at ecology, conservation and aspects of environmental science, including green energy. An understanding of the interdependence of all living things is central to Earth Books, and therefore consideration of our relationship with other animals is important. Animal welfare is explored. The purpose of Earth Books is to deepen our understanding of the environment and our role within it. The books featured under this imprint will both present thought-provoking questions and offer practical solutions.

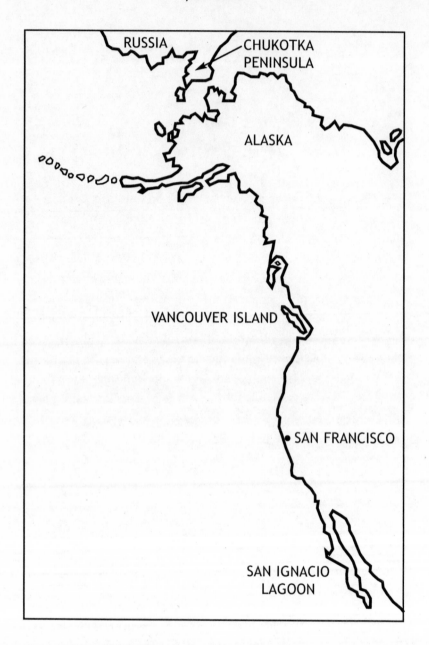

RUSSIA

CHUKOTKA
PENINSULA

ALASKA

VANCOUVER ISLAND

SAN FRANCISCO

SAN IGNACIO
LAGOON

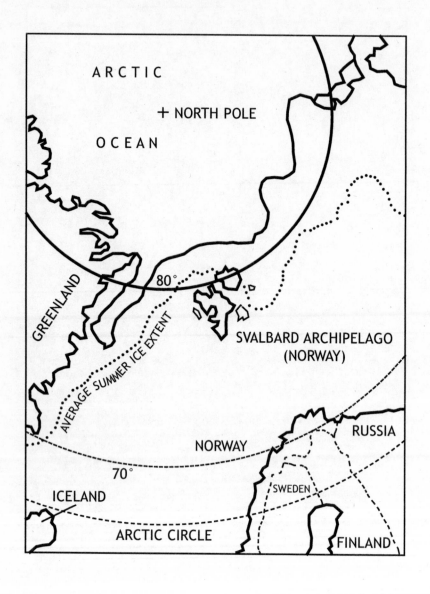